The Compendium of Renovating, Remodelling and Mending Clothes

- A Dressmaker's Guide -

By

Various

Copyright © 2011 Read Books Ltd.
This book is copyright and may not be
reproduced or copied in any way without
the express permission of the publisher in writing

British Library Cataloguing-in-Publication Data
A catalogue record for this book is available from
the British Library

GARMENT RENOVATING

By T. W. ALLEN

(*Author of " Clothes Cleaning and Renovating "*)

THE majority of tailors are compelled to undertake the cleaning and renovating of the garments of many of their customers, and although such orders may not be welcomed nor looked upon with much favour, yet they may be the means of more firmly cementing the bond between the tailor and his client.

A customer who has been thus obliged in an emergency is not likely so readily to transfer his patronage elsewhere as otherwise might be the case. Solely out of gratitude for a favour received, he would feel disposed to continue his support rather than withdraw it to the benefit of a competitor.

Apart from this aspect of the matter, the cleaning and renovating of garments can be made a profitable branch of a tailoring business, and, in addition, may be the means of getting into touch with individuals who may eventually become good customers. In any case, it is well to know how to clean clothing by removing marks and stains, as accidents in tailors' shops and workrooms are not unknown, and to be able to apply the remedy and repair the damage at once may mean a saving of time and money.

Of course, the cleaning of clothes is a special business of its own, conducted by large firms with branches in all parts of the kingdom, and tailors are among their best customers. It is not the object of this article to poach on the preserves of these people by endeavouring to explain their *modus operandi* ; neither would it be expedient to enter into a dissertation on the difference between dry cleaning and wet cleaning ; or expatiate on the merits or demerits of one or the other. My purpose is to show how to remove the more common and simple marks

GARMENT RENOVATING

and stains on clothes, when and where the more elaborate and expensive cleaning process is not convenient or necessary.

First, a few general rules on the subject will be laid down, followed by a number of particular remedies or recipes which perhaps are not comprised in the general treatment of the matter. A word of precaution, however, is necessary at the outset. Where the cloth is of a delicate texture, or of such a colour that there is a danger of the dye coming out, it is advisable in all cases to test the suggested cleaning agent on the inside of the garment, or on some other part where, should it damage the fabric, it will not be seen. Some dyes are very fugitive and unreliable as to fastness.

When clothes become soiled or marked in any way, it is a case of matter in the wrong place, and to remove this foreign substance one of four methods is usually employed, viz. by solvents; absorbents; acids or alkalies, or other chemicals; and by bleaching agents.

The common solvents are water, benzine, petrol, turpentine, chloroform, ether, alcohol (most frequently in the form known as methylated spirit), kerosene, and gasolene.

The principal absorbents are powder and similar substances, such as French chalk, pipe-clay, whiting, salt, fuller's earth, magnesia, starch, gypsum, brown paper, blotting paper, corn meal, flour, bran, sand, etc. Some of these, however, strictly speaking, are not absorbents, but they effect a similar purpose by imparting another colour to the article upon which they are employed.

Amongst the many acids and chemicals used are cream of tartar, acetic acid, cyanide of potassium, lemon juice, bichloride of tin, permanganate of potash, phosphoric acid, citric acid, hydrogen peroxide, oxalic acid, vinegar, and salts of lemon.

Bleaching is done by exposing the goods to various kinds of fumes, by applying certain chemicals, or by exposing them to the rays of the sun and the atmosphere.

The solvents, as the name implies, dissolve the foreign substance, which is eventually washed out by the solution. Water, both hot and cold, and in the form of steam, is a powerful solvent. Cold water will remove milk and cream stains, stains from sugar and sweets, and cocoa stains. Hot water is effective in removing fresh coffee stains. For greases—oil, paint, and wax—benzine, gasolene, and kerosene are very useful. For woollen and silk fabrics gasolene is probably the best, but not so with cotton goods. It is, however, very volatile and evaporates rapidly in the form of inflammable gas. In the case

GARMENT RENOVATING

of fine texture fabrics of delicate colour, the more powerful solvents should be avoided, and one or the other absorbents used, such as starch, magnesia, French chalk, or pipe-clay.

The absorbents are more efficacious when used on fresh stains while wet. Fresh ink stains, tea and coffee stains, and hot grease stains may be treated with absorbent agents. The stains may not be removed entirely by this means, but it will prevent them spreading, and is a preliminary treatment before using other agents. Some of the absorbents are sometimes used in addition to soap and water. For instance, fuller's earth occasionally replaces part of the soap in washing very greasy clothes, where it is not advisable to resort to strong soap or any strong alkali. Flour, salt, bran, starch, borax, chalk, silver sand, etc., are excellent agents for cleaning furs of all kinds.

The acids and chemicals are in some cases very powerful, and care must be exercised in their application. Acetic acid, diluted with water, is good for removing stains caused by alkalies. It increases the efficiency of alcohol, gasolene, and ether in some cases. It revives colours that have faded through various causes, especially blues, although, generally speaking, it does not prove so effective on dyed fabrics. After using oxalic acid solution, strong ammonia water is used to counteract the action of the acid. Ammonia is invaluable for eradicating stains from all wool fabrics and other materials made from animal fibres. It neutralises the effect of acids and fresh fruit stains, red wine and red ink.

For bleaching white flannel trousers and white woollen goods generally that have turned slightly yellow, sulphur fuming will have the desired effect. This process must be performed in a small room, fairly airtight, and, as the fumes are poisonous, it should not be attempted near a living-room. The articles must be quite clean and thoroughly wetted in hot water, wrung out, and hung on a line. Red-hot cinders on a shovel are placed underneath, and two tablespoonfuls of rock sulphur, or flowers of sulphur, are scattered over them. Another method is to ignite the sulphur by means of methylated spirit. In about an hour the sulphur should be burnt out and the fumes dispersed, and the garments should be a pale cream. If little change has taken place, the room was probably too large, or the garments too many for the sulphur fumes. In this case, burn more sulphur. Over-sulphuring will turn the garments yellow. As the fumes are poisonous, it is unwise to remain in the room while the fumigation is in progress.

In winter, stains may sometimes be removed by freezing.

GARMENT RENOVATING

The stain yields because the water is retained in the fabric for a long time. The removal of stains by means of sunshine and freezing, however, is only applicable to white cotton and linen materials, as both these methods affect the colours in silk and woollen goods. In the past cotton and linen bleaching was always effected by exposing the materials to the fresh air and sun for a lengthy period, the ozone in the atmosphere producing a perfect bleach.

It should be observed that many of the agents mentioned in cleaning and removing marks and stains are volatile and extremely inflammable ; hence, great care must be taken not to store them in or near a warm place, or use them in a room that is much heated, or near a light or fire of any description. This precaution is of the utmost importance, otherwise serious consequences may ensue. Moreover, after the garment has been cleaned it should be hung up, preferably out of doors, until all traces of the cleaning agent have disappeared by evaporation. This will also remove any unpleasant odour that may cling to it. It is advisable never to attempt to press a garment directly after cleaning, and before the chemical, or what not, has evaporated.

When removing grease spots on light-coloured materials it is well to begin to apply the cleaning agent some little distance from the stain or mark, and work towards the centre, otherwise a line of demarcation will be made by forcing the dirty part from the centre outwards. In order to prevent this, work in a circle round the stain from the outer edge, using sufficient benzine, petrol, chloroform, etc., to ensure sufficient driving power to preclude an unsightly ring of dirt by forcing it all to the centre of the stain.

CLEANING HINTS

For cleaning and reviving dark-coloured cloth or serge, steep about twenty ivy leaves in a pint of boiling water for two hours, and apply the solution with a brush or sponge. Laurel leaves treated in the same manner will have the same effect.

Two parts of spirits of wine and one part of ammonia will clean most fabrics, except brown. Cold tea into which has been dissolved a lump of ammonia is also an excellent cleanser for dark cloths.

To clean light-coloured cloth, mix equal parts of oatmeal and whiting, and with a pad of clean white flannel rub well into the material.

GARMENT RENOVATING

White waistcoats, white breeches, or a white flannel garment of any kind may be cleaned by applying powdered magnesia or powdered French chalk. This may also be used for keeping the hand cool and dry during the process of making. Cream or white serge may be cleaned by dipping a clean white cloth into a saucer containing ground rice, and applying vigorously. As the rag gets soiled, use a clean piece. If very soiled, a second application may be necessary. To free the garment from rice, well shake and brush out of doors.

Gold trimmings and gold lace which have become slightly tarnished can be cleaned with a mixture of cream of tartar and dry bread crumbled very fine. The powder should be applied dry, and the trimmings and lace brushed lightly with a clean, soft brush.

Scarlet tunics may be cleaned and marks removed by being rubbed with dry pipe-clay and then well brushed with a clean brush. Should this not prove effective, then the following mixture may be tried : $\frac{1}{4}$ oz. of salts of sorrel to half a pint of boiling water ; $\frac{1}{2}$ oz. of cream of tartar to half a pint of cold water. Each solution should be kept in a separate flat vessel. These quantities will be sufficient to clean two or three garments. The tunic should first be well beaten and brushed, and the solutions applied with a clean, hard brush. The solutions should be applied alternately, starting with the salts of sorrel, until the garment has been cleaned all over and any soiled marks removed. It is best to hang up the cleaned garments in the sun to dry, or, failing this, in a dry place, but not near a fire or stove.

The brightness of most scarlets, crimsons, and similar cloths may be restored by the application of a solution of bichloride of tin, followed by a local application of tincture of cochineal, if necessary. If crimson be required, a small portion of alum must be added ; if scarlet, cream of tartar with the cochineal.

A rubber coat may be cleaned with lukewarm water and soap, and if there are any spots or marks left, these should be treated with ether.

A mackintosh may be dry-cleaned by mixing together, in a large vessel, 4 oz. each of whiting, lime, white pipe-clay, and wood ashes. The garment should be wiped all over with this mixture, using an old towel ; then finished off by rubbing with a dry chamois leather.

GARMENT RENOVATING

Removing Stains

The most common stains met with are caused by grease of different kinds, and most of them may be removed by the application of benzine, petrol, chloroform, gasolene, or methylated spirit. Four parts of alcohol to one part ammonia and about half as much ether as ammonia, is an excellent mixture for removing grease. Eucalyptus oil will also remove grease or oil from most fabrics, however delicate, without injury of any kind. Magnesia or French chalk laid thickly over the stain and left for a day and then brushed off will often prove effective. Blotting paper or brown paper placed over the grease spot and pressed with a warm iron is another excellent remedy. This should be repeated with fresh paper until the grease disappears.

Heated silver sand will remove grease from furs. The sand should be poured over the fur, while the latter lies on a table, and rubbed in all directions. For white furs pour flour over the article and well rub in. Dip the hands occasionally in methylated spirits, and then plunge into flour and well rub in all parts. Shake out well and hang up.

Ink stains on cloth may be removed by rubbing with a ripe tomato cut in half. Afterwards sponge with rain water. They may also be treated with hydrogen peroxide or weak acids. Oxalic and tartaric acids are safe to use, but they may weaken the colour. When this is so, a weak ammonia solution will often restore it.

A grass stain on white flannel will yield to methylated spirits. It should be rubbed a little to loosen the stain, and while still damp, immersed in warm soapy water and washed in the usual way. Petrol and turpentine are no use for grass stains. Dry powdered magnesia applied to the stain and allowed to remain for twenty-four hours may prove effectual when the stain is slight; it must be brushed off and the garment well shaken.

One of the best remedies for removing paint stains is chloroform. Paraffin, benzine, turpentine, naphtha, and alcohol are also effective. Naphtha and chloroform are best for coloured and delicate fabrics. Equal parts of alcohol and liquid ammonia, one part sulphuric ether, and sixteen parts water will remove oil paint.

Pitch and tar stains should be first loosened by applying lard, butter, or other grease, and then washed in warm water

GARMENT RENOVATING

and soap. Turpentine, benzine, and alcohol may also be used with success.

A scorch mark, if not too severe, may be removed by rubbing with the flat side of a silver coin. Ammonia and water will remove rust. Vinegar will get rid of boot-blacking marks. For spots and stains on velvet turpentine and chloroform are effective, but care must be used with delicate colours. For stains on silk facings a little essence of lemon and turpentine applied with a rag will usually effect a change.

To clean white breeches mix pipe-clay and water into a thick paste, and then add a little powdered blue. Mix some of this paste with boiled milk until it is the consistency of cream, and lay it evenly over all parts of the breeches.

When all remedies have failed in endeavouring to remove stains on coloured garments, get a box of crayons and try to match the colour as nearly as possible. Dip the crayon in water and rub over the stain.

Miscellany

To waterproof woollen cloth, take 4 oz. of powdered alum, and $4\frac{1}{2}$ oz. of sugar of lead; dissolve in three gallons of water and stir twice daily for two days. When perfect subsidence has taken place, pour off the clear liquid only, and add to it two drams of isinglass previously dissolved in warm water. Take care to mix thoroughly. Steep the garments in this mixture for six hours, after which hang up to drain and dry. Wringing must be avoided. To stop a leakage in a mackintosh or weather-coat and reproof the part affected, rub beeswax on the wrong side of the coat, then pass a hot iron over the waxed material. This will melt the beeswax and so cover the bare part.

For restoring the pile of velvet, sponge lightly the back or wrong side with ammonia and water; then steam in the usual way. Faded plush may be brightened by brushing it lightly with a clean sponge dipped in chloroform.

To raise the nap on cloth, soak the damaged part in cold water, then lay the garment on a board and rub with a half-worn hatter's card filled with flocks. Then hang up to dry and lightly brush the nap the right way.

Gloss or shine on worn garments may be temporarily removed quite easily, but as it usually indicates a rather advanced stage of wear, it is not easily removed permanently. Ordinary pressing with hot iron and damp rag is one of the most effective

GARMENT RENOVATING

methods. Among the other suggested remedies, the following will yield more or less successful results. Apply a little oil of cloves, or a very weak solution of gum arabic, with a brush, lightly. Rub very gently with emery cloth, then sponge with a mixture of Castile soap, liquid ammonia, and water, rubbing briskly. In pressing afterwards, use a well-saturated "damp-rag." Rub with turpentine or a solution of ammonia, or some strong coffee. A teaspoonful of powdered nut-galls in a cupful of hot water applied to the gloss will remove it. Apply a teazle, or half-worn hatter's card filled with flocks, and so try to raise a slight nap; then brush the pile so produced the right way, and damp it off. This, however, must be done with great care, as the glossy parts are usually thin and will not bear much friction.

RENOVATION AND RE-MODELLING

MOST home-dressmakers find renovation a fascinating occupation—indeed, there are many who consider it more interesting than working in new materials. It can be a great money-saver if planned with foresight; but, on the other hand, it can be a sheer waste of time and money. For success it is necessary that the fabrics should be in good condition, with a reasonable amount of wear left in them; there should also be ample material to carry out your designs, and it should not be necessary to buy new materials or trimming—or, at any rate, the expenditure for these should be very small. I have known enthusiastic renovators to spend much time and money in making over materials which were shabby and almost worn out after a few weeks' wear in their new guise.

If renovation is a hobby of yours, then you should have it in mind when you make your original purchases of new materials; choosing them of good quality and of fast colour, and also, if possible, doubly reversible—that is, not only does the surface look the same from whichever end it is viewed (so that for economy's sake the different parts of the pattern can be placed either up or down), but also that both right and wrong sides are equally attractive, so that the wrong one may be used for the outside in the re-making.

RENOVATION AND RE-MODELLING

You will be wise to buy an extra yard beyond what you need for the original garment. You should select a simple style for the first time of making, and one with few seams, so that the material is not cut up unduly; this will facilitate the re-cutting for the second style, and fewer joins will be required to provide for new shapes of the different parts. In the original make-up do not use any ornamental or outside stitching, and avoid much trimming, either applied or in the way of pleats, gathers, etc., as these entail stitch marks and pressed folds which are often difficult to remove, and remain as a constant reminder of re-making. Also use a larger machine stitch than you would otherwise employ, as being easier to unpick. Make up as lightly as is consistent with firmness, and let the inner neatenings be light also. Another invaluable warning is, do not wait until the frock or other garment is really shabby before essaying renovation, or you cannot be sure of either a good appearance or of getting the desired amount of " wear ".

CHOOSING A STYLE

In selecting the second style you may choose a rather more elaborate one than before, if you wish; but in any case do avoid one in which there is great strain on any part. Also try to arrange the cutting so that those parts which originally have had much strain, as the front of a skirt, may be put in a less conspicuous position. From time to time Fashion favours a combination of contrasting colours or different fabrics, and this is fortunate for the renovator, for quite possibly she may have two garments which will combine successfully—in fact, the far-seeing shopper will have anticipated this when buying both materials.

UNPICKING

The best method of unpicking machine-stitched seams is to withdraw the under thread with a strong darning needle. This will not prove difficult if the stitch, as has been suggested, is fairly large. This method prevents loose ends of thread being left in the garment, and also the accidental cutting of it with scissors. When the fabric is a substantial one it will be found better to rip the seams with a safety razor. In this case you should either pin one end of the seam to a table, or get a friend to hold it, wrong side upward, and then begin to cut towards yourself from the farther end. Of course, great care must be taken that you cut the stitches only and not the fabric, but this is not difficult. The only drawback is that small pieces of thread are left in the material, but these can be drawn out with tweezers. When, however, the pieces of material are large, and there is no fear of shortage, you may save much time and patience by cutting the seams right out as close to the stitches as possible.

On no account re-make soiled material, so, should there be any stains, plan out your pattern roughly to see if these can be avoided—if not either send the whole of the material to the cleaner's or do the work of removal yourself. (See Chapter

RENOVATION AND RE-MODELLING

XXVI for methods.) Those places needing repair should be run round with white cotton so that they may be avoided in re-planning, or at any rate placed in an inconspicuous part. (See Chapter XXVI for repairs.) After this each piece must be pressed on the side which will in future be the wrong one. This should be done before cutting out, to ensure perfect accuracy. Any stitch marks, folds or crinkles must be pressed out with the aid of a damp cloth (as described in the beginning of Chapter XV), as, if they are first pressed dry, it will be most difficult to press them out afterwards, even with the aid of moisture.

The planning and cutting out should be done on the same principles which apply to new material, and due regard must be paid to placing the parts of the pattern on the correct grain, as in some fabrics this is not very easy when the selvedges have been removed.

INGENIOUS RE-MODELLING

It is surprising how nimble one's wits may become under the spur of necessity! Scarlet O'Hara illustrated this to perfection in " Gone With the Wind ", when she tore down a pair of handsome velvet curtains and hastily made them into a ravishing cloak! In a recent autobiography a lady of title described how in her childhood's days she and her sister lacked suitable frocks for a party to which they were invited, and finally these were provided by a resourceful nurse, who cut up a pair of frilled white muslin curtains and transformed them into two dainty, frilly, fairy-like frocks. Of course, the making of children's clothes from those of adults of either sex is an easy matter, and it is scarcely necessary to remind readers that a boy's suit may be cut from a man's overcoat or trousers; a boy's or girl's coat from that of an adult; a girl's frock from a woman's frock or skirt; a woman's blouse or child's frock from a man's shirt, etc. All these present no difficulty.

A Woman's Suit from a Man's

This is a piece of work which calls for ingenuity in planning and for tailoring skill; but it is one well worth while for the worker who has these qualities, and from personal experience I can vouch that the finished product need not proclaim its origin. (It is an advantage when the original wearer is well-built and the prospective one not above the average.) If the coat lining is suitable for re-use, it should be cleaned or washed after removal—but in any case this may be done, for, as linings for masculine garments are always of good quality, they will " come in " eventually for some purpose. Then the seams of the suit must be unpicked carefully, and also the buttonholes in the coat. If the cloth can be turned, so much the better, as the fronts will then be reversed, and the buttonholes can be either re-worked or bound. If turning is not possible, the slits must be fine-drawn (see p. 352, Fig. 173) and if pressed well they will be unnoticeable when the coat is unbuttoned.

The sleeves need care in planning, and if the

RENOVATION AND RE-MODELLING

pattern of the sleeve is cut with a full head, arranged in darts or pleats, small wedge-shaped pieces may have to be added at each side of the upper sleeve. Needless to say that these must match in grain and weave to a thread, and, if pressed well, the joins will be invisible. In planning the skirt, the trousers should be turned upside down. If more fullness is needed at the hem, pleats made from spare pieces may be inserted at the seams.

The above remarks refer to a lounge or jacket suit, but when the cloth is fine and thin, it is possible to make a frock from it, particularly if contrasting cloth is used for trimming. From a dress suit a very smart suit for a woman can be made, as the tails give extra material.

BLANKETS ARE CONVERTIBLE

More uncommon, but equally successful, are frocks, coats, and dressing-gowns made from blankets, or from large-sized table-cloths, etc. Let me enlarge upon this, for the idea is worth consideration.

One cold winter, when a new warm frock became a necessity, and my purse was thin, I hunted through the house for suitable material for a make-over. In exploring the blanket chest, I was struck by the very attractive texture of a blanket which must have been at least sixty years old. It was delightfully fine in weave, and age had denuded it of its fluffy nap, leaving a fabric with a hand-woven appearance. It was light in weight, too, so I despatched it to the dyer with a pattern of the desired colour—a shade of dead-leaf brown—with, it must be confessed, many hopes but more fears. But the result was better than I had dared to hope, and I made it up into a most attractive bolero and skirt—the former trimmed with a little wool embroidery to conceal an unavoidable small darn. The sole outlay for this was merely the cost of dyeing.

A Dressing-Gown

Another blanket I converted into a cosy dressing-gown. It was almost new, and had not been washed. Then why cut it up? Well, the reason was that a careless person—I won't say who!—had burnt several small holes in it with a taper, and as the consequent darns did not please me, and I urgently needed a dressing-gown, I cut one from the blanket and made it up in the regulation style with stitched edges to the revers and cuffs. I need not tell you what a treasure it is.

CRETONNE CURTAINS

I always like to apply the principle of devolution in both clothes and household furnishings. For instance, when new overalls or aprons are needed at the same time as new cretonne curtains, I cut up the old curtains into overalls, etc., and buy only material for new curtains. There is often a good deal of hard wear left in cretonne or linen loose covers even when they are too faded for their original purpose; but their faded condition is of no consequence when aprons for kitchen wear are

RENOVATION AND RE-MODELLING

required—and anyhow, a cheap patterned material used for them would quickly fade.

SMALL COTTON TABLECLOTHS

There are usually a few of these in use in most households. When mine begin to show signs of wear I turn them into aprons, instead of mending them. A thirty-two inch size is the most useful for

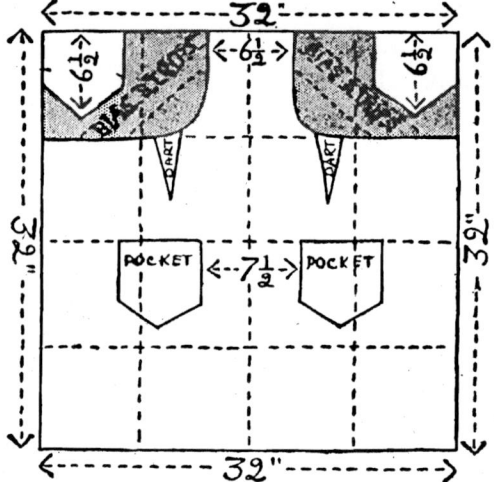

Fig. 161.—An Apron from a Tablecloth.

a medium figure, but for a larger figure the square should be in proportion. (Of course, a square of any other washing material—cretonne, crash, etc. —will serve.) Look at the diagram in Fig. 161, and fold your square as shown, *i.e.*, fold in half, then fold over again; then open out the square and fold twice the opposite way, and when the square is opened out you will find sixteen small folded squares. Now with coloured chalk draw according to the thick lines on the diagram. Cut the pockets from the spare pieces by the bib. Note the dart at each side of the bib. All figures will not need them, but if you use them they should be from 1 to 1½ inches wide at the top and about 2½ inches long.

Stitch the darts, press to one side. Hem the top of the pockets, turn in the raw edges, and stitch at a convenient height on the apron. Make narrow hems on the sides of apron and bib, and wider ones on lower edge and top of bib. Face the waist edges with bias strips cut from spare parts, and sew on tape strings (or strips of material) to tie at the back.

COTTON FROCKS, ETC.

Old cotton fabrics can often be transformed quite quickly into either petticoat-slips or overalls. If cut on slender lines, the sleeves may be removed and the armholes widened, also the neck cut down in front and back and the hem turned up a little—this will give a useful petticoat; while for an overall the sleeves, if wide and full, may either be set into wristbands with button and buttonhole fastenings, or may be cut to any length desired; unless it is preferred to remove them entirely and widen the armholes. Then the back should be cut down the middle from top to bottom and hemmed on both sides. The neck should be cut down all round, all raw edges should be bound with bias strips, and button and buttonhole fastenings should be made at waist and neck. One or two pockets should be cut from spare pieces and stitched on the front at convenient height. If the frock has a front fastening it is often possible to turn it back to front, especially if the front is at all shabby. The old bodice front may be cut off at the waist-band and at under-arm seams and shoulders. Then from the old back a bib may be cut, and this may be either pinned up or may have a strap of material sewn to each corner to be passed over the head. The old front of the skirt part should be cut from waist to hem and be hemmed on the raw edges. The skirt may be shortened if necessary. The apron may tie or button at the back.

TO MAKE BOLEROS AND COATEES

There is nothing to equal a bolero or coatee for cheering up a passée evening or afternoon frock. If it is short-sleeved it takes very little material, and when only small pieces are available it is often feasible to join these to the desired shape, if the joins are planned first, so that they become part of the design and there is no need to disguise them. Here are some of the sources from which I have seen good results: the best parts of an old skirt, frock or coat, if of suitable fabric; any old garment of velvet, satin, or brocade—even an old Victorian "dolman"! Besides these, old furniture brocades and hand-printed linens have possibilities, especially if the design is touched up a little in various parts with silks or gold thread. Of course, any striking material should be worn with a quiet-looking frock,

L (Dress)

and it is a good rule for one to be plain and the other patterned. If the bolero or coatee is required for winter wear and its material is thin, an interlining of domette, flannel, flannelette, or knitted fabric should be inserted, and the lining should be of silk, satin, or crêpe-de-chine—possibly the remnants of an old frock. Bits of fur may be used as trimming, and a chilly person will find a little upstanding collar of fur—merely a straight strip—a great protection from draughts.

I have seen a most attractive bolero cut from an old taffeta coat. The sleeves were cut off at the elbow, and the fronts were rounded so that the lower edge all round just escaped the waist-line. The whole of the fronts and back was worked over in large flowers in wool and silk, touched up here and there with gold thread. These poppy-like blooms were evenly spaced and carried out in bold stitches, leaving a good deal of the background showing inside the outlines. The sleeves were left plain except for a few lines of stem stitching in four or five colours round the lower edge. The maker had not intended this embroidery, but when she had cut down the coat she discovered several cuts in the taffeta, and therefore added the stitchery to conceal them—with very happy results.

TO MAKE BLOUSETTES AND WAISTCOATS

These attractive but deceitful little articles are quickly made for almost nothing. I say deceitful, for when worn under the coat of a suit or an odd bolero one imagines a complete garment, while in

RENOVATION AND RE-MODELLING

reality it is but a front or fronts attached to a back of net or other thin material. The home dressmaker's piece box will provide scraps of lace, satin, and other dainty materials for a blousette, and very often the back of a crêpe-de-chine or other blouse will be intact when all the other parts are outworn, and this will need but little adaptation for the same purpose. Rather more substantial fabrics are used for waistcoats, but, as there will be two fronts, even smaller pieces can be used, such as odd pieces of cloth, velvet, or brocade, etc. Plain materials may be embroidered or left plain, and if the latter, handsome buttons may be used with good effect.

Knitted Fronts

Only a very small amount of wool is needed to make what is apparently, when worn under a coat or jacket, a pullover. If sufficient wool of one colour is not available, two, three, or more colours may be used in horizontal stripes. Cast on a sufficient number of stitches to make a width of about 9 inches. Work a depth of $2\frac{1}{2}$ inches in knit one and purl one (or knit two and purl two) rib, then change to stocking stitch, or a fancy pattern, and work until, when you place the ribbing round the front waist and hold the knitting upward, the strip reaches the neck. Now shape the top like the front neck of a pullover, and work on until the side parts reach the shoulders, then cast off. Take up the neck stitches and cast on more at each end of the needle to make the first row of a collar which shall meet in the middle of the back neck, and be fastened there with press studs. Knit a roll collar to match the waist ribbing, or if you prefer a straight stand-up collar, this is equally suitable. Now take up the stitches on the left-hand side of the ribbing and knit a strip of garter stitch long enough to reach round the waist to the middle of the back, then work off in a point. Knit in the same way at the other end of the ribbing, but finish off the end with a buttonhole before the point. Sew a button on the left end.

TO WIDEN SKIRTS

To widen a narrow skirt often entails a good deal of ingenuity, and no hard-and-fast rules can be given. Here are methods which have proved successful, and may suggest others to the reader.

1. A skirt of four or more gores, too tight in its whole length, may be treated in this way. Unpick each seam, then press the fold of each turning (double) on the wrong side. Take a strip of material (either the same as the skirt or contrasting in some way—either in colour or texture) about 1½ inches wide and backed with lining, if thin. Tack the folds of the matching gores to this strip, leaving an even space all the way down. The width must be proportionate to the amount of enlargement needed, as the spaces must be equal throughout. A striped skirt should have the stripes cut with the stripes running across, or else be of plain fabric. Plain material could have similar strips, or of checked material cut on the bias, but a checked skirt will look best with plain strips. Bias velveteen, sold ready-cut by the yard, will also serve very well.

RENOVATION AND RE-MODELLING

Tack the folded edges down finely, then press the strip on the wrong side and stitch on the right side, either close to each fold or $\frac{1}{8}$ inch from it (Fig. 162),

2. An alternative method is better when the enlargement required is not the same for the whole length of the skirt. Unpick all the seams and re-fit the skirt with the turnings on the *right* side. Tack the seams according to alterations needed, then pin a strip

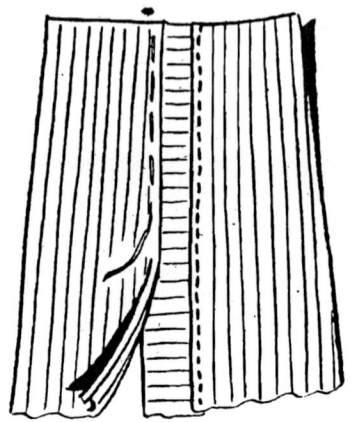

Fig. 162.—Widening a Skirt.

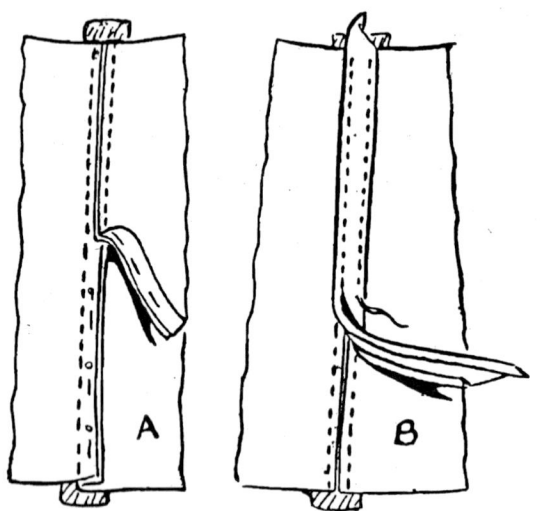

Fig. 163A and B.—Making Strapped Seams to Enlarge.

of lining about 1¼ inches wide under each seam, tack from the right side about ¼ inch each side of the tacked seam, then cut off the turnings, including the tacking (Fig. 163A). Now a take a bias strip of cloth (edges turned back and pressed if material is a fraying one, or cut with a knife on a board if very firm and close) and tack on the right side with the meeting edges of the gores exactly in the middle (Fig. 163B). Stitch the strip on the right side as close to the edges as possible. Braid might serve equally well, and it should be felled very neatly with silk on the extreme edges. If bias strips are used they must be stretched well under the iron in preparation.

3. If a skirt is too long as well as too tight, it is an easy matter to remove it from the band and raise it on the figure until it fits correctly round the hips; then the excess above the waist-line should be cut off, any necessary alterations made in the seams at the hips, or in the darts, and finally the skirt should be remounted on the waist-band and any needed re-adjustment made in the hem.

4. Here is an attractive method when the shape of the skirt allows it—for instance, a two-piece skirt with a seam at each side. Unpick the seams and insert a strip of material not less than 3 inches wide (without turnings) all the way down; after tacking, stitch down the turned-in edges of the skirt about ¼ inch from the turn. This would give a total extra width of 6 inches, and where this would be too much, the sides of the skirt pieces should be trimmed off and turned in afresh, so as to give the correct width

RENOVATION AND RE-MODELLING

measurements after the insertion of the pieces. If still more width is required at the hem, it may be given by making each strip wide enough (for about 10 or 12 inches from the bottom edge, plus turnings, according to fashion) to make an inverted pleat at each side. This entails adding 4 inches or more at each side of the strip. The join must come under the turned-back edge of the skirt piece.

5. For a skirt with seams at back and front a similar plan may be followed by inserting strips there. Certainly there should be pleats at the lower edge, their height being according to current fashion. There may be two pleats instead of one at each side of the opening, if the material is not bulky, and these would come on the top of one another.

Note. These inserted pieces may be of contrasting colour, or a skirt of plain colour could have them striped or checked. The stripes should be used horizontally. It is a good plan to make experiments in pleating in paper before cutting material, to avoid mistakes. When making these alterations the skirt hem should be unpicked for a few inches at each side of the seam, and a hem of the same depth arranged for on the inserted pieces, then, after pressing the seams, the hem may be re-adjusted and the pleats pressed again.

Widening on the Lower Part Only

When a skirt needs widening below the knees only, this may be effected by means of inverted pleats, either single or double, at each seam (Fig. 164A, B, and C); and in the case of wide gores vertical slits may be made also for pleats.   The same, or contrasting fabric may be used.   In a thin material godets

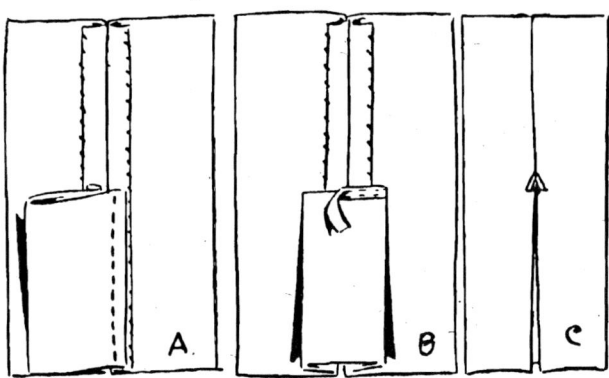

Fig. 164.—Inserting Pleats in Seams.

may be used instead of pleats (see Fig. 105A and B, p. 165, and instructions for making on pp. 164-5), and a tight-fitting evening skirt of silk or satin can

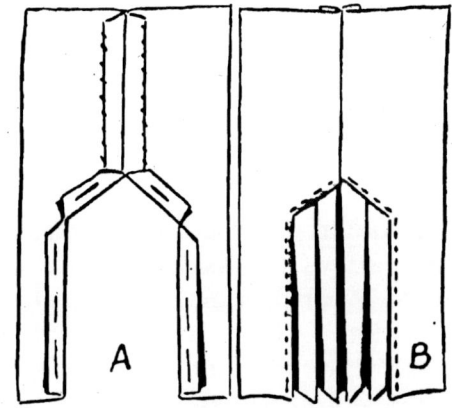

Fig. 165.—Another Method of Widening a Skirt.

RENOVATION AND RE-MODELLING

be renovated effectively by the insertion of ninon or georgette godets in several vertical slits.

Another method of inserting pleats is shown in Fig. 165. Here the two gores are cut away on each side of the seam as in A, and the turnings tacked back and pressed. A piece of material, cut on the straight, is laid in four pleats—two at each side with folds toward the middle. After being pressed they are tacked behind the turned-in edges of the opening and stitched as in Fig. 165B.

TO WIDEN A BLOUSE OR BODICE

In thin fabric it may be possible to give the required extra width by inserting two or three strips of lace or ribbon down the front (or fronts) and back, stitching these in by machine or joining them in with a faggoting stitch. Another plan is to cut away a strip from the middle of the front and to insert a sham waistcoat of different material, or a vest of tucked georgette or net.

TO LENGTHEN A SKIRT

A full gathered skirt of thin fabric may be lengthened in the following way :

If the material is a patterned one, add a straight band of plain material to tone, about 12 inches deep, to the lower part of the skirt; or cut off an even depth from the lower part and insert a straight band of another colour. This band should be rather narrower than the band of the original material below it. In the first method the lower part should be turned down on its upper edge and stitched over

L 2 (Dress)

the skirt at the desired height (the original material behind being cut away); while in the second method both edges of the added band should be turned down and stitched over the raw edges of the skirt. When the skirt is on a curve, great care should be taken

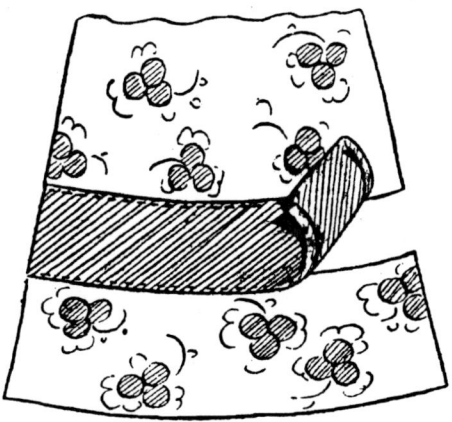

Fig. 166.—Lengthening a Skirt.

to get the band on the same curve as the lower edge of the skirt (see Fig. 166). In the case of very thin material, the edges of both skirt and added band may be pressed back, stitched once close to the turn, then joined by means of faggoting.

Add a Shaped Flounce

This method is only suitable for a fairly soft, though not necessarily very thin material, and it requires a good deal of extra fabric—exactly how much depends upon the particular style chosen. Cut off the lower part of the skirt so that the remaining upper part finishes at least 10 inches above the

RENOVATION AND RE-MODELLING

desired hem-line, then add a shaped flounce of the necessary depth. This method also serves well for combining two old frocks. The flounce would be cut from the second frock and the same material introduced as a trimming on the upper part of the first frock, perhaps as a yoke and sleeves.

For Fairly Firm Fabric

This is a suitable plan for thin woollens, substantial silks, cottons, etc. When the additional length required is not more than 1 inch and there is a hand-sewn hem in good condition inside (this is important) and not less than 2½ inches deep, proceed as follows:

Unpick the hem and press out all creases. Fold back the hem to the RIGHT side on the old turning and tack ¼ inch from the fold (Fig. 167A); then go to the right side, turn down the material below the tacking and tack through the three layers close up to the tacking (Fig. 167B). Press on the wrong side

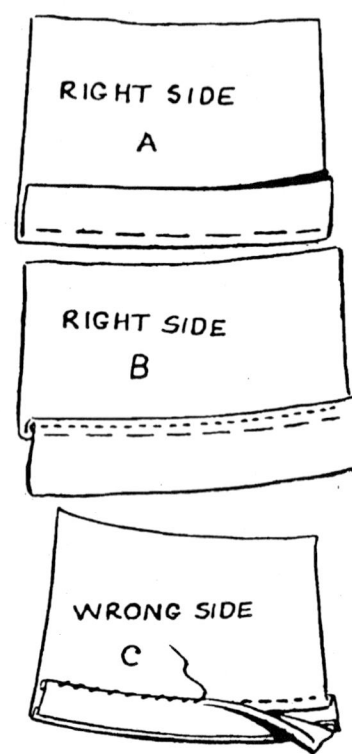

Fig. 167.—Re-making a Shabby Hem to Lengthen.

as flat as possible and stitch by machine on the right side just below the fold. Press again on the wrong side, then turn up the lower edge to the correct depth and face with a piece of lining or spare material cut to the shape of the lower edge, and sufficiently deep to be felled on its upper edge behind the first stitching (Fig. 167c).

RENOVATION OF KNITTED WEAR

NOT all knitters realise that there are many short cuts in their craft which will reduce labour and economise materials. I have often seen knitters laboriously pulling back a jumper of which they have grown tired or which has proved ill-fitting, when it could so easily have been altered in style without re-knitting, or enlarged or made smaller in order to improve the fit. Of course there are cases where re-knitting is the only cure. When this is the case, unpick the seams of the garment most carefully, to avoid breaking the wool. If they are sewn up by the edge loops with matching wool, you should begin unpicking where the seam was finished off. Use a blunt wool needle or a bodkin to find the last stitch. When this has been found, unpick a few stitches, then pull the wool gently, and when you have drawn out a few inches, cut it and straighten out the seam. The cut end will now be visible, and you can repeat this process probably for a good length of seam. Should there be a stoppage, the stitches should be unpicked one by one until the wool can be drawn out as before. When all seams have been undone, find the casting-off of the front or back and proceed to unravel the knitting. Do not pull the wool more than you can help, and do not make into balls, but wind round the back of a chair or a wide piece of card to produce skeins. Tie up each skein loosely at each end. Wash them quickly in a warm lather, holding them up by the tying threads. Dry quickly —in the open air, if possible, or otherwise before a good fire. When the wool is dry wind it into loose balls and avoid stretching.

You will now find that the yarn is thinner than it was originally, and also it will have shrunk in length, so that unless you decide to make a smaller garment, you will need extra wool. Do not try to match the old, but choose a different colour of similar thickness, and use this for trimmings, such as yoke, collar and cuffs, etc. Suppose that you have unravelled two garments of different colour but of the same ply, and you find that after washing the wool is thinner, you may, if the colours are harmonious, knit up the two together, and thus obtain a charming mixture effect. Silk and wool may often be combined attractively in the same way.

TO SHORTEN A JUMPER

There are two usual methods. (1) If the jumper has been knitted from the top downward unravel it from the bottom upward to the desired height above the ribbing, then re-knit this. (2) This serves whether the knitting has been done downward or upward. Cut off the garment at the required height above the ribbing and unravel the lower part. Take up the stitches and re-knit the ribbing. A better way is as follows.

Insert pins at the side seams to show where the top of the ribbing should come on the shortened

RENOVATION OF KNITTED WEAR

jumper. Then at one of the seams cut (with great care) an edge loop at the level marked. Pull the cut end very gently, and you will find you can trace the strand straight across to the other edge. Cut the loop there, and the lower part will drop off. Treat the other half of the jumper in the same way. If you wish to use the original ribbing, you may either unravel the unwanted part above it or else cut it off as just described; then take up both sets of stitches on no. 12 needles and graft them together. Should you wish the ribbing to fit more tightly than before, turn back a sufficient piece at each end and take up the discarded stitches on safety-pins. After taking up the remaining stitches on a no. 12 needle, knit a row on the stitches of the upper part, but take two together at intervals to reduce the number to correspond to the number on the ribbing. Now graft the two sets together. Sew up the sides of the ribbing, turn back the unwanted pieces and secure the loops left on the safety-pins to the back of the ribbing.

Note that this method of cutting knitting may be used for any other part of the garment.

TO LENGTHEN A JUMPER

If a jumper is too short between the armhole level and the ribbing, it is possible to add the desired length by means of stripes of a different colour. Cut off the back and front at the bust-line by the method described above, then take up the stitches of the upper part on needles the correct size, and with the new wool knit an inch either in garter stitch or a fancy stitch—that is, if the jumper is worked in stocking stitch, but if a fancy stitch this may be continued throughout the stripes. Pull back the wool of the lower part, wind it in skeins and place it on a rack above a bowl of hot water so that the crinkles will be steamed out. Now knit an inch or more, as desired, with the original wool to match the original part, and repeat these two stripes as

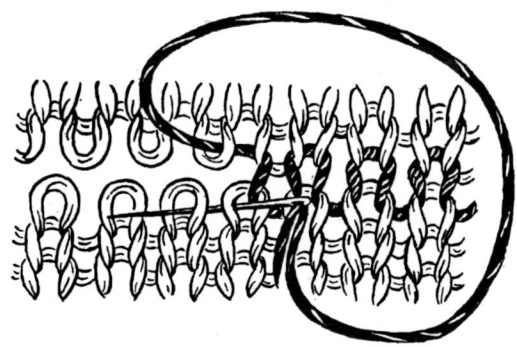

Fig. 168.—Grafting for a Join.

often as required to get the correct length, but contrive to finish with one of the jumper wool, even though it may be deeper than the others. Graft the last row of stitches to those of the ribbing, or else knit new ribbing. (It will be found a good plan to work out the number and depth of the stripes on paper by finding the number of rows to the inch, before beginning them.) It is desirable to add stripes to correspond on the sleeves at the same level, also collar and cuffs, of the new colour.

Grafting is shown in Fig. 168, above. If the knitting has been washed the stitches will be firm,

RENOVATION OF KNITTED WEAR

and may be joined as shown, pinned and tacked to a piece of paper; but if newly-knitted the stitches should be left on the needles.

TO WIDEN A JUMPER OR CARDIGAN

If the garment is tight round the bust only, and not round the lower part, unpick the under-arm seams from the armhole downward as far as seems desirable. Try on the garment and note the extra

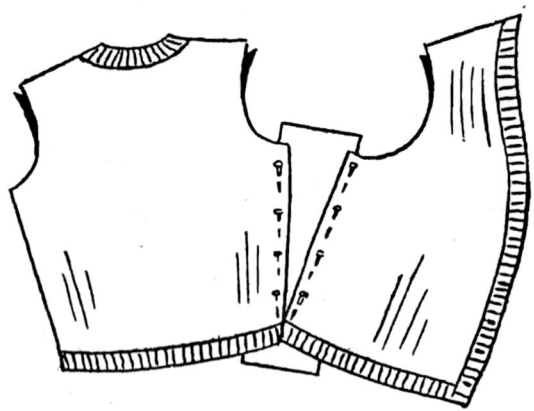

Fig. 169.—Widening a Jumper or Cardigan.

width needed at the bust-line. Cut a long strip of paper 1 inch wider than this extra width, and pin the edges of the under-arm seam to this strip, leaving the exact width needed at the top and then gradually narrowing the strip of paper off to nothing. Mark the shape between the knitted edges on the paper with pencil and take out the pins. Of course, should extra width be needed all the way down, the seam must be unpicked entirely, and the sides separated on the paper as much as is necessary.

Now knit two pieces to the required shape, using the same wool and stitch as the garment. Press well, then sew the pieces into the seams in the usual way, and press the seams (see Fig. 169). When the sleeves are tight in the upper part, wedge-shaped pieces may be inserted on the same plan, otherwise the armhole seam should be unpicked for 2 or 3 inches at each side of the inserted piece between the back and front, and the sleeve stretched to fit the armhole.

FOR A STOUT FIGURE

The ordinary type of jumper or cardigan proves unbecoming to the figure which is large in front in proportion to the back, which is often the case with a stout figure, and the garment is consequently tight across the bust and short from the neck to the lower edge. Here is the remedy.

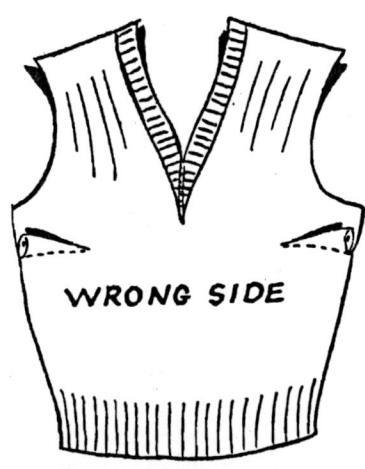

Fig. 170.—Darts for a Plump Figure.

Unpick the underarm seams, then take up a dart on each side edge of the front about 2 inches below the armhole. These darts should run straight across, and the amount taken up will depend on the figure (Fig. 170). Stitch them by machine

RENOVATION OF KNITTED WEAR

as you would stitch them in material, and be sure to taper them nicely, so that a poke is avoided. (However, if one does result, it can be got rid of in the following way. Make a circle of fine running round the poke, place it right side downward on an ironing blanket, lay a damp cloth over the circle and press with a hot iron, and allow the wool to dry before removing the running thread.) Press the darts up or down, but on no account cut them open. The side edges of the front will now be shorter than those of the back, and you must join up the underarm seams from the waist, leaving the excess on the back. When sewing in the sleeve, this excess will form a graduated turning which may be pressed back and caught lightly to the back threads of the knitting. If this method does not seem feasible, the back must be shortened as required, as described in the directions previously given for shortening a jumper. Note that darts may be placed in any other part where needed, and if well made they will be quite inconspicuous.

A PETTICOAT FROM A SKIRT

A very satisfactory petticoat can be made from a skirt, especially if it is a slim-fitting one with three or four seams. Suppose that you have one consisting of four gores of similar size. It may be possible to use this just as it is, after removing the waist-band and substituting one of elastic; but if the skirt is too wide for its new purpose, the seams may be taken in a little. If too long, a really shapely full-length petticoat (see Fig. 171) can be made in the following way :

TEACH YOURSELF DRESSMAKING

Put on the skirt and draw it up on the figure until you get the lower edge at the desired level, then pin the top all round to the under garment. Get someone to fit the lower part, taking in the seams if required. Measure the length in front from the front neck to the top of the skirt, and the width across the chest from armhole to armhole about half-way between neck and bust. Remove the garment from the figure and stitch any alterations. Now knit back and front yokes from any wool which will " go " with the skirt, even if of a different colour. For the front yoke cast on sufficient stitches to produce the chest measurement you took. Knit in stocking stitch—garter stitch drops too much—and decrease at both ends of the third row and of every alternate row afterwards until the yoke is about 3 inches narrower than the chest measurement you took. Continue without decreasing until the yoke, when attached to the lower part, reaches 2 inches below its desired position. Then work the remaining 2 inches in knit one and purl

Fig. 171.—A Petticoat from a Skirt.

RENOVATION OF KNITTED WEAR

one rib, using finer needles than before. Make the back yoke in the same way, but continue the stocking stitch for 1½ inches more than at the front, and work the last 2 inches as before. Note that instead of casting-on you may take up stitches from the top of the skirt for the yokes. If possible, use the original front gore of the skirt for the back of the petticoat to equalise the wear.

To complete the petticoat, knit shoulder straps 1½ inches wide in garter stitch, and stretch them well before sewing to the front and back yokes. If short of wool, the straps may be made of ribbon or double strips of silk or sateen. A hand-knitted skirt has been in mind in describing this renovation, but a machine-knitted one may be treated in the same way. If preferred, instead of adding knitted yokes, a short petticoat bodice may be cut in sateen with a back opening, and sewn to the wool skirt.

DISCARDED JUMPERS AND CARDIGANS

When these are of light colour they may often be adapted for night wear over thin lingerie. A touch of simple embroidery in wool may be added. A plain, short jumper with V neck may have sleeves removed, and may then be worn as a spencer under thin blouses. A hip-length, sleeveless jumper, with rather low neck will often serve as a vest, and if too short it may be possible to remove the ribbing on the lower edge and knit on the desired additional length.

A NEW WAY OF TREATING OLD "KNITTEDS"

Accidents often suggest novel ways of overcoming difficulties. I entrusted the washing of an outsize jumper in plain style to an inexperienced laundress, and it came back so shrunken that it was firm and close like cloth, with no " stretch " left in it. Enquiries disclosed that she had washed it in hot, soapy water, and dried it slowly. It was too small to be worn in that state, and it could not be unravelled, as it was much too felted, and I was at a loss how to deal with it until I hit upon the idea of treating it like cloth. So I cut from it a bolero with short sleeves, laying a paper pattern on it as though cloth were being used, and leaving the usual turnings. I made it up on the same method, but without neatening the outside edges. I cut a lining in some old silk and tacked it round the edges, but felled the under-arm turnings over each other, also the shoulder turnings. Then I cut off the turnings off the outer edges on the fitting-lines and bound the raw edges with silk braid.

The result was so successful that I have since shrunk knitting purposely to use in similar ways; for instance, a pair of knickers for a toddler can be made from a full-sized jumper. No lining is needed, but after the seams have been stitched the turnings should be pressed open, then tape or bias binding should be tacked over each raw edge and the edge on the turning should be stitched by machine, while the other edge should be felled by hand to the back threads of the knitting. The upper edge of the knickers should be faced similarly with a piece of sateen.

The above examples are only given as suggestions, and other methods will speedily be thought out by the ingenious needlewoman.

RENOVATION OF KNITTED WEAR

USES FOR OUTWORN GARMENTS

Knitted fabric, whether hand- or machine-made, should never be thrown away, however old, for in its final stages it can be used for a variety of purposes.

1. It may be tacked to thin silk or cotton and used as an interlining for coats.

2. After being washed and shrunk, pieces of various colours may be laid on an old sheet and their edges cut to fit until the whole surface is covered. The edges should then be tacked into place. Both sides should be covered with thin cotton material, preferably patterned, and the whole lightly quilted in large diamonds, after which the edges should be bound with a bias strip of the same, or contrasting, material. This makes a cosy quilt for a bed, and may be made in any size desired.

3. Kneeling pads may be made by sewing several layers together and binding the edges with broad braid.

4. Seat cushions for chairs may be made with several layers of knitting covered with cretonne, etc. They may be buttoned down at intervals like mattresses, if liked that way.

5. When the arms or seat of an armchair become somewhat flat they may be padded up with pieces of knitting of graduated size, and then, when the desired result has been obtained, the knitting should be covered with a piece of thin material (a piece of an old garment will do), which should be catch stitched lightly to the upholstery. Of course, this presupposes that the chair has a loose cover. Por-

tions of knitting may be unravelled, and then used for padding up small depressions to the desired shape.

REPAIRING THIN PLACES OR HOLES

If possible, the repair should be done before a hole has developed, so, while a garment is in use, the vulnerable parts, particularly cuffs and elbows

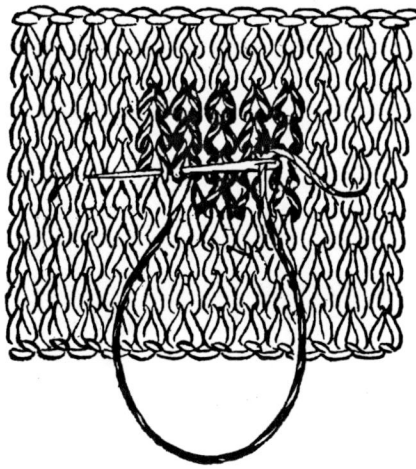

Fig. 172.—Swiss Darning.

of sleeves, should be watched. Thin places may be darned on the wrong side, using matching wool—dividing it if it is too thick for its purpose; or it may be possible to match the colour in darning wool. Place the thin part over an " egg ", but do not stretch it. Then darn upward and downward through the back loops of the knitting, with a **wavy** edge at top and bottom, and leaving the wool **there** rather loose

RENOVATION OF KNITTED WEAR

to allow for shrinking in the wash. Do not darn across unless the place is very thin; but in that case it is best to turn the knitting to the right side and try to imitate the knitting stitches as much as possible. A better effect may be obtained by tacking the worn part, wrong side downward, to a piece of card, then working over the stitches as in Swiss darning (see Fig. 172).

When there is only slight thinness, darning may not be necessary, but a piece of thin net should be tacked on the wrong side to cover the worn part, allowing a good margin of net all round. The corners of the net should be rounded off, and then the edges should be herringboned with silk to the back threads of the knitting. If the elbows show signs of strain and the sleeves have a head with a symmetrical curve, you may take out the sleeves and transpose them, thus bringing the strain to a new place. (When the elbows have become baggy they should be shrunk as described for the top of a dart.)

A More Decorative Way of Repairing

If the defective spot, be it hole, thin place, or stain, is in a suitable position for ornamentation, the best thing is to work an embroidered motif or spray of flowers in coloured wools over it. I once put away a cardigan for a few weeks, and on taking it out found it moth-eaten on the left front near the shoulder and also on the lower part of each sleeve. I tacked a piece of net under the holes on the front and worked a spray of multi-coloured flowers over them and through the net; but on the sleeves the holes were too numerous to be treated similarly, so I cut the knitting across just above the elbow, turned up an inch, and herringboned the raw edge to the back threads of the knitting. A good pressing followed, and the result was most effective.

CARE AND REPAIR OF CLOTHES

WHEN the home dressmaker has satisfactorily replenished her wardrobe, her work is by no means over—that is, if she is to get full value out of her clothes in regard both to appearance and durability. Their care is a continuous process, and cannot be confined to stated periods. Each time they are taken off they should be looked over and any necessary repairs or cleaning noted, and then carried out as quickly as possible, for delay always makes stains, etc., more difficult to remove. This daily lookover soon becomes a habit, and if nothing else is needed, a brushing of suits and cloth frocks, and a shaking of thin frocks, are generally called for. A stiff brush is required for cloth and firm materials, a softer one for thin fabrics and velvet, and velvet pads for silk and satin, etc. After each time of wearing it is also a good plan to air the discarded garments over a towel airer, either in the open air or near a moderate fire.

Any stains or grease spots should be removed at the earliest opportunity; and even should your garments be free from them, yet those of cloth and substantial fabric are improved by a general sponging-over with a cleanser from time to time. There are many excellent cleansers on the market, in the way of liquids, soaps, and cloth balls, and they should be applied according to the instructions which accompany them. But there is a good homemade cleanser which will serve the double purpose of stain-remover and general reviver.

HOME-MADE CLOTH CLEANSER

Shred 2 oz. of Castile soap into a pan containing one pint of water. Boil until the soap is dissolved, then add 2 oz. of lump ammonia, 1 oz. of glycerine, 1 oz. of ether, and 2 quarts of water. Mix well, put into bottles and cork tightly. Dilute with water before using, as required. (It is the best plan to use a piece of the same material as the garment when applying this mixture, and if this is not forthcoming, then to use the nearest you can get.)

If the stains do not yield to the action of the cleanser, try one of the remedies which follow. But although all have been tried and found efficacious, yet it cannot be guaranteed that they will be successful in every case. Differences in the texture of the material, or in the nature of the dye used, may prove a deterrent. It should be borne in mind that all strong acids, such as oxalic acid, must be used with caution, and they should first be tested on the turnings of the garment, for there is always the chance that the colour might fade. As a general rule, after using oxalic acid the material should be sponged with ammonia, followed by the application of warm water.

A Stronger Cleanser

When simpler methods have proved unsatisfactory try the following :

CARE AND REPAIR OF CLOTHES

Dissolve 2 oz. of oxalic crystals in one pint of water, then bottle and cork tightly. When required for use dilute with twice its own quantity of water. Moisten the stain by means of pieces of cotton wool dipped in the solution. Repeat until the stain disappears, then sponge with ammonia, followed by warm water. Peroxide of hydrogen is often successful on silks and thin woollens.

REMEDIES FOR STAINS
Ink

There are many reliable ink removers on sale, but all may fail at times, as has been explained in reference to home remedies. Here is the simplest remedy for ink-stains, and I have seen it bring out a small bottleful of ink and leave no trace behind. On the other hand, sometimes it has failed for an unknown reason. It should be remembered that if the stain is allowed to dry it is extremely difficult, and sometimes impossible, to remove it. It is best therefore to put the stained part in lukewarm water until milk or other remedy can be obtained.

1. Whether the material is linen, silk, or wool, white or coloured, put the stained portion into milk and leave for several hours. If not successful, then try again or use one of the other treatments suggested. In either case, wash out in warm water first.

2. Use tomato juice in the way described for milk.

3. Moisten the ink-stains with turpentine and leave for half an hour, adding more turpentine if the fabric shows signs of drying up. Then rub the stained part between the hands as if washing.

Now sponge with cold water, whether successful or not, and then, if the stain has gone, rub dry with a piece of the same material.

4. Wet thoroughly with peroxide of hydrogen. Rub with a piece of self material, and when the stain has gone sponge over with weak ammonia and rub dry with a piece of the same material, but dry.

Fruit

Fruit-stains often prove most difficult to remove, though some yield almost at once to warm water or milk, especially when they are tackled immediately. A method which is often successful is to soak the spot in chloroform, and then in ammonia. Repeat several times, if necessary, then sponge gently with warm water.

Mud

Do not attempt to remove mud while it is wet. When dry lift off what you can with a penknife, then brush well, and afterward rub with a slice of raw potato, followed by a sponging with ammonia. Instead of potato, pure alcohol may be used. (This latter should always be used in the case of silk.)

Paint

If the paint is wet, remove at once with a piece of self material and then rub with a fresh piece until the mark has gone. If it is obstinate, rub with chloroform, or with a mixture of turpentine and ammonia. Finish off by sponging with warm soapy water, and rubbing until dry with a piece of self material. If the paint is hard, saturate the spot

CARE AND REPAIR OF CLOTHES

with turpentine and ammonia and renew as required until the spot is soft.

Machine Oil or Grease

Use ether, benzine, or turpentine. (Either of the first two should be used for silk or delicate fabrics.) Take a piece of the same material or similar, dip it in one of the liquids and apply in a circle wide of the stain; then gradually work up to it and rub as required. (This is to avoid a ring mark.) When the grease has disappeared rub until dry with a piece of the same or similar material—the wrong side of another part of the garment will serve. When the grease is only slight, place the stained part between two pieces of blotting-paper and pass a warm iron over the paper next to the stained side of the material. This method often drives the grease completely into the lower paper, but should a mark remain, remove it with benzine or ether.

Tar

Cover the spot with oil of eucalyptus. When softened, remove with benzine or methylated spirit, and finally sponge with warm water.

REPAIRS

These should be done before you press the garment or before it is sent to the cleaners.

Buttonholes

When these are broken, turn the part right side downward on an ironing blanket, draw the edges of the buttonhole together and press on the wrong side under a damp cloth. Then carry two strands of buttonhole twist (if this has been used for the buttonhole) round the edge of the slit, and with fine matching silk (finer than the original silk used) work all round with buttonhole stitch over the two strands, but making the stitches shorter, and taking them between the original stitches. If the bar is broken, cut it off, and work a new one. Press on the wrong side.

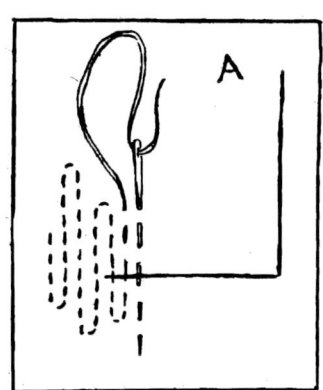 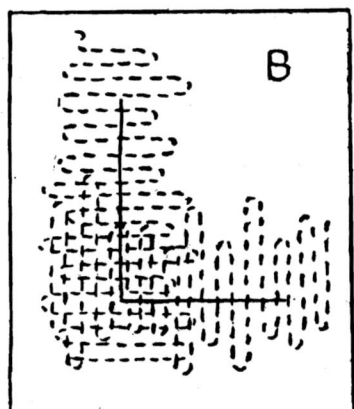

Fig. 173.—A Three-Cornered Tear.

A Three-cornered Tear

If the garment has a lining, unpick this behind the damaged part, then tack the tear, right side downward, to a piece of thin card, drawing the edges of the tear together to meet exactly. Thread a long fine needle with fine matching silk (or a strand of the material if this is fine and loosely woven) and darn across the torn edges just on the uppermost threads, as no stitches must show on the right side,

CARE AND REPAIR OF CLOTHES

working from left to right and starting from a little beyond the closed end of the tear. Let the stitches end in wavy lines (see Fig. 173 A). Make two or three lines of darning beyond the corner, then cut the silk. Start again at the other closed end and work as before (see Fig. 173 B). If you think the angle of the tear needs greater strength, darn across the two sets of darning stitches diagonally, though this is not done in the illustration. On the right side scratch up the cloth a little with a needle over the darn, then press on the wrong side.

Note that there is a mending tissue, and also a mending solution, on the market, by which small patches may be applied over a tear, either without darning or after darning as just described. These are sold under trade names, and are usually most satisfactory.

Torn Pocket-ends in Coats

Make a buttonhole bar in strong silk across each end (see Fig. 76, p. 129), or work a small arrowhead in these positions, with the broad end at the pocket opening (see Fig. 174).

Weak Places

When a place begins to show signs of weakness without the threads being broken—for example, the elbow of a coat—any bagginess which may have formed there should first be shrunk out (see Chapter on Shrinking). A small circle should next be run in silk to enclose the baggy part, and then this fullness shrunk away with a wet cloth and hot

M (Dress)

iron. After this the weak part may be darned across the back threads on the wrong side with fine silk. (It is best to tack the part face downward on a thin card as for the three-cornered tear.) The silk must not be drawn tightly, and the lines of

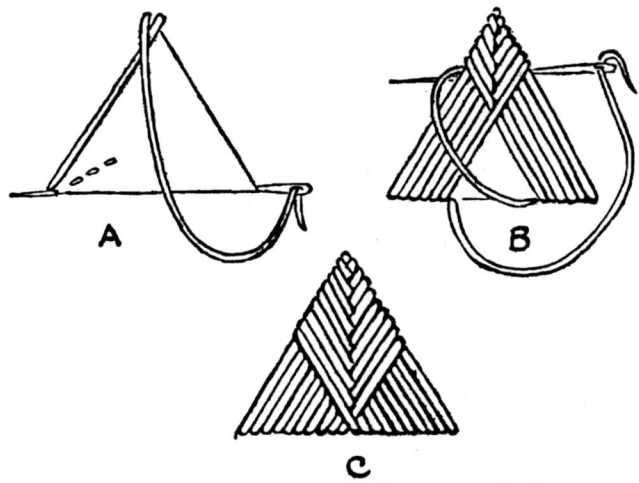

Fig. 174.—Sprat's Head or Arrowhead.

stitches should end irregularly to avoid a ridge on the right side. Instead of this, a piece of fine net might be tacked on the wrong side, the corners rounded off, and then the raw edges of the net lightly herringboned to the cloth with silk.

PATCHING

Always avoid a patch in a conspicuous place, if possible, as it is difficult to make one perfectly invisible. The simplest method is to use one of the tissues which are sold for this purpose, by which

CARE AND REPAIR OF CLOTHES

patches are applied with a hot iron without sewing. But however they are applied, patches should always match the damaged part in grain, also in pattern when there is one. If possible, the patch should not be of new material, but should have had the same exposure to the air as the garment, and it may be necessary to cut a patch from an inconspicuous part (perhaps the turn-up of a skirt or the front facing of a coat) and to replace the part taken away by a new piece, either matching or as near so as possible.

A Fine-drawn Patch (Fig. 175)

First draw on the right side of the garment with tailor's chalk a square or oblong to enclose the hole or tear, ruling by a thread. Then draw the patch to the same size, matching the enclosure on the garment in grain. Place the garment over a board or piece of glass and cut along the lines with a sharp penknife and a ruler. Cut the patch in the same way. Remember that the patch must not be even a shade smaller than the hole. Place the material right side downward on a piece of thin card and, without stretching it, tack finely all round. Then drop the patch in, secure with a large cross in the middle, draw its edges to meet those of the hole, and tack finely all round, seeing that the corners are perfectly exact. Now work through the meeting edges as described for the three-cornered tear. Finish off in the same way. Note that this method is only suitable when the cloth is firm and non-fraying. When it is more loosely woven, particularly when it is of the hopsack order, the following method is good.

A Darned-in Patch

Cut a piece of material 4 inches larger each way than the hole. It should be square or oblong, and

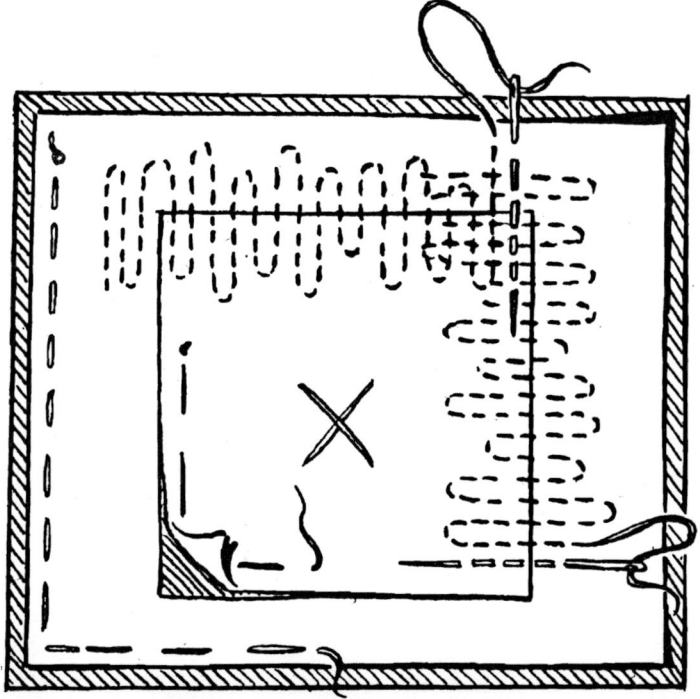

Fig. 175.—A Fine-drawn Patch.

should match it in grain—that is, the warp threads of both should run the same way, and if there is a nap (which is not likely), it should run the same way in both patch and garment. Fringe the edges of

CARE AND REPAIR OF CLOTHES

the patch all round for $1\frac{1}{2}$ inches, and about $\frac{1}{4}$ inch from each corner on all sides draw out a few more threads, so that the corners are no longer sharp. Now tack the hole onto thin card, right side upward, and tack the patch exactly over the hole, matching the grain. Thread up in turn each strand outside the patch into a needle and darn into the surrounding material, following its weave. The best way of doing this is first to darn in the needle only, leaving the eye close up to the patch, then to thread the strand through the eye, and pull out the needle by the point. Leave the edges of the stitches irregular, then draw the strands to the back of the material and cut off each. When finished lay the patch right side downward and press from the wrong side.

Darning Tweeds

Some tweeds are very easy to copy with the needle. In that case a worn part may be reproduced easily, either by using warp threads pulled out of a spare piece or from the turnings. If this cannot be managed, it may be possible to buy darning wool to match. Take a piece of thin net behind the garment, then darn through both tweed and net to reproduce the pattern. If the tweed is not thick it is best to tack it to a piece of thin card. Of course a good final pressing is needed.

Holes in Thin, Patterned Fabrics

These may be repaired invisibly in two ways.

1. Cut a patch about 2 inches larger each way than the hole, matching the design perfectly, and

round off the corners. Now apply this patch to the under side of the garment with the special liquid sold for the purpose.

2. To be quite successful the pattern of the material should be large and bold. Cut out a largish piece of the fabric matching the part where the hole is, then cut round the edges of the different parts of the design as far as possible, leaving a turning of about $\frac{1}{8}$ inch. Place over the damaged part and tack finely and plentifully so that the patch does not move. Now begin to fell on the patch all round, turning in the raw edges bit by bit as you do so, and changing the colour of the sewing silk as the colour of the pattern changes.

Another way, instead of felling the edges, is to cut them off close to the design and then to work fine satin stitch over the raw edges with matching silk.

CARE OF COAT LINING

If a coat lining is soiled it is a good plan to remove it and wash it; and when it is at the same time outworn it should be replaced by a new one—probably an old frock of rayon, crêpe-de-chine, or thin silk would provide the material. If you find that you have not sufficient of one material a second one may be used for the sleeves, or perhaps for the lower parts of them, where it will not show. The new lining should be cut from the old one and inserted as described in Chapter XIX. But while the coat is without lining it is a good opportunity to brush it well, inside and out, and to sponge it all over with cleanser. Necessary repairs should also

CARE AND REPAIR OF CLOTHES

be made, and the coat then pressed according to rules given in Chapter XV. If the padding round the armholes and on the shoulders has worn thin it may be renewed or added to with extra layers cut to the original shape, tacking these lightly into place and then fraying out the edges with the opened points of the scissors. When it is desired to build up the shoulders, pads should be bought or made and inserted, after which the lining should be sewn in as described in Chapter XIX.

TO REMOVE BAGGINESS

A cloth skirt is liable in course of wear to develop a bulge at either back or front, or both. Run a circle very finely with silk, large enough to enclose all the bagginess. Place this face downward on an ironing blanket and cover with a large piece of the same material as the skirt, or similar, which has been wrung out of water. Apply a hot iron all over the baggy part with a dabbing movement, not allowing it to stay long at each dab, but being sure that the whole area of the bagginess is touched by the iron. Allow the steam to escape, then repeat the process several times. Then remove the wet cloth and hold the iron over the exposed part very closely, but without touching it. When dry, if not sufficiently shrunken, repeat the treatment. Finally press with the iron, but take care not to stretch the material which has just been shrunk. Then turn to the right side and rub the part downward (particularly if there is a nap) with a piece of the same material—another part of the skirt will do.

If the side seams appear to be out of shape owing to stretching in wear, it is a good plan to unpick them and to straighten the fitting-lines with chalk and a long ruler, after which the seams should be re-stitched on the chalked lines and pressed. To help to keep either the front or back gore in shape cut a piece of strong lining the shape of the upper part of the gore, and reaching below the area of the former bulge. Hem the lower edge lightly or notch the raw edge, then fell in the turned-in edges at the waist and down the seam turnings.

TO REPAIR TORN INVERTED PLEATS

Sometimes inverted pleats in a skirt seam tear away at the top. Here is a remedy. Tack the pleats as they should be and press them. Take a piece of the same material, if you have any, otherwise velvet or silk of the same colour will serve. Cut a triangle in canvas, each side measuring not more than 1½ inches. Place this on a piece of the chosen material, turn back the edges, tack, and press them. Then machine as shown in Fig. 176. Press again, then tack over the top of the seam opening and slip stitch neatly

Fig. 176.—Repairing Torn Inverted Pleat.

CARE AND REPAIR OF CLOTHES

into place. If untidy at the back, face the damaged part with a triangle of lining.

GARMENTS OF THIN MATERIALS

These, when tumbled and crushed, look a sorry sight; but discretion is needed in pressing, and only a light iron and moderate heat should be employed. It is really better to try steaming before pressing. Place the garment on a coat hanger in a steamy bathroom and leave for several hours. After this you will probably find that all creases and crinkles have smoothed out—if not, you can then go over the frock lightly with a moderate iron. But remember that after either steaming or pressing a garment should be allowed to dry very thoroughly or it will crease at once, more deeply than before.

STORING CLOTHES

As a rule clothes are better hung than folded, and they should be placed on padded hangers, while if not in general wear, or delicate in colour, they should be covered. Old nightdresses make good covers as the lower edges may be buttoned together or fastened with press studs. When special sizes are needed they may be made from old sheets or tablecloths. Full sleeves should be stuffed with tissue paper. A frock with frilled skirt should be hung upside down so that the frills fall over, as then they will look fresher when worn. Hang a lavender bag in each garment for moth prevention. There are many good moth preventives, but generally their smell is both unpleasant and clinging.

Furs

These are best stored in special moth-proof bags; failing these, newspapers may be stitched up into bags with moth balls inside them, and then the edges of the paper should be pasted together to enclose the furs and exclude the air. Furs not so stored are best hung in a wardrobe and taken out daily for inspection, and also beaten with a cane in the open air very frequently. Valuable furs should be put into cold storage for the summer months.

Folding clothes

If you must store clothes in drawers because of lack of space, use the longest ones you have so as to avoid many folds in the garments. Any necessary folds should be arranged in such a position that if creases are formed they will be inconspicuous when the garment is worn. Keep the frock, etc., right side out, and make large rolls of tissue paper to extend large sleeves or draperies. Very soft frocks, such as those of lace, crinkly fabrics, and uncrushable velvet, may be stretched out to their full width, then rolled downward and laid like that in a drawer, inserting rolls of paper in any folds.

WARNING

It is most important, and it cannot be impressed too strongly, that on no account should any garments which are soiled, spotted, or damp be put away for even a few days, as it is such things which attract moths, and which they attack first. Washing frocks and blouses should be washed and rough-dried. The wardrobe, cupboard, or drawers should be free from dust and perfectly dry, and a moth preventive should be sprinkled in all corners. A cover (one made from an old sheet will serve) should be laid over the contents of any drawer.

MENDING

NOT VERY MANY years ago the mending of clothing and household linen was considered an art, equally as important as creating new garments and accessories. Although we have departed a long way in the opposite direction, we are now, strange as it seems, returning to the road that was, and are keenly interested and aware of the necessity and importance of the once-considered-wearisome tasks which our forbears had to do.

Under MENDING, one has to consider DARNING and PATCHING. DARNING is the strengthening or replacing of the worn or broken ends of fabric by weaving in thread with a needle, while PATCHING is fitting in a new piece of material to take the place of that which was either torn or worn away.

DARNING

Darning a Thin Woven Place

When only a few of the threads are worn, a darn will suffice, if the surrounding material is in good condition. Threads of the fabric drawn from hems or seams may be used—if possible use the warp or lengthwise threads, because often they are the stronger.

This darning is done on the right side with running stitches. (See Chapter 15.) Follow the weave of the material, putting in the weave of the warp or lengthwise grain first. Be sure to darn well beyond the thin places and do not draw threads tightly—this will allow for any strain or possible shrinkage—but do not have perceptible loops at the edges.

MENDING

After the warp threads have been rewoven, weave the crosswise or weft grain, closely following the weave of the fabric.

One of the most important phases in completing the darning of woollens is the steam pressing. Use a dampened, worn, Turkish towel and steam the darn on the right side, but do not allow the iron to rest in one spot. (See Chapter 3 on "Care of Fabrics.")

Darning Lost in the Nap or Pile of Woollens

This method may be used for making invisible darns or joins in cloth.

The darn is worked on the wrong side of the material, using a fine needle and strong fine thread instead of the thread drawn from the material. Linen or hair may be used, as hair is much stronger than any thread. The material is held over the left hand, as for hemming (see Chapter 15), with the edges together. Put in the needle about $\frac{1}{8}$ of an inch from the edge of the tear, in a slanting direction, and bring it out about $\frac{1}{8}$ of an inch on the other side of the tear, not letting the stitch show through on the right side, but more a surface stitch on the wrong side. Weave backwards and forwards in very close rows, allowing a little ease. If there are any broken threads, weave these in at the same time.

The hair will remain embedded in the material and the tear will be invisible after steam pressing and brushing the nap on the right side.

NOTE.—For all napped material steam on the wrong side with dampened, thin, Turkish towel.

Darning a Straight Tear

This is the kind of darn used to repair a rent in any material where the edges fit into one another. This may be either a lengthwise or crosswise tear. The broken threads must on no account be cut away, but should be worked in. As previously, use the warp threads, if possible, drawn from one of the seams or hem of the garment. Weave backwards and forwards, as in illustration, using running stitches, following the thread of the goods and bringing all loose ends through to the wrong side. The stitches should come well beyond the tear, the distance depending upon the material and the position of the tear on the garment.

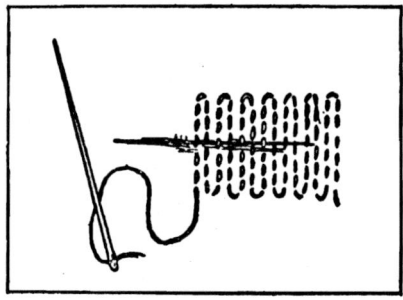

ILLUSTRATION 6

They should not be drawn tightly and there should not be any perceptible loop at each turning, unless new thread is being used.

Continue darning, following as near as possible the actual weave of the fabric until well past the tear.

> NOTE.—In some instances, one may have to use many small pieces of thread, especially for a tear in a woollen garment. This is no detriment. Just weave a little farther past the tear and leave a loose end.

Darning a Straight Tear with a Machine

Tack a piece of tracing or other similar paper on the wrong side of the fabric, being sure the two torn edges are close together. Loosen slightly the tension of the machine

MENDING

and work back and forth across the tear, the same as when darning by hand.

Darning a Diagonal Tear

A diagonal darn must have two sets of threads crossing each other, as both the lengthwise and crosswise threads are torn. (See Illustration 7.) The principle by which this is accomplished is the same as darning a straight tear. After one set of threads has been completed, weave another set of stitches at right angles to the first.

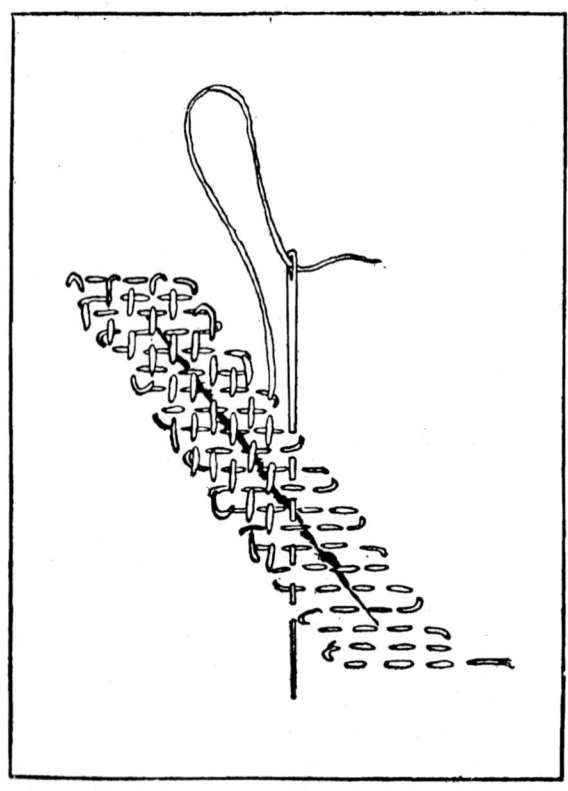

ILLUSTRATION 7

Darning a Three-cornered or "Barn-door" Tear

This is the same as two straight tears combined. After completing the lengthwise grain tear, weave the crosswise tear. The stitches at the corner will overlap and give added strength.

Darn and Patch Combined

The darn and patch combined is used especially for badly worn spots in woollen garments.

Baste a piece of material similar to the fabric, or one as near like it as possible, on the wrong side of the garment, allowing a good leeway past the worn spot. Work running stitches backward and forward on the thin spot, catching both fabrics.

PATCHING

When any portion of a garment is too worn to be darned, the worn spot must be cut out and replaced by another piece of fabric. It is very important that the piece of material match the fabric of the garment, in nature, weight, and colour. A new piece of material may be too heavy in comparison with the remainder of the article. Never use new material that hasn't been washed or cleaned; it is liable to shrink later. Fabric may be faded in the sun if necessary.

Hemmed Patch

A hemmed patch is the best to use for plain cottons, linens, and rayons.

Cut a square or a rectangle of the material for the patch, depending upon the shape of the worn portion, with the sides cut with the grain of the material, and sufficiently large so there will be 1 inch beyond the thin part.

Pin the patch on the wrong side of the garment, the right side of the patch to the wrong side of the garment, the threads of both matching, and the worn portion in the centre of the patch. Baste the patch into position.

Following the threads, cut away the weakened material about the hole until a square or rectangle is made. Mitre the corners by making a tiny diagonal cut $\frac{1}{8}$ to $\frac{1}{4}$ of an inch

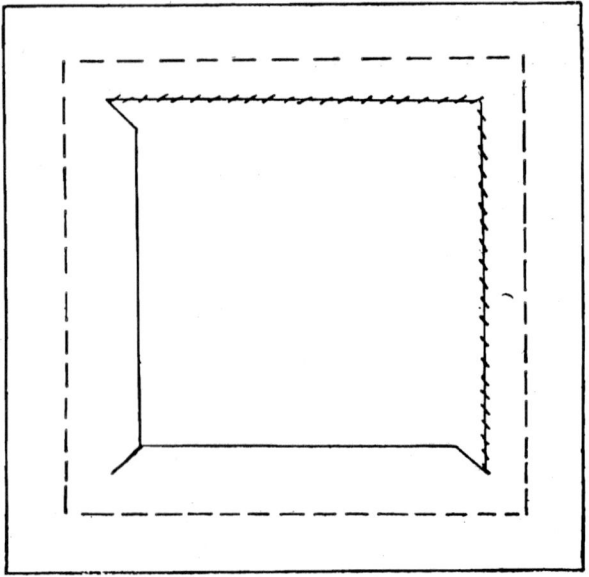

ILLUSTRATION 8

deep. Turn under the four sides and baste to the patch, making all the sides equidistant from the sides of the patch.

Turn to the wrong side of the garment, turn under and baste the raw edges of the patch.

The edges of the patch may be sewn on the machine, but hand hemming is advisable for old or thin material, the needle and thread suited to the weight of the fabric.

If the patch is to be completed by hand, hem the right side first, adding two or three extra stitches for strength at the corners.

Top Sewing a Patch

This type of patch is suitable for all materials except woollens, especially where there is a stripe or design to match.

It is placed on the right side of the garment so the design

ILLUSTRATION 9

or stripes of the patch exactly match those of the garment. (See Illustration 9.) Cut the patch as for hemmed patch, covering the worn portion, and place it on the right side. Pin the patch in place and baste in position.

NOTE.—If the patch is to be completed by hand, seam or overhand the patch and garment together, holding the patch toward the worker to make a flat seam.

MENDING

Turn to the back and cut away the material around the worn place as for hemmed patch.

The seam may now be flattened as in Illustration 10, and the eight edges overcast, or the raw edges may be blanket-stitched or overcast together, or the raw edges may be turned under and hemmed to the garment.

Darned Woollen Patch

The patch is placed at the back of the worn portion, the

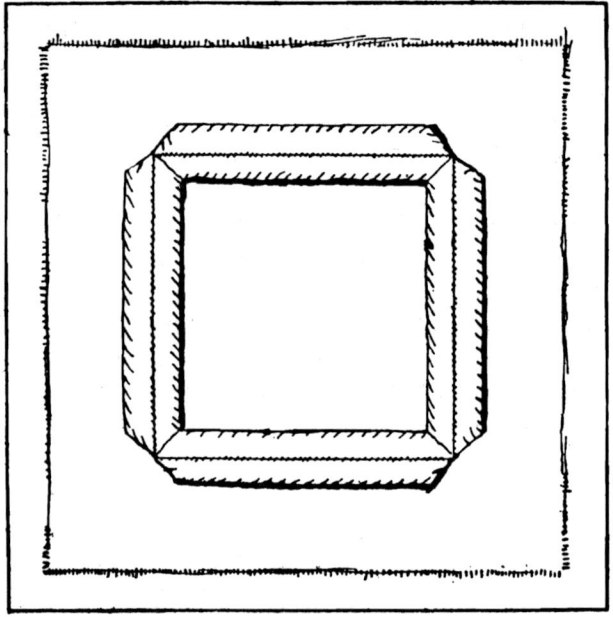

ILLUSTRATION 10

same as the hemmed patch, but the corners are not mitred nor the raw edges turned in.

Each of the four front edges is darned as for a straight tear, with the stitches overlapping at the four corners.

Finish the back of the patch with overcast stitches and

steam on the right side using dampened cloth and iron, or steam iron.

REPAIRING KNITTED ARTICLES

Darning a Thin Knitted Place

When the loops of a knitted article are not actually torn, but have been worn thin, the weak stitches may be strengthened by new stitches worked exactly over the worn ones.

Be sure the darning or worsted needle is not too large, or it will tear the threads, nor the thread too heavy. Naturally, it should match the fabric to be strengthened, in nature and colour.

This darning is done on the right side, starting well beyond a worn spot. Bring the needle through from the back to the front, between a knit stitch, leaving an end of yarn on the wrong side to be woven in later. Follow the actual outlines of the knit stitch, inserting the needle and taking up two horizontal threads, first up and then down, working over the knit stitches. For the second row, turn the work upside down and again work from right to left, following the outlines of the stitch. Continue in this manner until a square or rectangle of darned knit stitches has been formed.

Knitted Patch

When the knitted loops are torn, the stitches that are damaged must be replaced by new ones.

As in the case of a woven patch, a square or rectangle is made beyond the torn or worn stitches. This requires care. The horizontal loops at the top and bottom edge of the hole must not be cut, but the threads pulled out and from 2 to 4 loops disengaged on either side, so the vertical loops may be turned back in a straight line on the wrong side, where they are sewn in place. (See Illustration 11.)

MENDING

In a knitted patch, the actual patch has to be knitted on to the garment. Working on the right side, pick up the stitches at the bottom of the hole—put the needle in from the back so as not to cross the stitches—attach the yarn, and using the loose end with the yarn, knit four or five

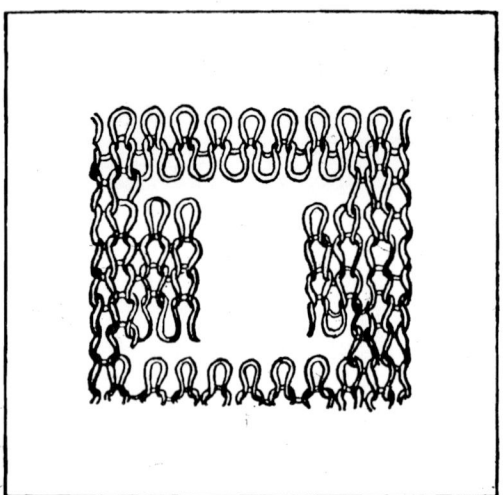

ILLUSTRATION 11

stitches. Continue working stockinette stitches; that is, knit one row, purl one row, for the necessary length of patch, ending with a purled row.

Place the loops on the top of the hole on another needle, then weave the stitches on the two needles together by the following method:

1. Pass the needle through the first stitch on the front needle as if to knit, draw the yarn through, then slip the stitch from the needle.

2. Pass the needle through the second stitch on the front needle as if to purl, draw the yarn through, but leave the stitch on the needle.

3. Pass the needle through the first stitch on the back needle as if to purl, draw the yarn through, then slip the stitch from the needle.

4. Pass the needle through the second stitch on the back needle as if to knit, draw the yarn through, but leave the stitch on the needle.

Repeat these four steps until the stitches on both needles have been used.

> NOTE.—Do not draw the yarn too tight nor have it too loose. The joining should look like a continuation of the fabric.

Sew the two sides together on the wrong side.

Snag on a Sweater or other Knitted Article

If the yarn isn't broken try to ease the knit stitches back into place without breaking the yarn. If the thread is broken, the two pieces will have to be joined together as explained for Knitted Patch. Use the actual broken thread to graft or weave the loops together if no other thread is available.

Mending Stockings

Darn stockings on the right side, using thread the same colour and nature as the hose, and a fine needle. A larger needle will pierce the stocking and make bigger holes. For runs and split seams, use small overhand stitches.

REMODELLING AND RENOVATING

NEEDLES AND PINS, threads, a sewing machine, a tape measure, scissors, a foundation or commercial pattern, and perhaps a replica of one's own figure, as well as materials, old and new, can do wonders towards maintaining a happy disposition.

"To a woman, the consciousness of being well-dressed gives a sense of tranquillity which religion fails to bestow."

MRS. HELEN BELL
(quoted in Emerson's letters)

American women are considered the best-dressed women in the world, but in many instances they have to develop that ingrained something which European women seem to have from birth. The utilization of every scrap of material, whether old or new, is second nature with them. Nothing is thrown away unless every last ounce of good has been extracted. There is much satisfaction from taking a garment that has been discarded and remaking it into a beautiful creation of which one can justly be proud. It is the joy of creating, the same thrill that comes to an artist when he has completed an inspiration. For no matter how simple the blouse, if one has put her best into its making, the same uplift is there.

There is often good service left in discarded garments or in the material of which they are made, so before one plans to buy clothes for any member of the family, take an inventory of the clothes closet. This is sure to produce garments that have not been worn for some considerable

REMODELLING AND RENOVATING

time; old suits and coats, dresses out of style, dad's shirts worn at the collars, and a dozen other garments needing that special attention, waiting like a butterfly to come out of its chrysalis and appear in all its glory.

It should be understood that remodelling doesn't necessarily mean that the whole garment has to be made over. According to Webster, remodelling is "to model or fashion anew," while renovating means "to make new" or "to restore to freshness and vigour."

The question is, why haven't these garments been worn? Clothing which is satisfactory as to styling, fit and colour is never discarded unless in need of cleaning and repair.

Let us break this down a little further and see what might be done.

The garment may be any of the following:

1. Ill-fitting at any or several of the following places: armscye, shoulder line, bust, waist, hips, neckline, sleeves, length of skirt, etc.
2. Worn in certain places, or have spots or stains which can or cannot be removed.
3. Material stretched out of shape so that the garment persistently hangs badly.
4. Colour not suited to the individual, and the design and interest not suited to her personality.
5. Out of style.
6. Broken or pulled seams.

Let us assume that the garment is a ready-to-wear and therefore there are no scraps. Naturally, one doesn't encounter the same difficulty if the garment was made at home or if it was dressmaker made. The material is good and the colour is becoming. The difficulty lies in the fit.

Fitting is not altering, it is an adjustment of the garment to your figure.

Is the style of the garment one that demands snug, easy

or loose fitting? Garments of cloth should generally fit snugly, except where the style warrants loose fitting. Silk and rayon dresses are fitted looser than cloth, and all transparent fabrics should be fitted looser still.

We will take some of the fitting problems in turn.

1. What can be done with uncomfortable shoulders?

The shoulder seam should be a ruled line directly on top of the shoulder. On a round-shouldered figure, however, it may be placed slightly to the back. (See Chapter 5 on "Measurements for Shoulder Line.") Unless the shoulders are fitted correctly, the garment will never be comfortable.

The Slant of the Shoulder

The slant of the shoulder varies with individual needs. In the garment it may be too square or too tapering. The shoulder line may be too long or too short. This is where a foundation pattern would be very useful. (See Chapter 9 on "Patterns.")

Directions for Re-fitting

Put on the waist or dress with the right side outside and centre front and the centre back exactly in the centre of the figure. Stand in a normal position. It is important that the grain of the material run straight across the chest, straight across the bust, straight across the back, and straight up and down. Before noting where any adjustments are to be made, smooth, not strain, the material into place.

So that the garment will not slide down the centre front and back, pin it to an undergarment or to your own dress form. It is advisable to pin it on the crosswise grain of the material so that there will be no possibility of stretching the material out of shape.

Shoulder too tapering; that is, too much depth.

1. If only a slight alteration is necessary.

REMODELLING AND RENOVATING

If the length of the shoulder seam is correct, but the shoulder line is a little too tapering, rip the shoulder seam not quite to the armscye, at least not to begin with.

Now fold the front shoulder under to the desired position of the shoulder seam line, and lap it over the extra material at the back shoulder seam line, being sure there is no strain across the front or at the shoulder. If there is, it may be necessary to refit the armhole.

2. If the shoulder depth is great.

If the shoulder line is much too tapering, it may not be altered satisfactorily unless the back of the garment is wide enought to lift the armscye and straighten the grain with a centre back dart.

Shoulder line too square; that is, not deep enough.

1. If only a slight alteration is necessary, rip the shoulder seam and adjust at the neck edge.

2. If considerable adjusting is necessary, this may be done only if the shoulder-line, neck-base intersection to waist measurement is long enough.

Rip the shoulder seam and the upper part of the cap of the sleeve. Again fold the front under to the desired position of the shoulder seam as in Diagram 56, and lap it over the extra material at the back shoulder seam, being sure there is no strain. Pin into position. If much alteration is necessary the armscye may have to be fitted out too, also some of the depth slashed from the cap of the sleeve.

To Reshape the Armscye

Never cut out the armscye without marking it first. Find the end of the shoulder bone and place a pin on the armscye line. Then take a tape measure and place it over the shoulder so that it marks the curve of the upper half of the armscye, front and back. (See Illustration 25.)

The underarm curve will be thrown out of place if one tries to pin it, so let the crease made by swinging the arms

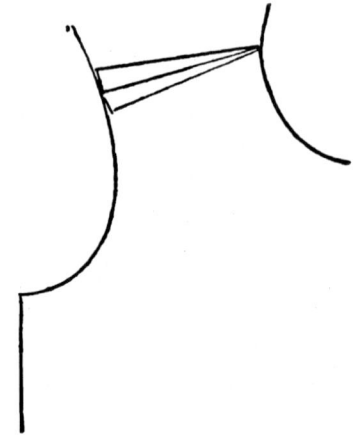

DIAGRAM 56

be your guide. Slash the underarm of armscye, remembering seam allowances.

To Reshape the Cap of the Sleeve

It is advisable to take out the sleeve if the cap has to be altered. (See "Caps of Sleeves" in "Pattern Drafting," Chapter 9.)

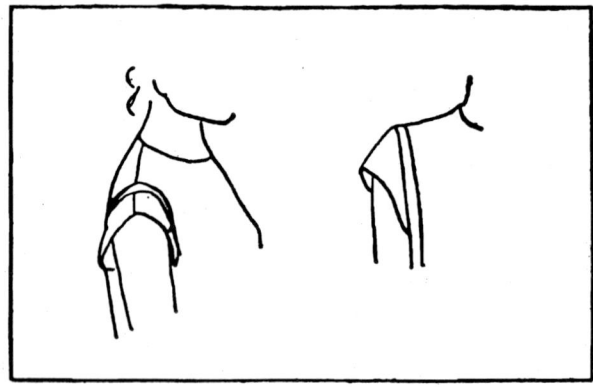

ILLUSTRATION 25

REMODELLING AND RENOVATING

Shoulder Line Too Short

This is one of the hardest offenders to rectify. Here we have a lack of material.

It may be necessary to insert pieces of material taken from the hem of the garment or the inside of belt, etc., add insertion or use other devices to broaden the shoulder line.

It may be possible that there is extra fullness incorporated in gathers, shirring, tucks, etc.

There may also be a good allowance at the armscye seam, or there may be shoulder darts which might be opened to give added width.

Each garment will have its own particular problem which can be solved with a little ingenuity.

Shoulder Line Too Long

When the shoulder line is too long it hangs down over the shoulder giving the wearer a very sloppy appearance. This may be corrected in many ways, depending upon the type of garment, the amount to be fitted out, the needs of the individual figure, and the length of the cap of the sleeve.

1. Take out the sleeve and reshape the armscye as stated previously. It may not be necessary to change the underarm curve. Be sure to check for strain across the back.

Measure the necessary depth of the cap. (See Chapter 5 on "Measurements.") It may not be necessary to lengthen the cap of the sleeve, but if it is, the depth cut from around the armhole, front and back, would generally be the amount that would have to be added to the top. This would necessitate the changing of the type of sleeve, because the cap would have to be made deeper by cutting out the upper part of the sleeve. (See Illustration 26.)

2. Rip the shoulder seam, and for soft material, shirr the front and ease in the back to the correct length of the shoulder

line, the shirring to be carried down to nearly ½ the depth of the armscye.

3. For a person with a full bust and narrow shoulders,

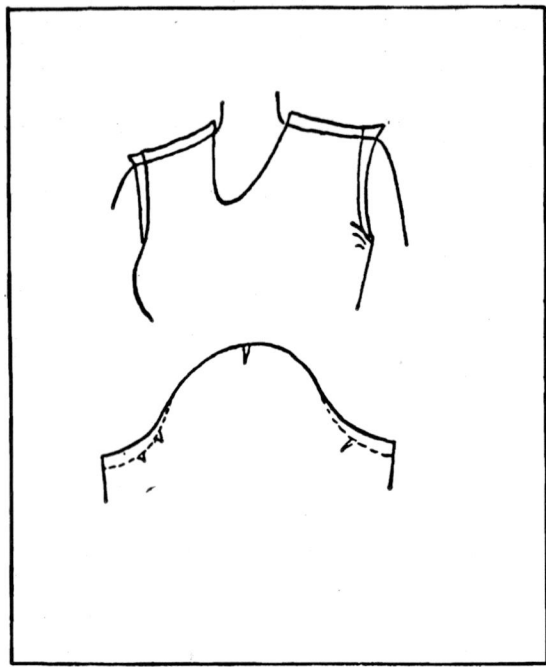

ILLUSTRATION 26

rip the shoulder seam, and make a shoulder dart in the front, and at the back; cut out the upper part of the armscye as in number 1, or make centre back neck darts if necessary. The neckline may also have to be refitted.

4. For tailored clothes, rip the shoulder seam and darts, and alter where necessary.

NOTE.—

1. In each of the last three cases, it may also be necessary to lengthen the cap of the sleeve as in number 1.

REMODELLING AND RENOVATING

2. It is always advisable to recheck the basted alterations when the figure is seated, to assure enough ease over the shoulder bones.

ALTERATIONS AT THE NECK

Alteration of Shoulder Line for Long Thin Neck

Diagonal wrinkles will run from the armhole toward the neckline. (See Illustration 27.)

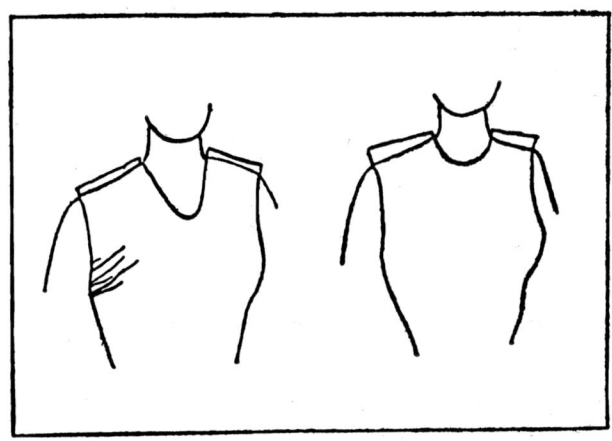

ILLUSTRATION 27

Rip the shoulder seam and take out the sleeves. Smooth the material up toward the shoulder. It may be necessary to alter both the front and back shoulder seam lines the same amount; or the amount taken up may be different. This changes the size of the armhole at the upper portion.

The armscye line should be checked and altered if necessary, and the top of the cap of the sleeve should be changed, as explained under "Shoulder Line too Square."

Poorly Fitting Necklines

1. If the dress is too wide across the back and draws

across the chest in front, the excess fullness is fitted out by means of tucks or small darts at the centre back. This will make the back of the neck smaller and shorten the shoulder seam over the arm.

NOTE.—Be careful that the grain isn't drawn out of line.

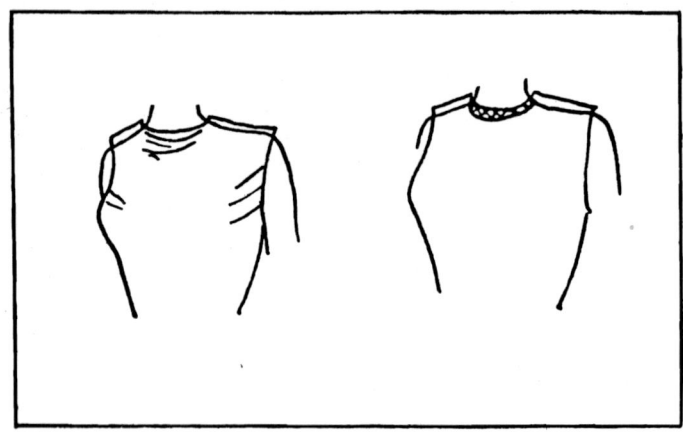

ILLUSTRATION 28

2. If there is a large unbecoming neckline in front, see if it isn't possible to put in a front neck dart, change the neckline, or wear a vestee or jabot to cover it.

SHOULDER LINE FOR SQUARE SHOULDERS

If a person has square shoulders, the garment may draw across the front in diagonal wrinkles, and there will also be wrinkles at the neck. (See Illustration 28.)

First clip the neckline to ease out the neck wrinkles. Rip the shoulder seam and smooth out the front, then adjust the shoulder seams, as explained previously. It may also be necessary to alter the armscye and the cap of the sleeve.

REMODELLING AND RENOVATING

SLEEVES

After fitting the garment and learning where the sleeve errs, rip out the sleeve from the armscye, and also the sleeve seam, using a razor blade.

1. Sleeves are Too Tight

The upper part of the sleeve in ready-to-wears is often too tight for a figure with a large upperarm.

(a) If the seam allowance is large enough, restitch the sleeve seam, making sure a sufficiently wide seam remains, so there is no chance of a split or pulled seam.

(b) Set a strip or gusset into the sleeve seam, using a piece of material from the belt or hem.

(c) Add a shirred or tucked strip through the centre, starting from the top of the cap, the piece to be taken from the belt or hem.

(d) Make short, or ¾-length sleeves (becoming to a person with a full arm) from long sleeves, using the extra material to add a strip for widening or for a gusset.

(e) Put in an entirely new sleeve of contrasting colour or texture.

(See Chapter 9 on "Drafting Patterns"—"Sleeves.")

2. Armscye Too Tight

Read about the shaping of the armscye under "Shoulder Line too Square" (page 215). Check the bust and back width, and the underarm to waist length before altering. If the sleeve draws across the upper arm, the under portion of the armhole is too high. Rip the sleeve and reshape the armscye and the cap of the sleeve to correspond.

3. Cap of Sleeve Too Narrow

If a cap fits tight around the upper part of the arm, and the garment appears to draw at the front and back, the cap of the sleeve is too narrow.

(a) Add a strip down the centre as for long sleeves.

(*b*) If sleeves are sufficiently wide, cut new short or ¾-length sleeves, and a new wider cap.

> NOTE.—It is impossible to alter tailored sleeves if the lower part of the sleeve is too narrow.

4. Cap of Sleeve Too Wide

This is readily adjusted. Rip the armscye and adjust in the fitting or recut from the foundation pattern. Be careful of the grain. It must be straight, lengthwise, from shoulder tip, and straight across, parallel to the floor. (See Diagram 2.)

5. Sleeve Cut on the Wrong Grain

If a sleeve is uncomfortable and twists on the arm, it is very probable that it is cut off grain. Look at the material closely, and note whether the grain of the upper portion of the sleeve runs straight across and straight lengthwise from the shoulder tip.

The only remedy in this case is to put in a new sleeve of contrasting texture or colour.

> NOTE.—Some tight-fitting sleeves are cut on the true bias, but they will "give."

6. Length of Sleeve

(*a*) To Make Short Sleeves from Long

Cut off the sleeve at the elbow, then turn under the desired amount suitable for individual needs. Pin into position and check for necessary length. Cut off an equal amount from the other sleeve, then baste and press, making the hems the desired width.

Three-quarter-length sleeves may be altered in the same way.

If a more fitted sleeve is desired, cut out the excess in the sleeve seam.

(*b*) To Shorten Coat Sleeves either because of the length or because the cuff is slightly frayed

Rip the lining free from the material at the bottom of the

sleeve, using a razor blade, take out any hems, and steam press. Fit the coat for the necessary length and pin. Turn the hem and steam press, cutting away any material that is not required. Two inches is ample, but less will suffice if the sleeve was worn. Catch the sleeve lining to the seam in several places. Next pin and baste the lining to the sleeve at several points about ¾ of an inch above the hem to keep the lining in position. A rayon lining should not fit tightly. Baste the hem of the lining and slip stitch it to the sleeve edge about ½ an inch from the bottom.

Armscye Too Loose

A dress may bulge at the armscye in front or it may be too large all around.

When a dress bulges at the front curve of the armscye, it is usually on a figure with a full bust.

Rip the lower portion of the front armscye and the underarm seam. Slightly smooth the material over the bust and pin in an underarm dart. The front armscye will now be deeper than the back. Material from hem or belt will have to be used to build up the front.

Armscye Too Deep or Dress is Worn Under the Arm

A too deep armscye may be remedied, provided the sleeves are full and long.

Rip the sleeve and, before altering the cap, measure the necessary length and width of the cap for alteration. (See Chapter 9 on "Pattern Drafting"—"Caps of Sleeves.") Now reshape the cap, and with the piece reversed, fit a patch into the underarm.

If necessary, reshape the shoulders as suggested previously.

NOTE.—The original cap may not be too deep. Be sure it is long enough so that it doesn't send the grain askew. If no adjustment can be made at the cap, a piece of material might be taken from the length of the sleeve, then a band of trimming added, or the sleeve might be changed to a short or ¾ sleeve.

This is also applicable if the underarm is worn out both at the sleeve and in body of the garment. Patches or gussets may be applied.

If the garment warrants it, either a raglan or a dolman cut would remove worn portions; then sleeves of contrasting material could be made, repeating the fabric either on welts of pockets, the belt, or applied vestee.

Waist Too Tight Across the Back

1. Check for large seam allowances at the armscye and centre back, but be sure there will be no strain if ripped.

2. If there is any material from the belt or hem, insert a piece down the centre back to widen. This might be necessary for a round-shouldered person, then add darts at the neck centre back.

Waist Too Tight Through the Bust

Check the seams at the underarm, and darts, shirrs or gathers for any allowance which might be used. Or add bands or vestee of contrasting colour down the front.

ALTERATIONS IN LENGTH OF SKIRT

Before any adjustments are made, consider the correct length for individual requirements. Very short and very tall figures have the greatest difficulty with ready-to-wears.

Ask these questions: Does the skirt allow for freedom of movement? Does it draw when I sit down? Can I step easily? Is the hemline even at the bottom?

REMODELLING AND RENOVATING

A skirt may appear to hang perfectly when it is first worn, then gradually it dips at one place or another. In the cheaper ready-to-wears, the amount of material used, rather than the correct position of the grain, is paramount.

Skirt Too Short

For a tall figure, add a border at the bottom, or it may be possible, if the waist to hip measurement is a little wide, to drop the skirt and make a short yoke from pieces taken from

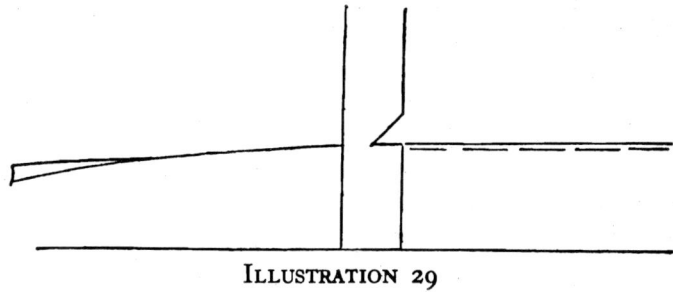

ILLUSTRATION 29

the belt, or of contrasting material, adding some of the same material to the yoke of the upper garment.

To Alter a Dress Hem

Rip the hem and press out the seam crease. Keep the binding, if any, to use again.

Put on the skirt, stand on a wide stool or table, and have someone mark the desired length of skirt from the floor. Use a yard stick and mark the length at intervals with pins parallel to the floor. Fold the fabric at the pin line for the hem and fasten with pins placed at right angles to the hem. Baste close to the fold, then remove the pins, and press on the wrong side according to type of material. Use a gauge as in Illustration 29 to mark the desired width, then trim the edges, and hem or sew on the binding.

There is also a commercial skirt marker which one may

use. The marker is set at the desired height from the floor, and by means of a contraption the skirt can be marked at intervals. However, if one has no one to assist, she can mark her own hemline by the following method :—

Wear the skirt and stand near a table. With a piece of tailor's chalk, being careful that all marks are parallel to the floor, mark around the skirt at the height of the table. It is above the markings where the alterations in the length of the skirt are to be made.

Take off the garment, and from this line, at very close intervals, measure the desired length. Complete the hem as stated previously.

Skirts Too Tight Through the Hips and Waist

(See Chapter 9 on "Pattern Drafting of Skirts" for necessary waist and hip allowances.)

No skirt should be the actual hip measurement, and no tight-fitting garment at the waist (back) should be worn by a person with a sway back.

1. The easiest way to remedy either a too tight waist or hip is to be able to take out the seams, and adjust by fitting.

2. Let out the hem and raise the skirt until the necessary allowance is added at the hip for that particular type of skirt. Adjust the hem.

If there is no hem allowance, finish the bottom with a border or a binding and repeat the design somewhere in the waist, across the yoke, or down the front, etc.

3. For a short figure, where there is no extra material at the hem, add a panel down the front of contrasting material or colour for a redingote effect and repeat this line in a vestee or bands down the front.

Often a ready-to-wear does not need any serious alteration, but it is over-elaborate or has too much detail, in which case

REMODELLING AND RENOVATING

perhaps some of the flowers, bows or buttons may be eliminated. Or the collar is the wrong shape for one's face. The best features of the wearer are those to emphasize. Note some of the garments in the better magazines. These will give you some good pointers. Learn to be critical. Keep your eyes wide open.

REMODELLING THE ENTIRE GARMENT

GENERAL directions for discarded garments have been considered. Now we shall discuss how one may make over garments in their entirety.

Some may be remodelled solely from one garment, or the material from two garments may be utilized, or we might require a small amount of new material to make sleeves or a vestee, or to use for trimming. We might also unravel yarn and knit new sleeves or the whole front of a jacket.

Let us consider coats and suits.

Is it worth one's time and effort to remodel a "grown-up" coat, or change a man's suit into one for the small son or for one's self?

There are several angles to be considered, the first of which is the condition of the material. How badly is the garment worn? Am I able to buy material of similar quality to-day, and for what price? If I remake the garment will it last two years without worn places?

A garment with fewer but larger pieces is better for our purpose than one made up of many small sections. Then again the material might be turned to the wrong side to hide any pronounced defects.

Having decided that the material is worth the labour, inspect the fabric for worn or faded spots or stains which will not disappear with cleaning. Decide which side of the material to use. Patch pockets, bands, etc., leave a lighter shade when removed.

Preparation of the Material

It is better to rip the entire garment apart, if at all possible. This, of course, depends upon several factors.

REMODELLING THE ENTIRE GARMENT

(*a*) Is the material in the used garment sufficient without having to resort to the use of the old lapels, etc.?

(*b*) Would the making of the garment be simpler if some of the tailoring were kept intact?

(*c*) Would the cutting out of the new pattern be more complicated if one tried to adhere to some of the previous lines?

Personally, I consider that ripping the entire garment and starting from scratch is much more simple than trying to adjust some of the pieces.

For ripping a garment, use a safety-razor blade and remove all threads. Clean the material according to the correct method for the particular fabric. (See Chapter 3 on "Care of Fabrics and Garments.") It isn't necessary nor better to send the garment to the cleaners. This adds to the expense; besides, after the garment is ripped the seam lines are left. Whereas, if the pieces are washed at home with care, and the garment has full seams, more material may be utilized.

If wool, steam press the pieces perfectly flat on the side to be used as the wrong side.

The Importance of the Grain of the Material

Read Chapter 6 on "Grains of Material."

The same principles must be followed when using reused material as when making a garment from a new piece of fabric.

It is advisable to mark both the lengthwise and crosswise grain of each piece with a basting thread and leave the threads in the material until the garment is completed. This will help you to keep on the grain while you cut, and also prevent the fabric from pulling off grain while fitting. Remember, a garment is never satisfactory if it is cut wrong on the grain. It is better to have a narrower coat or skirt.

Choosing a Suitable Pattern

Choosing a suitable pattern is where a knowledge of

pattern drafting may be used to good advantage; for this is where it is necessary to cut one's coat according to the amount of cloth on hand; one may encounter difficulties when using a commercial pattern especially if one isn't sure of how to make changes in width and length. Of course, a reliable commercial pattern of good design, basically simple, of a style suited both to the material and the use, can be used if one is able to cut it from the sections. Of course, the material may be pieced, but avoid conspicuous piecing wherever possible.

POSSIBILITIES OF A MAN'S TAILORED SUIT

Naturally, one can do more with a suit with two pairs of trousers, either when repairing or entirely making over. It is advisable not to rip a man's suit if there is any possibility of either you or a tailor being able to renovate it.

1. "A stitch in time saves nine." How true! If there are thin spots at the knees or elbows, a darn to reinforce the spot, using thread drawn from a seam of the garment, will be practically invisible. It is advisable, where possible, to follow the weave of the material. (See Chapter 4 on "Mending.")

2. If the bottoms of the sleeves or the trousers are frayed, turn new hems to remedy. Be sure to allow sufficient material, so the hems stay in place. Half an inch in the sleeve or trouser length will scarcely make any appreciable difference.

3. Reinforce buttonholes where necessary.

4. If the coat is broken through at the elbows, replace the under section of the sleeve with a new section cut from the extra pair of trousers.

REMODELLING A MAN'S SUIT WITH ONE PAIR OF TROUSERS

Suit for an Older Boy

Before ripping the entire suit, study the pattern sections. It may be necessary to use the lapels as they are. Rip the

REMODELLING THE ENTIRE GARMENT

Illustration 30

shoulder seams and collar, also the sleeves, but don't rip the two front sections until certain the lapels have not to be used.

Naturally, if the two front sections have to be used as they are, the pockets will require some consideration. It is possible to place a patch pocket over the slash made from a welt pocket, and so adjust the position of the pocket. Also, the right side of the material will have to be used.

The previous instructions with regard to the treatment of the material, the consideration of the pattern pieces and the grain of the material are applicable in all cases.

ILLUSTRATION 31

The original canvas interfacing may be used to line the lapels, also the original tape, if the whole garment was ripped.

As the size and style of the suit one wishes to make vary with individual needs, no two garments will be placed exactly the same on the pieces.

NOTE.—Take care of the larger, more important sections of the pattern first, the sections of the pattern for the

REMODELLING THE ENTIRE GARMENT

new garment matching sections of the old wherever possible. Pin all the sections on the material first, carefully watching the grain. Some of the smaller pieces may have to be pieced, but these can be made practically inconspicuous if the grain is matched, and the seams pressed before using.

Complete the garment as stated in Chapter 14.

Small Boy's Suit

An English type collarless coat and short trousers with the drop front are the easiest for tailoring.

There will be material to spare; in fact, with some manœuvring one may obtain two pairs of trousers.

It is advisable to rip the entire suit and use the material on the wrong side.

Woman's Tailored Suit

Before deciding to make a woman's suit from a man's, there are several factors to be considered. If a suit with only one pair of trousers is to be used, the man must be larger than the woman, the style of garment she wishes to make must be suited to the material, and the lines resemble as nearly as possible the original suit.

Men's suits differ slightly as to styling. Generally, there's a seam down the back, two darts at the waist, and two side pockets and a breast pocket. Of course, if there are two pairs of trousers, much of the worry over fitting the material pieces to the pattern is eliminated.

The previous directions for ripping, preparing the material, and pattern suggestions apply equally well when making a woman's tailored suit from a man's woollen suit.

The lining might be made from a used silk or rayon dress, a discarded pair of silk pyjamas—if one is fortunate enough to possess such a luxury—or a silk or rayon housecoat.

ILLUSTRATION 32

REMODELLING THE ENTIRE GARMENT

Before using any used material for the lining, pull the fabric to determine its strength, hold up to the light to see if there are any weak spots. If pyjamas or housecoat are used, there will be sufficient material to make a matching blouse.

The original canvas interfacing may be used to line the lapel, also the original tape. If the canvas is too heavy, use muslin, which must be pre-shrunk before using—just wash the material and press while damp. It would also be advisable to wash the canvas, since that will give it added life.

One of the difficulties presented in remodelling a man's jacket is the fastening. However, material might be saved by piecing a strip, exactly on the grain, to cover the buttonholes. As this becomes the button, or left side, of a woman's coat, it is not discernible.

As was stated previously, if one is able to draft her own pattern, half the battle is won. Of course, a reliable commercial pattern is perfectly satisfactory, if one is able to cut it from the material.

When planning, follow as near as possible the sections of the man's jacket; that is, the front pattern sections for the woman's coat from the front of the jacket, and the back from the back. There will be no difficulty with a two-piece sleeve and the original facing for the lapels. (See Illustration 33.)

NOTE.—
1. It is not advisable to cut two similar pieces at once. One is apt to overlook a thin or worn spot, or the position of the pockets. However, be sure to change the side of the pattern when cutting the second section.
2. For further details about completing, see Chapter 14.

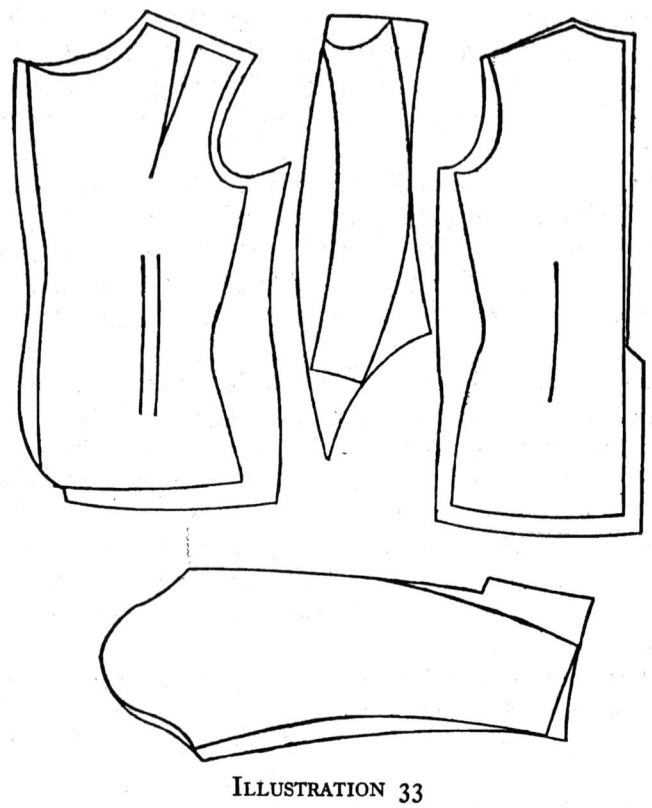

ILLUSTRATION 33

A Skirt

The type of skirt depends upon whether one pair or two pairs of trousers is available, and how much the suit is worn. A straight skirt with gored side seams, and straight seams at the centre front and back, and darts at the front side and the back side, with pleats added for more fullness at the centre front and back, or a four-gored skirt may be made from one pair of trousers. (See Illustration 34.)

From two pairs of trousers, a six- or eight-gored skirt may be cut.

REMODELLING THE ENTIRE GARMENT

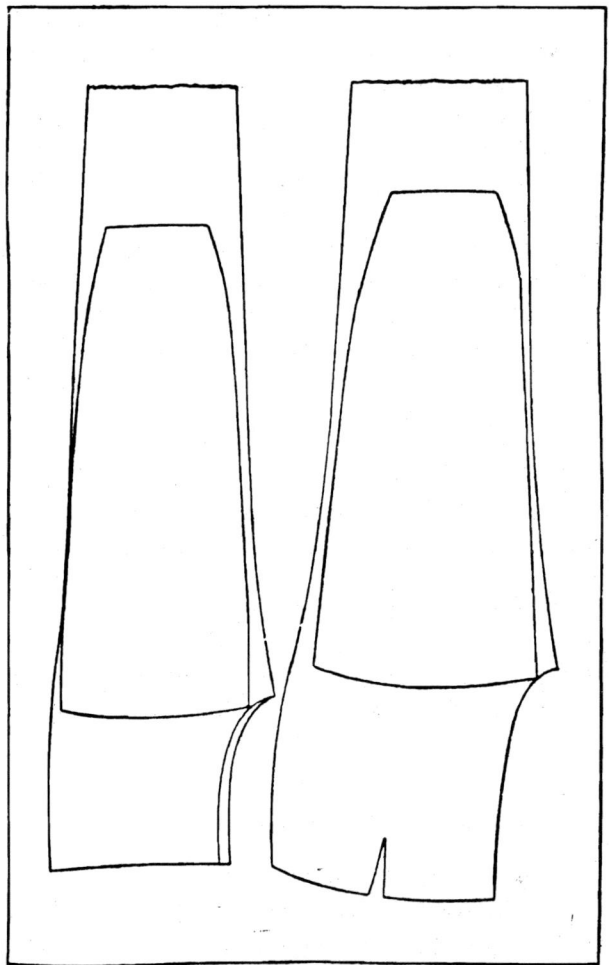

ILLUSTRATION 34

Since the seat is the widest part of the trousers, and when only one pair of trousers is available, place the top of the skirt toward the cuff and the bottom toward the seat.

When using two pairs of trousers, and especially if there

are any worn places, it is better to adjust the sections of the pattern to the material, sometimes the top of the skirt to the cuff, and sometimes the bottom. Of course, this depends upon the nature and nap of the material. It may not always be possible to do so.

Probably, too, the elbow of one of the sleeves is worn, then the undersection of a sleeve will have to be cut from a section of the trousers. Or the knee of the trousers may be thin. There are many eventualities. Always use your own judgment. There can be no set rules. Adjust the pieces of the pattern until the best result is obtained, then pin into position. The above illustration will aid when cutting out, but it isn't the only one.

A Girl's Dressmaker Suit

A suit for a small girl lends itself very readily to home dressmaking. There will be more than ample material.

Girl's or Woman's Slacks from a Pair of Trousers

In order to be able to cut a pair of woman's slacks from man's trousers, the man must be considerably larger than the woman; but there will be no difficulty for a girl's pair of slacks. (See Illustration 35.)

POSSIBILITIES OF A MAN'S OVERCOAT

Having decided that the overcoat is too worn to be repaired, consider what might be made with the material. A shorter coat for young son, as in Illustration 36, is an excellent suggestion.

Follow the general directions for making over a man's suit. Plan the front sections of the coat carefully, and if the pockets are not worn, the same ones might be utilized, or a new welt might be sewn on.

Draft the pattern or select a commercial pattern to suit.

REMODELLING THE ENTIRE GARMENT

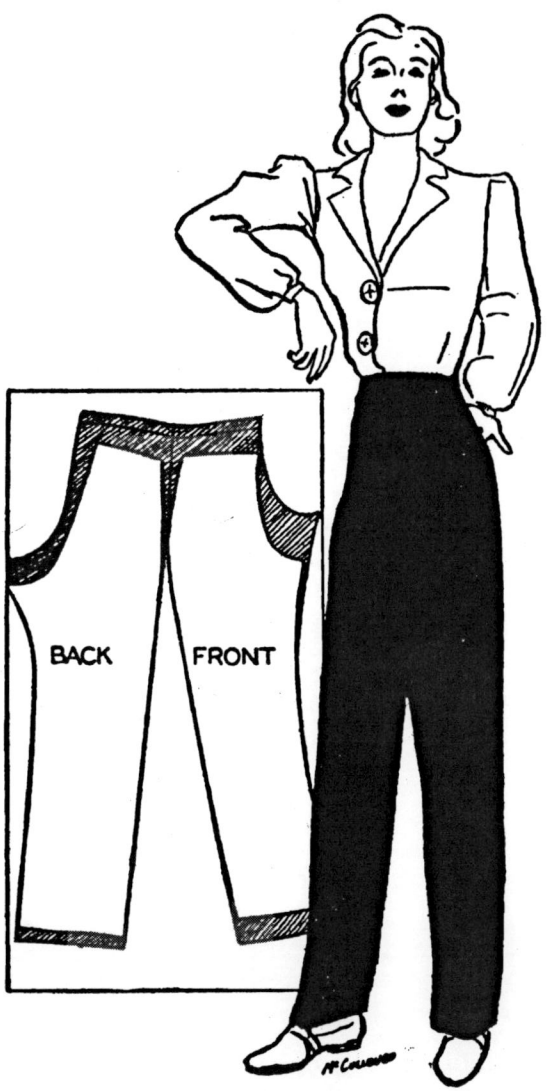

ILLUSTRATION 35

ILLUSTRATION 36

A Boy's or Girl's Topcoat

Rip the entire coat and prepare the pieces as before suggested. Use the original canvas. Choose or draft a simple but stylish-looking coat for either boy or girl and complete as in Chapter 14.

REMODELLING THE ENTIRE GARMENT

POSSIBILITIES OF A WOMAN'S COAT

The material in the coat is good, but it is very much out of date.

When planning the new design consider the style and the material. Look through fashion magazines for some inspirations. Could I cut a short coat to better advantage, or should I buy material for a skirt and make a jacket? Would it be better to combine the material with some other? In these days of mixed colour schemes this method can be very attractive. Could I use the old facing to give width to the new coat, adding sections from the underarm down, then use contrasting material for new facing? Would it be advisable to knit in sleeves, or knit the complete back?

Read the directions about making a woman's jacket from a man's. The general directions are the same; also turn to Chapter 9 on "Pattern Making"; it may assist you in your choice.

COMBINING RAVELLED YARN AND USED MATERIAL

There are many and very effective ways to combine materials and yarn, with either harmonious or contrasting colours used. A good-looking jacket with knitted sleeves is an asset to any wardrobe, and would look most intriguing with knitted mittens or gloves to match.

It is very simple to knit sleeves from a given pattern.

HOW TO KNIT A LONG SLEEVE FROM A PATTERN

NOTE.—A simple one-piece sleeve should be used.

1. Make a piece of fabric of the yarn, using stockinet stitch, in order to ascertain how many stitches there are to the inch in that particular fabric.

This is called taking a stitch gauge.

Cast on 20 to 30 stitches, depending upon the weight of

ILLUSTRATION 37

the yarn, and knit a piece of stockinette stitch about 2 inches wide. It is advisable to steam the piece of fabric—do not pin it—then, using a steel rule or a tape measure, and in the centre of the fabric, count the number of stitches to the inch. Count the ½ stitches where necessary; e.g., 5½ stitches to the inch.

2. Measure the width of the sleeve at the wrist and multiply it by the number of stitches to the inch. This gives the number of stitches to cast on at the wrist.

REMODELLING THE ENTIRE GARMENT

3. Decide what texture stitch will be appropriate with the material that is to be used for the rest of the jacket; it may be stockinette, ribbing, or any other texture stitch.

4. Measure the widest part of the sleeve and multiply the measurement by the stitch gauge. This gives the necessary number of stitches at this point.

5. Subtract the number of stitches required at the wrist from the necessary number of stitches for the upperarm. This gives the number of stitches to increase on both sides; $\frac{1}{2}$ the number on each side of the sleeve.

6. Divide the number of stitches, which have to be increased on each side of the sleeve, into the distance over which the increases have to be made, to learn where to increase.

7. The Cap of the Sleeve.

The direction follows after Knitted Sleeve Without a Drafted Pattern.

KNITTED SLEEVES WITHOUT A DRAFTED PATTERN*

Long Sleeves

FORMULA.

1. The wrist measurement plus 1 inch, or the measurement around the knuckles of the hand, × the stitch guage = the necessary number of stitches for the cuff, more to be added if desired.

2. Add 1 inch of stitches on the first row after the cuff is completed.

3. Upperarm measurement plus 2 inches × the stitch gauge = the necessary number of stitches for the width of the sleeve. ($1\frac{1}{2}$ inches added to the width for an average child.)

* Taken from *The Complete Book of Progressive Knitting* by Ida Riley Duncan, Liveright Publishing Corporation, 1940, p. 105.

4. Difference between the wrist stitches (after adding the extra inch of stitches) and the number of stitches necessary for the width of the sleeve = the number of times to increase on sides of sleeve.

5. Divide the number of times to increase into the distance over which increases have to be made to learn where to increase. (Should be completed between 3 and 4 inches below the armpit.)

6. After increasing the necessary number of stitches, knit even to the desired underarm length.

7. Number of stitches first bound off for the cap of the sleeve = the number of stitches bound off at the back and front underarms.

8. Knit 2 together at the beginning and end of every other row until the distance around the cap measures the same as the armhole.

9. The average length of cap for an adult is $5\frac{1}{2}$ inches from the first bind off.

10. Approximate number of stitches along the top of the cap equals 3 inches of stitches for an adult, 2 inches for an average child.

NOTE.—This is a fitted cap.

The completion of the cap of the sleeve depends upon the style of the garment and the needs of the individual. (See Chapter 9 on "Pattern Drafting"—"Sleeves.")

KNITTED FULL CAP GATHERED INTO THE UPPER
PORTION OF THE ARMHOLE

NOTE.—More width is added to the cap by changing the curve; this is accomplished in knitting by not decreasing so often.

1. As with the fitted cap, the number of stitches bound

REMODELLING THE ENTIRE GARMENT

off at the underarm corresponds to the start of the curve at the back underarm.

2. Instead of knitting 2 together at the beginning and end of every other row for the depth of the cap, knit 2 together at the beginning and end of every 4th row, until the desired depth of cap is reached, then knit 2 together across the remaining stitches, and bind off.

Note the depth of this cap will be longer than $5\frac{1}{2}$ inches, the depth depending upon how much fullness is desired.

KNITTED SLEEVES WITH DARTS AT THE SHOULDER

This type of cap must also have added width.

1. Bind off the number of stitches to correspond with the start of the curve at the back underarm, then knit 2 together at the beginning and end of every 4th row, until the actual depth for a fitted cap is reached—$5\frac{1}{2}$ inches.

The number of darts depends upon individual needs and the type of material. They should be even on each side of the shoulder seam, and, in knitting, may either be fitted out or darted out as when sewing. For the latter, continue as for a full cap, gathered, until you have the desired length of cap, probably 7 inches, then make darts at the desired places instead of gathering the top.

2. To fit out the fullness, decreases must be made at regular intervals.

If four darts are desired, two on each side of the shoulder seam, divide the number of stitches that remain after the actual depth for a fitted cap has been reached by five. This will mark the position of the four darts. Place markers at each of these four places, and knit 2 together, every other row, before the first two, and after the last two, until between 2 and 3 inches of stitches remain. If a wider top is desired, decrease every 4th row until the cap fits into the armhole.

KNITTED SLEEVE WITH BOXED TOP

(See "Caps and Sleeves" in Chapter 9 on "Pattern Drafting.")

This is the same as the cap with fitted-out darts, except, after binding off and knitting 2 together at the beginning and end of every 4th row for the depth of an ordinary cap, a square or rectangular effect at the shoulder is made.

For a square effect, divide the number of stitches that remain by 3. Bind off the first $\frac{1}{3}$ of the stitches, knit to the end of the row, turn, bind off a $\frac{1}{3}$ at the other end, then knit the centre until the length is equal to the stitches that were bound off.

If rectangular effect is desired, bind off less than $\frac{1}{3}$ on each side, and knit the centre stitches for the smaller length.

Sew the top of the sleeve.

To knit other types of sleeves, see "Sleeves in Pattern Drafting" (Chapter 9) and knit as explained for *Long Sleeves*.

If the front or back of a garment for an adult or a child is knitted as in Illustration 38, measure the shaping from the pattern pieces as suggested for the long sleeve. Make a stitch gauge, and if necessary draft a simple pattern. It is imperative that the pieces fit into the material pieces; these cannot be steamed to fit, as is often the case with knitted garments.

POSSIBILITIES OF USED SKIRTS

There is nothing like remodelling for exercising one's powers of ingenuity. Sometimes it is wise to spend a few minutes visualizing the effects one might achieve.

Skirts which are too small or worn in spots may possess just the right material for creating a chic waistcoat, a jerkin, or a bolero; or combined with another material or yarn of harmonious or contrasting colour or texture, a very be-

REMODELLING THE ENTIRE GARMENT

ILLUSTRATION 38

coming jacket. Any of the above are very stylish and will aid one to vary her wardrobe. (See Chapter 9 on "Pattern Drafting.")

POSSIBILITIES OF DISCARDED DRESSES

Don't discard anything that can be made over. A garment which is pulled at the seams, stretched out of shape, or is out of style may not be worth remodelling, yet the material of which it is made is good and would give satisfaction if used for another garment.

What may be made from silk, rayon, or wool dresses, or rayon or wool housecoats? Dresses, lounging pyjamas with yoke effect similar to a skirt to take care of the length of the trousers, blouses, children's dresses or lingerie.

First rip the garment or garments. It is sometimes advisable to combine two materials, figured or plain rayon or silk, silk and wool. Using two discarded dresses one may make a stunning garment. (See Illustration 39 for a combination of two colours.)

Never use cotton and rayon together, unless they can be cleaned separately. Their treatment is so different when laundering. Scrutinize fabric carefully for any thin or defective places. Save the zippers, snaps, buttons, hooks, and eyes. Clean as stated in Chapter 3, "Care of Fabrics and Garments." Draft or choose designs which are simple.

Cotton house dresses may be used for neat little cotton frocks for school or play. Play suits and sun suits require little material, and there are aprons, pinafores and blouses. The colours may be combined, or they may be finished with contrasting pieces of bright new material, to enliven sombre colours, at the collar, cuffs, and belt.

POSSIBILITIES OF MEN'S SHIRTS

If the collar and cuffs are worn, turn the collar, being careful that the fronts are absolutely even, also turn the cuffs. New collar and cuff sets may be bought for white shirts. If the elbows are worn and the rest of the shirt is good, shorten the sleeves—the same as when shortening a woman's sleeve—and don't stiffen the collar when laundering. The shirt will then be wearable during the summer.

Child's rompers, boy's blouses, girl's blouses, simple

REMODELLING THE ENTIRE GARMENT

ILLUSTRATION 39

little dresses, aprons and pinafores may effectively be cut from the material of a man's shirt.

For making a boy's sport blouse, use the lowest buttonhole of the shirt for the lowest buttonhole of the blouse, being careful to place the top buttonhole in the correct position. The back of the blouse can be cut from the shirt tail. Short sleeves may be cut from the upper portion of the sleeves, or the original sleeve may be wide enough for long sleeves after the worn portion has been removed.

REMODELLING FOR CHILDREN

When remaking larger garments into clothes for children, select designs which are simple, comfortable yet attractive, and keep boys' clothes masculine. Select or draft a pattern with not too much fullness, then sufficient material is assured. If more fullness is required, pleats, etc., may be added. Be sure the material over the elbows, seat and knees is strong. Stitch with good thread and adjust the machine to suit the thickness of the material.

RENOVATING HAND-KNITTED AND MACHINE-KNITTED GARMENTS

TO SHORTEN A HAND-KNITTED SKIRT

ALL HAND-KNITTED SKIRTS should be begun at the bottom so that the tension of the stitch is assured before the vital fitting areas, the hips and the waist, are reached.

It is impossible to shorten a hand-knitted skirt started at the bottom by unravelling it from the bottom. No knitting can be pulled out backward. But if the skirt cups at the back, it may be lifted up, and the extra length taken from the top. However, if it fits satisfactorily, shorten in the following manner:

Having decided on the length of skirt—one that meets individual needs and the type of garment—place a pin horizontally to mark the length. Now break a thread at the desired length, just the same as when snagging a stocking, but continue to pull the thread and draw it out as far as possible before breaking the other end.

After the thread has broken the knit loops will remain. Now take a crochet hook, not a knitting needle—a number 4 or 5 steel hook, if available, is suitable for almost all emergencies—and slip stitch in all the loops.

Continue pulling out the thread and slip stitching in all the loops until the whole skirt has been shortened. Finish the bottom of the skirt as it was previously—probably two rows of single crochet around the bottom to prevent it from rolling.

NOTE.—Don't be afraid to pull out the thread. The loops will stay in place until you are ready to slip stitch them.

TO LENGTHEN A HAND-KNITTED SKIRT

Break a thread as near the bottom as possible. Pick up the stitches on the same circular knitting needle that was used to knit the skirt—always picking them up from the back so the loops will not be twisted—and this time knit down. Steam press the bottom of the skirt.

NOTE.—The joining on stockinette stitch will not show.

TO REKNIT WORN SLEEVES OR ALTER OTHER KNIT SLEEVES

It isn't necessary to take out the entire sleeve if it is very worn at the elbow or cuff. Just break a thread above the worn portion, unravel the yarn backwards, then pick up the stitches, knit and shape the sleeve in the opposite direction.

NOTE.—When knitting the sleeves at the elbow, it is advisable to use another finer strand of yarn with the used yarn to give added strength. This other strand need not be taken all the way across the row, but a rectangle may be made, where the strain occurs at the elbow. Leave the finer yarn when the desired place has been reached, then on the way coming back lock the two strands together by twisting one round the other.

Long sleeves may be shortened by the same method.

IF A SWEATER IS TOO SHORT FROM THE UNDERARM TO THE WAIST

Take out the side seams, not quite to the underarm. Do not use a safety razor blade. Break a thread carefully and pull the yarn out.

Reknit one portion at a time. Break a thread just above

RENOVATING KNITTED GARMENTS

the ribbing. Again knit downwards, decreasing instead of increasing at the waist.

NOTE.—One cannot break a thread in ribbing and knit downwards. The effect is not the same. It is only in stockinette stitch where exactly the same effect is produced.

TO REPAIR HAND-KNITTED GLOVES AND MITTENS

If the fingers or thumbs have been worn thin or have holes in them, either darn over the thin places or pull out and reknit where necessary.

TO REPAIR HAND-KNITTED SOCKS OR STOCKINGS

Break a thread as explained in discussing skirts and reknit the necessary part.

Darning knitted articles is explained in the chapter on mending.

REMODELLING MACHINE-KNITTED GARMENTS

As most machine-knitted dresses and sweaters are cut to shape, not knit to shape, it is impossible to unravel them. However, after the garment has been fitted, and the seams and the position of the hems marked, BEFORE CUTTING, machine stitch several times just inside the edges to be cut so the material won't unravel, then cut and sew on the machine, the same as any woven fabric.

If father's sweater is too worn for him to use, but is large enough so that portions may be utilized for small son, use the knitted cloth as a woven fabric, but, as when remodelling other machine-knitted garments, machine stitch just inside the edges to be cut several times, and then cut the pieces and sew as for any other garment.

TO RECLAIM WOOL YARN

Many used garments have lots of good yarn in them which, when salvaged, can be made into articles practically as good as new. Nearly all hand-knits may be unravelled. However, any hand-knit which has matted, or an angora sweater, etc., must be treated as a machine-knit.

Method

First wash the article (squeeze) in suds of lukewarm water and neutral soap chips, granules or flakes. Use two sudsy waters if necessary, then rinse in clear water of the same temperature.

Dry the garment in a shady, airy place, flat on the ground if possible.

Unravel the ribbing around the armholes and neck of a sleeveless sweater, if it has been put on after the portions of the garment were knitted. Unpick the seams carefully, not using a razor blade or scissors—I have seen too many casualties that way.

Most of the sweaters with set-in sleeves are knitted from the waist up; raglans from the neck down. As one must unravel yarn from the end of the knitting, not from the beginning, it is necessary to know how the garment was knitted. If the garment was not knitted by the person who is doing the unravelling, it might help to look for the top of the knit stitches. The actual loop of a stitch, the widest portion, is uppermost when knitting.

1. Wind the yarn loosely at the same time that it is unravelled around a piece of strong cardboard or wood at least 12 inches long, leaving the end visible.

2. Use your own discretion about the amount to wind around the cardboard to make a hank—that greatly depends upon the type of yarn. It is better, however, not to have the

RENOVATING KNITTED GARMENTS

hanks too big. Break the yarn and fasten the two loose ends together.

3. With a piece of white string, fasten the hank in several places, then remove it from the cardboard.

4. Repeat the above until all the yarn has been unravelled and wound into hanks.

5. Wash the hanks in lukewarm suds and thoroughly rinse again. This removes any kinks and soil which might have adhered between the stitches.

6. Squeeze out the excess water, but do not twist.

7. Shake carefully so that the strands do not become entangled, and hang in an airy place to dry.

NOTE.—The only satisfactory way to use reclaimed yarn for knitting is to make a stitch gauge and knit from measurement. Do not try to use stereotyped directions. This is merely a hit and miss proposition. Knitted garments should fit just as well as any other.*

* *The Complete Book of Progressive Knitting*, by Ida Riley Duncan, Liveright Publishing Corporation, 1940, contains concrete formulas so that one is assured of a perfect fit for any garment.

Remodeling Your Clothes

A WOMAN who is adept at remodeling her clothes will get a great deal of satisfaction out of this type of sewing. Not only is there a saving in actual cash, but there is also a fine sense of accomplishment in having increased the life of a garment. You will certainly find it worth your while to go through your closets to see if there are any clothes which might be recut, re-trimmed, or even combined with others to make a new outfit.

WHAT IS WORTH MAKING OVER?—To be sure that your time and effort will be used to the best effect, examine the things you want to make over. Hold them up to the light to see whether the material is in good condition. Woolens attract moths and you may discover pin-point holes. Silk, rayon, and cotton clothes may have small tears. If there is still enough sound material, however, clothes with slight damages can always be salvaged. Some materials can be turned and used on the wrong side. In many cases a new pocket or a bit of embroidery can be added to cover up a place which has a tiny hole or tear if the rest of the material is still sturdy enough to give good wear.

SELECTING YOUR PATTERNS—When you are remodeling a dress it is essential to get a pattern that is neither too complicated nor calls for large pieces of material. For instance, if you are going to remodel a two-piece dress that has a narrow skirt, do not buy a pattern with a princess line or a wide flared skirt. The same principle applies if you are making over a jacket with set-in fitted sleeves—do not buy a pattern with raglan shoulders or wide puffed sleeves. The pattern you buy for your new dress must not include any pieces that are larger than the pieces of your original garment. Of course there may be a place or two where you will have to do a little inconspicuous piecing, or you can add new contrasting material. But do remember, as a general rule, not to buy a pattern where more material is required than you have at hand.

PREPARATION OF MATERIAL—Garments should be washed or dry cleaned before you start to rip them apart, as it is always more pleasant to work with clean material.

Rip the seams with a one-edged razor blade, or with a small scissors clip the threads at short intervals and pull apart gently. Used material may not be strong enough to stand quick

ripping of the seams, so do it carefully.
When the garment is ripped apart, it should be pressed. If the material has a definite right and wrong side, make some mark on the wrong side of each piece to identify it and keep it from getting mixed up later on when you are cutting. Also, before pressing mark the "straight" of the material on the right side with tailor's chalk or long bastings, to aid you in cutting from the new pattern.

PIECING INSUFFICIENT MATERIAL— If it is necessary to piece material which is not large enough, do this in such inconspicuous places as the top of the back waist at the point where it joins the front seam under the arm. A piece can be inserted to make a skirt wider either by a whole gore the full length of the front or the back or both sides of the skirt. A skirt can also be pieced at the side seams. If you find that a little piece has to be added when you lay the pattern on the material, stitch the piecing together into position and press the seams out flat on the wrong side before you start to cut out the pattern. The piecing will not be noticeable if you make sure that the materials joined together run the same way on the grain, that the designs, if there are any, match, and that the seams are flat and have not been puckered by stretching when they were stitched together.

Sometimes it is better to use contrasting material for remodeling. You can use a garment which has done its original service and is ready to be cut up for remodeling, or you can buy a piece of new material which looks well with the old fabric you are using. A sleeve, vestee, bolero, or bands on a blouse or skirt can be effective in contrasting material if there is not enough of the original garment material for a complete remodeling job.

CUTTING—Now that the material has been cleaned, ripped apart, and pressed, spread it out right side up. Place the pattern pieces over the pieces of fabric, making sure that each is placed on the straight of the goods. Then, before you do any cutting, check again to see if and where you will need to piece. It is better to take the time to do this before you cut than to discover too late a short piece that you overlooked.

SUGGESTIONS FOR MAKE-OVERS— Clothes closets and dresser drawers invariably contain many articles of outmoded or outworn clothes which are still in very good condition and are merely waiting to be rejuvenated. Every sewer has her own specific ideas about what should be done with the usable things that she discovers. These general examples may help you with your own special make-over problems.

Turning a man's shirt into a blouse—Collars and cuffs may be frayed, the buttonholes may be torn, or maybe Dad just doesn't like the color or stripe in his shirt. It will make an attractive tailored blouse for the lady of the

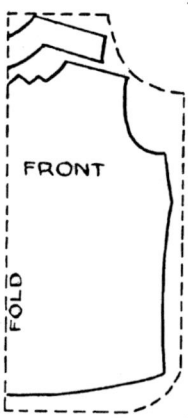

REMODELING YOUR CLOTHES

house. Use a basic blouse pattern and lay it on the ripped parts of the cleaned and pressed shirt. As a rule the front of a woman's blouse is cut from the back of a man's shirt and the back of the blouse is made from the front pieces of the shirt.

If you do not want a buttoned-down-the-back blouse, select a pattern which can be seamed down the center back. You can also use the shirt fronts for your blouse front by reversing the buttonholes, and sewing buttons over the buttonholes which were in the man's shirt. (A woman's blouse buttons from right to left.)

By following the same general directions you can cut down one of your own discarded blouses to make a pretty blouse for your daughter. Buy a pattern for Little Sister and cut out the blouse as described above.

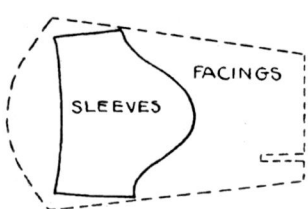

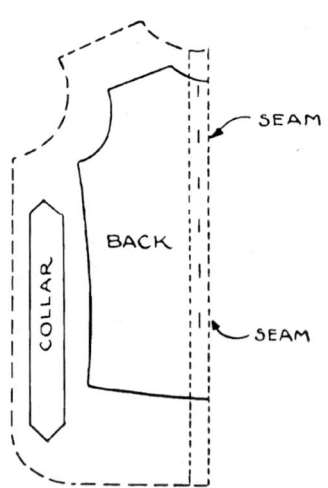

Child's dress—No little girl can have too many dresses, and when you consider how quickly she outgrows them it may be wise not to invest too much in new clothes. Here is where ingenuity can be used in cutting down Mother's or Big Sister's wardrobe. If there isn't enough of one material, a charming dress can be made by com-

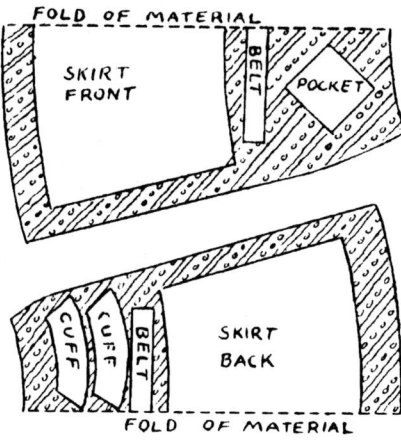

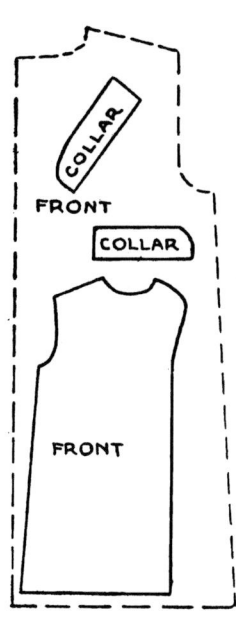

bining two materials. The accompanying illustrations offer a suggestion for the resourceful sewer.

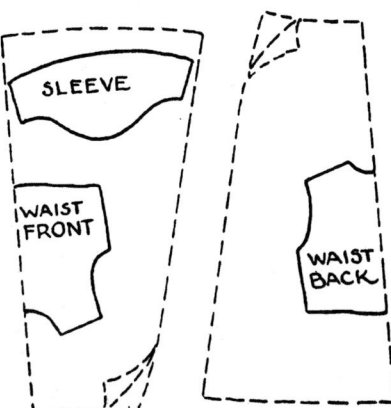

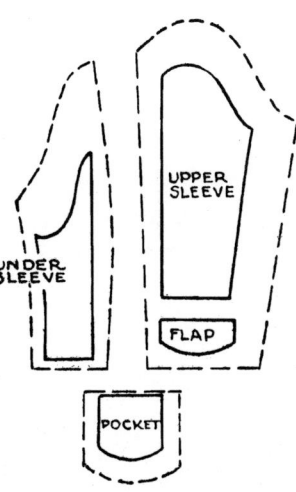

Small child's coat—Your schoolboy can have a fine coat made from his father's or older brother's worn or outgrown coat if you avoid too large a check or plaid. Small boys just aren't the size for those patterns.

can be made over from one which her older sister has outgrown.

Making a man's suit into a woman's suit—This is one of those make-over tricks that women like to brag about. If the man in your family has outgrown a suit or is tired of it,

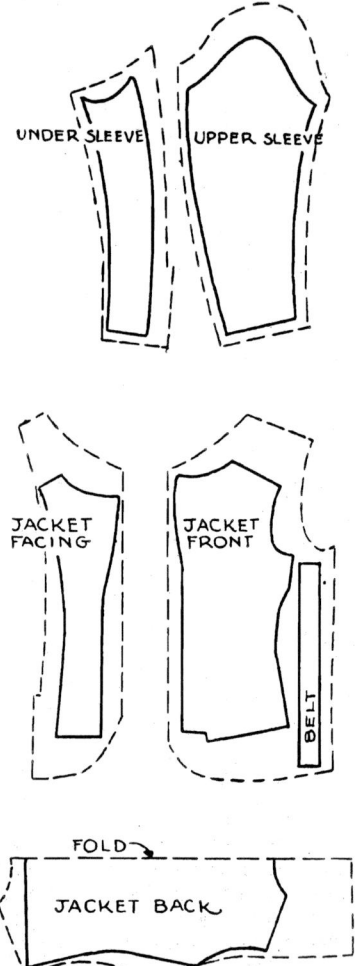

The illustration shows how to cut down a man's coat, but the same principle applies to a little girl's coat which

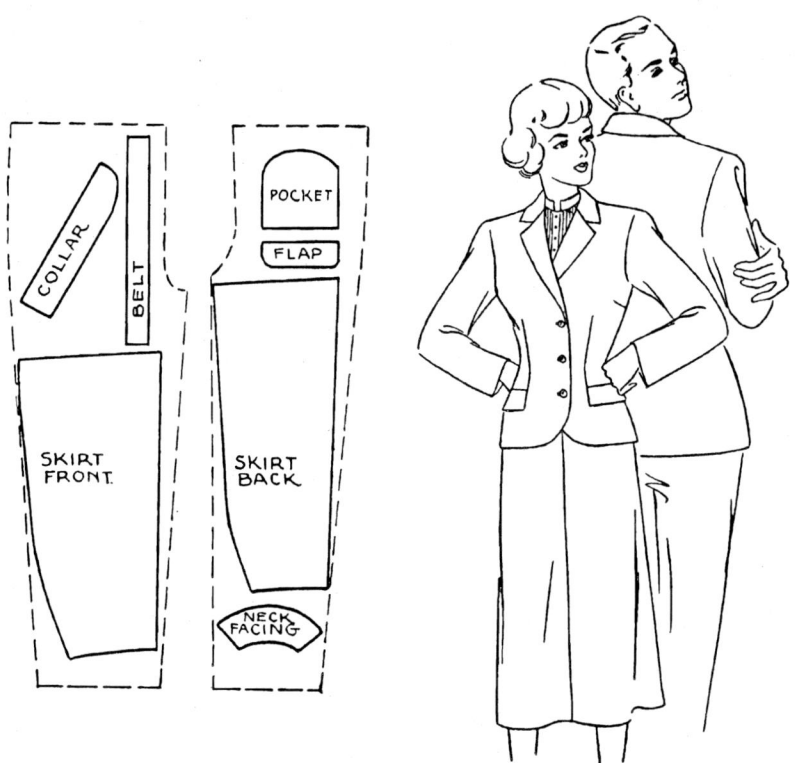

claim it before the moths do. Buy a pattern for a simple tailored suit, cut your pieces, and follow the sewing directions which come with the pattern. The jacket for your suit can be the popular hip length or waist length, depending on your figure and the current fashion trend. Stitch the old buttonholes together by hand and sew buttons over them. Make your buttonholes on the right side of the jacket.

One dress from two—Do you have two dresses which are partly worn? Perhaps one is threadbare under the arms or shrunk from washing or dry cleaning. Perhaps you are just tired of the other dress and want something new. Here's the place to use your imagination and combine the two dresses. Use a simple pattern with very little trimming, for combining materials can make a dress look "dowdy" unless you consider the same points as you do when choosing material for a new dress. For a slender person, the top of the dress might be of one material, perhaps a print, and the skirt a harmonizing plain color.

Evening dress cut shorter—Do you have an evening dress which just hangs

REMODELING YOUR CLOTHES

in the closet because it no longer looks well on you? If so, you can recapture its value for dress-up occasions by shortening the hem line and adding a touch of trimming at the neck and sleeves. This remodeling job is simple, quick, and inexpensive, and you'll still have a dress for social functions without its being limited to the strictly full-length formal.

OTHER REMODELING POSSIBILITIES—The scope of remodeling possibilities is so unlimited that nothing in your wardrobe need be wasted. You can transform one of your skirts into one

for your young daughter. A pleated skirt can be turned into a slim trim one. A tight skirt can be made more comfortable for walking by slitting one or both sides.

If you have a two-piece suit with a jacket you do not like you can cut down the jacket and make a bolero of it, or remove the sleeves and convert the jacket into a jerkin.

When a dress has sleeves which are too tight or are worn-out, you can remove the sleeves and make a jacket or bolero of contrasting material to wear over this sleeveless dress. If the dress is of wool, it might be turned into a sleeveless jumper to be worn with a variety of blouses. A third suggestion is to make bishop sleeves of a solid color to fit the cutout armhole.

REMODELING YOUR CLOTHES

If you're handy with knitting needles you can replace the worn-out sleeves in a woolen blouse or jacket with knitted woolen sleeves, and they can be so chic!

A bathrobe for Junior or even Little Sister can be made by cutting down Dad's or Mother's bathrobe. For Mother or Daughter a practical bathrobe can be made from a discarded candlewick bedspread.

Men's shirts when they become worn under the arms, on the collars, or the cuffs, needn't be discarded. Use the shirt backs and the two fronts to make aprons for the children and yourself. They can even be made into rompers and sun suits for the baby.

Lingerie can also be made over. A nightgown can be cut down into a slip or a petticoat, a bed jacket, or a little girl's nightgown. A slip with a torn lace yoke or straps, or one that has become too short, can be made into a petticoat merely by removing the top and stitching an elastic or tape around the waistband. The evening slip which is no longer used need only be shortened and hemmed to make a daytime slip out of it.

The upper and lower parts of pajamas may not always give equal wear. As a rule the trousers wear out first. If this is the case, don't discard the pajama jacket; instead, make another pair of trousers. They don't have to be the exact color or design as the jacket —in fact, a pajama set can be most attractive if the top contrasts with the bottom.

Your clothes closet is probably concealing a variety of clothing which you can use as some clever remodeling— all you need is imagination and patience.

REMODELING

ADVANTAGES AND SCOPE

1. **Relation Between Renovating and Remodeling.**—The previous chapters concerning the care of clothing have dealt entirely with renovation by means of laundering, dry cleaning, and freshening or changing the color, but there is also the phase of renovation that begins with slight rearrangements and grows into the subject of remodeling. The renovating and the remodeling of clothing, therefore, are very closely connected, but remodeling requires more definite changes, even to the recutting of a garment.

2. **Satisfaction Gained from Remodeling.**—If making two blades of grass grow where one grew before is a feat to be proud of, then surely the making of a comfortable, becoming, and attractive dress from a garment discarded and seemingly useless is cause for rejoicing, and the woman who achieves this bit of success is perfectly justified in the pride and satisfaction she feels in her accomplishment. There is no doubt about the fact that it takes more brain power and work to produce a successful make-over than it does to make a lovely gown from sumptuous new material, for the pieces of material to be made over have certain set limits beyond which we may not go, while new material stretches out yard upon yard to lure the scissors.

3. **Economy in Remodeling.**—Not only does a successful make-over bring satisfaction to a woman's creative ability and the joy of conquest to her keen intelligence, but it has a most pleasing reaction upon her sense of economy, for it is gratifying to any woman to be able to dress attractively at moderate cost. To do this, she must know how to put to good use every garment in her wardrobe. No woman should look with disdain on the work of remodeling, for it is indeed praiseworthy for any one to give thought and effort to the

REMODELING

making of pretty, attractive things out of clothing that has already seen considerable service, and it is an acquirable art, just as much as is the making of tempting dishes for one meal out of food left from a previous one.

4. A woman possessing the skill or developing the ability to make over garments successfully, can usually have a greater number of outfits each season than would be possible otherwise. Where economy is an absolute necessity, this procedure is of invaluable assistance. Then, too, the ability to make over clothes enables the woman of limited means to buy better materials than she would be justified in purchasing if the usefulness of the material depended on only one development of it; or, the money saved in this way may be added to the rainy-day fund or used for purchasing another new frock or something else especially desirable. It is true that many dollars are saved each year by women who are clever enough to make over their previous seasons' gowns.

There is nothing clever in wastefulness. It is a habit that fails to give the acquaintances of any woman an impression of her social importance; nor does it convince any one that her financial standing is unquestionably secure. Rather, extravagance in dress conveys to thinking persons a feeling of doubt as to a woman's intelligence. Thrift, intelligent application of knowledge, and skill with the hands are really worth-while factors in life and are recognized as such by persons qualified to judge.

So, in the interests of economy, the wise woman reconciles her desire for a smart new outfit with what is already on hand, in this way gaining the satisfaction of putting to use her ability to obtain the maximum of wear from garments purchased or made. "Maximum of wear" does not mean the continued use of a garment that has lost its style value, but rather an intelligent adjustment of a partly worn garment so that both its beauty and its usefulness are increased, and it becomes a worth-while addition to even an already well-supplied wardrobe.

5. **Association vs. Changes in Design.**—Probably every woman has a certain amount of sentiment in connection with her clothes. In some, this is more pronounced than in others, and with such women the question of association should not be overlooked in considering the aspects of remodeling. When one possesses a dress

REMODELING

or a suit that has been particularly becoming, there are undoubtedly attached to this garment many pleasant recollections of happy hours and peace of mind when it has been worn. In this case, the desire to retain the garment as it is far outweighs the desire to transform it into a more up-to-date garment of entirely different effect. However, it is usually possible, by means of slight changes, to make sufficient concession to current fashion and at the same time to retain the good points of the dress which have endeared it to its owner.

6. Remodeling the Well-Made Garment.—Somewhat different from the matter of sentiment for a garment because of its associations is the question of the hesitancy that restrains some women from remodeling a well-made dress simply because it is well made. They look with awe upon any suggestions of such a procedure, seeming to feel that the garment's original excellence entitles it to a long lease on life. As a matter of fact, once it is badly out of date, no degree of excellence of construction can give a garment the value that a thorough remodeling will. It is a great mistake to keep such garments unaltered for any great length of time, for good construction in a gown is usually accompanied by good material, which should be made to give the greatest possible usefulness. But it is difficult to make them over satisfactorily after the color becomes passé or the weave of material is no longer popular.

7. Aims in Remodeling.—In all remodeling, whether for economy or for the satisfaction of producing a useful garment from a useless one, the aims to be kept in mind are *desirability, serviceability*, and *becomingness*. They are of about equal importance and are so closely related that it is difficult to consider one apart from the other two. For example, a garment is desirable if it is becoming and promises to be serviceable. It cannot give great service unless it is becoming and of a design that is desirable. And, of course, it is not probable that a dress would be becoming without being desirable and serviceable.

REMODELING

PREPARATION FOR REMODELING

MAKING A SURVEY OF YOUR WARDROBE

8. At the beginning of each season, make a critical survey of all of the clothing you have on hand, including dresses, coats, suits, blouses, skirts, and the smaller accessories. Do not make merely a mental review, but take the garments into a good light where you can study them. Make yourself ready as though you were going out, arranging your hair becomingly and wearing a well-fitted corset, underwear that conforms with the fashionable silhouette, and good street or dress shoes. Then try on each garment in turn, and observe its lines in relation to the current fashion. Note particularly what parts need to be changed or freshened, and determine whether or not cleaning is necessary and whether adding a new piece of lace or a frill, or taking off the belt, or adding a new one would remove a worn or unseasonable appearance. Simply diagnose the case of each garment—dissect it, so to speak, and note just how it may best be improved, or where a touch of becoming, seasonable color would add to its appearance.

9. **Classifying Your Wardrobe.**—In the light of your discoveries, classify all garments as good, possible, or impossible. Assemble them in groups, as follows:
   1. Those requiring only slight freshening up, such as brushing or cleaning, tightening of fastenings, a little mending of trimmings, etc.
   2. Those needing some new material, new trimming, buttons, or lining to put them into condition.
   3. Those that must be ripped and made over.
   4. Those that are of no value to you.

The garments in the last group should, by all means, be passed on to some one who can make use of them, for there is nothing more unkind nor unjustifiable than the hoarding of garments that are entirely valueless to the one who possesses them but that might clothe and make presentable some other human being. Instead of allowing good materials to lie useless or to make breeding places for moths, find some one who can make use of them.

In making this classification of your wardrobe, be very wise in your decisions. Do not attempt to improve a garment by merely

REMODELING

renovating it if it needs a complete remodeling; and do not give the time to remodeling unless you are reasonably sure that the finished garment will justify the expenditure of your time and effort.

CLEANING AND MENDING MATERIALS

10. After you have classified all garments, go over them carefully, giving each the brushing, cleaning, and pressing that it requires. Very often proper cleaning will so freshen a garment that it will seem like new. If cleaning is all that is required, refer to *Laundering and Dry Cleaning* and follow the method that is best fitted to the garment in question.

Garments that are not to be remade must have any necessary mending done, such as the tightening of hooks, eyes, snaps, or buttons. If buttonholes are in bad condition and are large enough, they may be freshened by binding them with silk or braid. In the case of a coat that must be relined, much effort can be saved by removing the old lining, pressing it, and using it as a pattern in cutting the new lining. Frayed hems may be freshened by turning them a little deeper, or by cutting them off and adding a facing. Worn facings should be replaced by new ones. Other helps in the matter of mending are given in the volume, *Home Sewing*, where the different kinds of mending and their uses are discussed in detail.

STUDY OF POSSIBILITIES

11. Styles.—Having definitely decided which garments are to be remodeled, the next step is to study prevailing styles for their lines in order to produce the most attractive and modish effects possible. The illustrations in current fashion magazines are always rich in suggestions for whole costumes as well as details that may be adapted. When you find a design that appeals to you, study it carefully, keeping in mind all the while the size and shape of the pieces you have from which to cut the garment. A great deal of planning is often necessary, but it will be found in many cases that, by making very slight changes, the desired effect as a whole may be produced.

12. Materials and Colors.—Good fashion publications give also information in regard to the newest colors and materials. While

REMODELING

it is sometimes impossible or impractical to change the color of the material to be made over by dyeing it, yet a new effect may be produced by adding a touch of a seasonable color, thus detracting attention from the color and weave of material that speaks of a previous season. But when a new color is to be combined with an old color or material, a somewhat soft tone should be chosen. Colors in good materials ripen with age, and must not be "killed" by a bright, harsh, new material.

13. Each season brings forth also new combinations of materials and colors in the same costume, a fact that offers many advantages in the making over of garments. Different materials of the same weight, as tulle, chiffon, and lace, or of different weights, as satin and chiffon, or velvet and Georgette crêpe, may be used together, as may also two similar materials of the same color, or a plain color and a checked, striped, or figured material. In combining a checked, striped, or plaid material with a plain one, the plain material should match one of the colors in the check, plaid, or stripe, usually the predominant one. A striped or figured silk of medium or heavy weight might be combined with a plain Georgette or chiffon, or a plain silk might be made up with a striped, figured, or printed, sheer silk fabric. If you use a plain color to match a stripe or plaid, rather than one to match the body of the garment, use the plain color sparingly to avoid making the dress appear "top heavy" with trimming.

Black and white combine well with many colors. Often two plain harmonizing colors may be used together in the same costume. When different materials are combined, the colors must, as a rule, be subdued in order to produce an harmonious combination, and the proper balance must always be maintained.

14. Current styles will present very few difficulties, so far as the making is concerned, to the woman who understands garment construction, and the remodeling will be a simple task once she realizes the great need of exercising good judgment in combining just the right colors and materials in made-over garments. A little more discretion and a little more skill are required for make-overs than for new garments. This phase of dressmaking, however, requires only forethought and knowledge of sewing principles and what is considered good taste in colors and combinations of colors and materials.

REMODELING

15. Trimmings Suitable for Remodeling.—In remodeling garments, trimmings play a very prominent part, it being possible, in many cases, to create entirely new effects. When in vogue, narrow ruffling, plaited and plain frills and jabots, plaiting, puffing, and smocking are all good as trimming. Cording, piping, shirred and tucked bands, hand embroidery, hemstitching, picoting, braiding, and braid-bound edges are often employed. Then, in accord with the mode and the season, come embroidery and lace edgings and bandings, appliqué, fringe, fur, beads, and buttons. Still other features, some of them acting as both trimming and essential parts, are listed in Art. 18. Study the mode for trimmings just as carefully as you do for constructive features, lines, colors, and fabrics.

16. Dressmaking Accessories.—Just as each season's fashions call forth new materials, trimmings, and colors, so do they make necessary different features of dressmaking accessories as aids to developing the current silhouette. Manufacturers of such accessories are thoroughly awake to the ever-changing vagaries of fashion and never fail to have practical, and frequently most unique, articles ready for the dressmaker's assistance. The professional dressmaker, of course, keeps in close touch with the producers of such articles, and there is nothing to hinder the home dressmaker from doing the same, for the accessories are without doubt an invaluable aid to fashion and style and they are never exorbitant in price, considering their usefulness and the usual simplicity with which they may be applied.

Of particular value are bias tapes in various colors of silk and cotton, cords, braids, weights, weighted tapes, and the innumerable varieties of hooks and snaps and other fasteners. Every woman who sews should make it a part of her routine to study these aids to good dressmaking, fashion, and style just as she studies fabric, color, and design. Practical dressmaking accessories can be procured at the notion counter of any well-equipped, dry-goods store, and their advent is usually announced in the advertising columns of publications devoted to women's interests.

REMODELING FEATURES AND THEIR APPLICATION

17. Construction Features for Remodeling.—Changes of fashion are indicated by the size, shape, and length of the sleeves, the collar or neck finish, the position of the waist line or lack of waist line, the

REMODELING

length of skirts, and the location and means of obtaining skirt fulness, all of which are construction features that change and determine the fashionable silhouette. Such changes, however, are seldom sudden or radical. Students of fashion can readily recognize them and watch their progress and development. By keeping in touch with them and watching the interesting evolution of dress ideas, the home dressmaker will find that the possibilities of dressmaking and remodeling will be made more profitable, and real pleasure will be experienced in doing work of this kind.

18. Features or sections of garments that may be altered or added to give new life to garments may be easily decided on, yet a classification of these features, as well as an idea of their usefulness, is here given to serve as a handy reference.

Blouses and dresses, skirts, and coats are considered separately, with lists under each of the construction features, trimming features, or accessories that may be added or changed to improve the appearance of them.

Dresses and Blouses

Appliquéd sections	Capes	Folds	Puffing
Aprons	Caps on Sleeves	Frills	Revers
Bands	Chemisettes	Girdles	Sashes
Belts	Collars	Inserts	Scarfs
Berthas	Cuffs	Jabots	Sleeves
Bibs	Fichus	Overblouses	Stoles
Boleros	Flounces	Peplums	Vests
Bretelles			Yokes

Skirts

Applied bands or straps	False hems	Panniers	Set-in plaits and tucks
Applied plaits and tucks	Flounces	Pockets	Suspenders
	Godets	Ruffles	Tunics
Draperies	Overskirts	Set-in bands or straps	Yokes
	Panels		

Coats

Applied bands	Capes	Peplums	Sleeves
Applied plaits or tucks	Collars	Pockets	Stoles
	Cuffs	Revers	Straps
Belts	Godets	Scarfs	Vests

19. Subtlety of Fashion Changes.—To arrive at the best results, the real significance of the features of fashion should always be correctly understood. While some of these features are always to

REMODELING

be found in dress, and while it is known that just so often does practically every feature of dress return to use, seldom, if ever, are they identical in form or application with earlier presentations, and the successful dressmaker is she who is quick to grasp these changes in construction or application and make ready use of them.

Thus, when fashion announces a radical change in a garment, as, for instance, the advent of full, flaring skirts when close-fitting ones have been the vogue, a person is not unlikely to think at first that a wide, flaring skirt of several seasons back may be used without alteration; yet, upon examination, it will be discovered that this old model cannot be worn in its original form. Nevertheless, it is true that it may be more readily altered to conform to the new dictates of fashion than a garment cut on straighter lines.

Similar conditions will be found true of practically every other feature of dress, for even when it is only a question of the fulness in sleeves, the length of the shoulder may be the point on which the smart, new appearance of the garment depends.

20. Blouses and Dresses.—At all times, the constructive features of garments serve some purpose, but, in remodeled garments, their purposes increase in number. Yet this fact should not be noticeable, if the garments are to have the coveted appearance of newness. Consequently, although there is a subtle reason for the presence of a bib collar on a blouse or a band on the bottom of a dress, the best of one's dressmaking skill should be brought into play to guard the secret. Any added feature, having a reason all its own, should be chosen and added so that it is a part of the design and is in harmony and perfect balance with the other parts of the garment.

21. The uses to which the blouse and dress features may be put are here explained, the terms being mentioned in alphabetical order.

Appliqué has always been enthusiastically sanctioned for use in milady's wardrobe, be she little or grown-up. And since appliquéd trimming or sections appear on the smartest of gowns as they come from the designers, surely they can, if properly used, be appropriated to cover an ink spot or a burnt place or to lengthen a sleeve or a hem.

Such things as *aprons* had too many possibilities to be connected with work hours, world without end. Now, Fashion occasionally turns to aprons to furnish interest in party gowns, incidentally offer-

REMODELING

ing a means of supplying front fulness, or of covering a spotted skirt, or of furnishing a reason for a belt over a one-piece dress that is one piece in effect only.

During some seasons, *bands* of self-material or another material, cut either bias or straight, are in fashion on frocks and suits. The make-over possibility in these features is readily seen, especially when some means of lengthening is necessary or when two materials are combined.

Beaded lace, embroidered, or *braided robes* may be used over worn foundations, really making a thing of beauty out of a shabby dress that has been cleaned and mended.

Belts, as well as *sashes* and *waist-line ornaments,* are largely instrumental in effecting style changes and freshening up dresses, giving an appearance of newness to every type of dress. Likewise, they can be used to conceal figure defects, to reduce the appearance of size in a large figure, or to increase the proportions of a slim figure.

Berthas serve to give width to narrow shoulders and to conceal the upper part of sleeves or badly shaped armholes.

A *bib* furnishes an excellent means of building up a neck that has formerly been low in front or accidentally cut lower than intended. Also, bibs share with collars and vests in the success they have in freshening up a dull and worn past-season blouse or dress.

Boleros are excellent when it is desired to cover the entire bodice portion of the waist.

Bretelles, which are cape effects extending from the belt in front over the shoulder to the belt in back, serve practically the same purpose as berthas, conceal bad shaping or piecing in the front of a waist, and give a pleasing vest outline. With the aid of bretelles, chemisettes or vests can be cut in such a way as to give an appearance of reducing a large figure or increasing the proportions of a slim one, or to effect new openings.

Capes may be employed for practically the same purpose as fichus.

Caps on sleeves are useful in showing fashion changes, in lengthening sleeves, or as a clever means of piecing materials.

Chemisettes may be used to change collar and neck finishes and to freshen up a waist or a dress.

Collars sometimes materially change the style of a garment, as in substituting a low collar for a high collar, and there is no question about a collar giving a new, fresh look to any waist or dress.

REMODELING

Cuffs lend new character to sleeves and can be used to advantage in lengthening or shortening, or as a means of effecting a new fashion. *Fichus* are useful in concealing narrow shoulders, ugly seams at the back, worn or slightly soiled appearance at the neck and shoulders caused by perspiration or other wear, and extreme thinness. They also serve to equalize a figure where the shoulders are narrow in proportion to the hips and to effect a pleasing appearance in a maternity garment.

Sometimes *folds* of material play the same part as bands. The chief differences are that they are double, as the word implies, and that they may not be so wide as bands.

A *frill* on a blouse or a dress is, in some cases, the main feature of interest. Its position may be at the neck, on the sleeve, or down the front, and, besides acting as a trimming, it may cover up a seam, add length, or conceal a bad finishing.

Girdles, depending on their width and character, frequently give the desired style tone to a garment, and wide girdles likewise allow of piecing or serve to conceal lack of material for waist or skirt lengths.

The addition of a *jabot*, after the manner of a front frill, has the power to mark a dress or blouse as belonging to a certain season when jabots are the style.

Now and again *inserts* of lace, embroidery, or novelty materials, find their way into blouses and dresses, and certainly there is no better way of joining small pieces of material, or enlarging garments at the seams.

Overblouses help to combine two materials and give an appearance of completeness to a costume. They likewise serve to conceal piecings and partly worn underblouses, and can be made to conceal defects of figure.

Peplums are strong features in fashion changes, and may be made, by their length or fulness, to reduce or increase in appearance the size of the hips and to cover ugly piecing or bad shaping in skirts. Peplums are useful when two materials are required for making-over purposes. They give an appearance of completeness to very plain dresses and are useful for extremely slim figures.

When *puffing* is in style, it furnishes a means of lengthening or enlarging, and also of concealing seams or piecings.

Particularly when mannish effects are in vogue, *revers* are adapted for use on frocks. The altering of a tailleur so that it

REMODELING

carries this style is all that is essential to bring some dresses up to date.

Sashes serve much the same purpose as girdles and belts.

Scarfs may be made to serve the same purpose as fichus.

Often dresses and blouses can be dated by their *sleeves*, so changes in these features are very important. Then, too, sleeves can always be added or subtracted as well as altered.

Stoles conceal soiled or ugly shapings at the neck and front, and have a tendency to give length and slimness to short, stout figures.

Vests freshen up soiled neck and front appearance, conceal bad shapings, and can frequently be used as a method of increasing the size of a garment.

Yokes may be used to change the shape of a garment or as a trimming application.

22. Skirts.—Features for remodeling skirts may be made to serve as follows:

Applied bands or *straps* conceal piecings or worn places, and make the combining of materials attractive.

Applied plaits and *tucks* conceal piecings, make a pleasing application where two materials are combined, and may also be used to conceal worn places.

Draperies, while they serve a purpose similar to overskirts and tunics, have the added advantage of concealing the defects of a figure, reducing the appearance of a large figure, and increasing the proportion, or appearance of proportion, in a slim figure.

False hems and *novelty hem finishes* make possible the adding of necessary length to skirts and are likewise used to advantage in the combining of two materials.

Flounces add length, give a bouffant or flaring effect when this is desirable, and may be used to change radically the shape of a skirt or the proportions of a figure.

Godets give width and a circular effect; they are also good as trimming when increased size is desired.

Overskirts allow of the combining of two materials and may be combined with a close-fitting skirt that is to be used as a foundation.

Panels make possible greater width of skirts.

Panniers serve much the same purpose as overskirts, either of which may be used advantageously when Fashion decrees that a bouffant effect in skirts is desirable.

REMODELING

The addition of *pockets* on a skirt when it is made over can make a skirt present an entirely different appearance. They also can cover worn or soiled spots.

Ruffles, so far as usefulness is concerned, belong in a class with flounces.

Set-in bands and *straps* serve a purpose similar to applied bands and straps and, likewise, are useful in increasing width or length.

Suspenders, when in fashion, may be used to change the style effect of skirts. They also make possible the wearing of blouses that could not be worn otherwise.

Tunics serve a purpose similar to that of draperies and overskirts.

Yokes on skirts give additional length and allow of new shaping at the waist and hips. They may be of a character to reduce or increase the appearance of hip measurements and are useful where two materials are combined.

23. Coats.—The manner in which features for remodeling coats may be utilized is as follows:

Applied bands, *plaits*, or *tucks* are useful as trimming to cover seams, piecings, and worn places.

Belts are useful where changes in fitting are necessary and where a radical change in the style of a garment is desired without resorting to complete remodeling; as, for instance, a belt may be added to a loose or a semifitting coat to give it a closer waist line.

Capes serve a purpose similar to that of collars, being likewise useful in concealing shoulder width, sleeve and armhole shaping, and in developing a decided style tendency, such as increased width to the upper portion of a figure.

Collars are useful in freshening up a garment or in changing its shape or style, as a trimming application, or a means to good taste, where two materials are to be used.

Cuffs add length and give style changes to sleeves.

Godets serve to give width and a circular effect to coats when Fashion demands this silhouette.

Peplums will lengthen the appearance of a coat and can be made to increase the proportions of slim figures or reduce the proportions of large figures.

Pockets, when in vogue, may be used to give an effective and a smart touch to a coat.

REMODELING

Novelty *revers* are sometimes used on coats instead of the usual conservative revers, and these are often helpful in taking away any scant appearance in the front.

From time to time, *scarfs* are considered the finishing touch to a coat. When this is true, no feature could be more acceptable, because they can entirely conceal an out-of-date collar or neck finish. The way they fall down the front also conceals a too-snug or an ill-fitting front.

Sleeve piecings and alterations may often be concealed by trimmings that have a certain style or fashion value.

Stoles are employed in much the same way as collars and also as a means of decoration when they are finished with hand embroidery or braiding. Frequently, stoles are very good for stout and mature figures where there is need of long lines from the shoulder to the waist or to the lower edge of a full-length or slightly shorter coat.

Straps applied to a plain coat give a Norfolk effect, as do also applied-plait sections. Such features may be used also to conceal piecings and seams.

Vests serve to freshen up a coat, make possible the elimination of a worn or badly constructed closing, increase the size of a coat, or act as a trimming effect, giving a certain dressed-up appearance that cannot be obtained from a coat with regulation single-breasted closing.

24. Veiling Garments.—The veiling of garments is a great help to remodeling. Thus, if a half-worn dress of silk, satin, brocade, or taffeta is at hand and the desire is not to recut it, it may be veiled with net, chiffon, all-over lace, Georgette, or fine voile, according to taste and the current mode. In this way, a very handsome gown may be inexpensively made.

Any color may be veiled with the same color, either in a lighter or a darker tone. Light blue, amber, canary, salmon, heliotrope, maize, cerise, and rose may be veiled with black or white. A more difficult problem is to veil one color with another; in fact, good judgment is required to do it successfully. As examples, green, rose, pale yellow, turquoise, or red may be used either under or over gray; yellow may be veiled with brown; rose, vivid red, and green, with dark blue; and gray, rose, mauve, and white, with green.

Over plain colors, two-tone changeable chiffons, voiles, and Georgette, matching in one tone or the other the color of the founda-

REMODELING

tion dress, may be used. A plain dress of white or black or of a color sufficiently vivid to contrast sharply with it may be veiled in black; and when a black or a white foundation is veiled with black, a third color, such as Chinese blue, peacock blue, emerald green, corn color, gold, old rose, or scarlet, may be used for the waist-line finish or as a part of the trimming. When a brilliant color is veiled in black, the color itself may be used in the trimming.

GENERAL RULES

25. The rules and hints relating to remodeling in this chapter are necessarily made as broad and flexible as possible, and should, therefore, be applied discriminately to individual requirements. By so doing, you will find it an easy matter to work out minor details that will be suitable to the needs of each garment.

Following is a summary of helpful general rules for remodeling. Study these carefully and apply them wisely.

26. Treatment of Materials.—Always prepare carefully new material that is to be combined with old fabrics, treating it to a sponging process or to steaming, if necessary, so that it will not contrast too definitely with the old material. A procedure of this kind is generally more necessary where fabrics of the same quality and weave are combined than where different qualities and weaves are used together.

Thoroughly clean and press old material to be used.

Make use of the dye pot. Good materials, discarded because they are faded or streaked or of a color no longer fashionable, may be restored by a few cents' worth of dye and a little time. Complete directions for using come with each package of dye; also, the preceding chapter is given over entirely to this subject.

27. Selecting Patterns.—Before selecting the pattern you are going to use, look through your fashion magazines, for these will suggest many ideas.

Two-fabric designs, especially, offer no end of possibilities.

Use simple patterns. Old material, unless very rare, seldom merits the outlay of time and energy necessary to make an elaborate garment.

28. Utilizing Remnants and Materials On Hand.—Learn to make the most of remnants. These may often be purchased for a small

REMODELING

sum, and, when used with old material, produce very desirable effects.

Very often a half yard or more of material is left from a dress. Keep this until you are able to combine it with another similar remnant, or to use it with used material.

Not infrequently the materials from two old dresses may be used to develop one new frock, provided they blend in color and harmonize as to design or pattern. If, however, new material is to be combined with that of an old dress, it is best to select a quiet or subdued color that will not glaringly proclaim its newness and thus mark the garment as unquestionably made over.

29. Ripping Apart Garments.—Save time by cutting close to seams instead of ripping, if the material in the seams will not be needed.

If it is necessary to save the material in the seams, you must, of course, rip them. There are several methods of ripping machine stitching, but the one to use generally is governed by the fabric and the length of the stitch. A method that is usually satisfactory consists in pulling one end of the thread (upper or lower), drawing it up as far as possible before breaking it, and then drawing one end of the remaining thread in the same manner.

Another method is to use a sharp knife with a small blade, or a safety-razor blade, drawing the material apart so that the stitching may be cut through the center. In this method, it is necessary to go over the ripped section a second time to remove the clipped threads. In ripping, care must be taken not to clip the material nor to stretch any bias or irregular edges.

30. Recutting.—As a rule, it is an easy matter to cut down—that is, to make a closer-fitting garment from a full one. But when the change is the reverse, the task is more difficult, and in this connection it is necessary to employ various methods of lengthening, of broadening, and of concealing pieces and places where materials are combined.

Recutting and contriving require patience and ingenuity, particularly if the material to be used has a figure of any kind, is a plaid or a stripe, or has an "up and down." In such cases, it is necessary to follow very closely the grain of the goods, as well as the figures, plaids, and stripes, matching them when necessary.

REMODELING

With plain material, the exercise of such great care is not so necessary, for if some of the pieces are a little bias, or are used on the crosswise grain of the goods where they can be covered with trimmings, the difference does not amount to so much. If the material used is plain and has no right or wrong or up and down, the possibilities for making over are greater than when matching must be done.

In any event, do *not cut anything until all pieces have been planned for.* Sometimes the pieces can be arranged a second time to much better advantage than at first. A good plan is to begin by picking out the longest pieces of the pattern and choosing the material for them, and if piecing must be done, it is always best, when possible, to piece lengthwise of the material.

Mark thin or badly worn spots with thread or chalk. Then avoid these in cutting, if possible. Carefully darn them if their use is unavoidable.

When there seems to be no way of remodeling a garment for an adult, try to plan a way of using it for a child. As a rule, a garment can be cut down to a child's size with a smaller outlay of time and energy than would be necessary to remodel it for an adult.

31. Remaking.—New seams help to "perk up" an old garment, so often recutting and making new seams will make a garment as good as new.

When piecing is necessary, it may be done so cleverly in many cases that no one need be the wiser. Tucks and folds are invaluable when used to this end. Also, lace insertion or entre deux may be so used as to make trimmings a feature of the piecing. Braids and bandings cover a multitude of seams.

It is necessary, in combining two materials, to exercise great care and thoughtfulness so as to acquire the right proportions and balance. The lines must be such that the design is "tied up" or held together, thus avoiding a "patchy" or spotty effect. A well-thought-out make-over is frequently even more effective than the original dress.

32. Trimmings.—Choose trimmings with a view to smart effect, avoiding those whose quality is so fine that the contrast with the material will emphasize its age.

The opposite grain of a material, like bengaline, may be used as a trimming. The right and wrong sides of crêpe satin may be combined with good effect.

REMODELING

In remodeling or freshening a garment, it may be necessary to resort to left-overs in trimmings, such as silks, chiffons, nets, laces, and pieces from the scrap bag, particularly if they are of bright colors; and if you have the whole array of garments and trimmings before you, you can see just what you have of each kind—the weight, color, and quantity—and can then intelligently adapt them to the required purpose and possibly procure new things that will combine to better advantage with what is at hand.

Fig. 1

When the collarless dress begins to show wear across the shoulders, it need not be discarded. Merely supply it with a becoming collar and matching cuffs of Georgette. The type of collar shown in Fig. 1 is particularly becoming to the slender figure.

33. Need of Consistency.—The principal point to remember regarding garments that are much worn is to make as little unnecessary alteration as possible, for ripping apart means an expenditure of time and labor and usually unwarranted expense in buying new materials. The art of making over lies in disguising the fact that the garment is remodeled. The ultimate effect, even on much worn garments, should be the mark of inspiration and not that of necessity. If a woman feels that they are just old things and that anything will do, the finished product will very likely be disappointing; if the material is worth making over, it is worth the effort that would have to be put forth in making a perfectly new dress.

EXAMPLES OF REMODELING

USING UNSEASONABLE SUITS

34. Preparation For Recutting.—As a suit made over usually emerges from the process as a dress, one must invariably dismiss all idea of using any of the seams as they are. The severing of its parts must be complete, for coat shoulders are broader than those of dresses, and all seams have a perverse way of coming at the wrong places.

REMODELING

Before ripping the suit, however, examine it carefully to decide whether or not the condition of the material is such that it will warrant a considerable amount of time being spent upon it, and also to determine the relation of the sections of the suit to the pattern pieces of the design you wish to copy. If the answers to these questions are favorable, it is safe to go ahead with the original plan of developing a dress from a suit that can no longer be considered either smart or becoming.

In this, as in all cutting of garments, lay the pattern pieces on the material and be sure you know that each piece is accounted for before you do any cutting.

Fig. 2   Fig. 3

35. Making One-Piece-Dress Effects.—If a dress of one-piece effect is the end in view, it may be accomplished by covering the necessary joining of the blouse section to the skirt with a belt, either of the material or of leather. Very often the addition of a

REMODELING

contrasting material, plain, figured, or plaid, is a great help in eking out the available material, particularly if the coat is one that is cut in narrow pieces.

If original thought and really sincere effort are put to the task, the very limitations imposed by the size and the shape of pieces, often lead to the development of effects that are very desirable and that would not have been conceived otherwise. This is particularly true in the case of the two dresses illustrated in Fig. 2.

If the suit is not badly out-of-date, but a change seems, nevertheless, desirable, the coat may be worn as it is, and a blouse of harmonizing plain or figured silk material may be attached to the skirt, after the belt and upper section of the skirt have been cut away. Fig. 3 suggests a one-piece possibility of this kind.

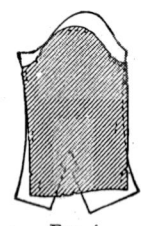

Fig. 4

36. Sleeve Possibilities.—Suit sleeves often present perplexities because of their two seams. These seams need not be objectionable, however, even in the dress sleeve. In preparing the sleeve for recutting, rip the full length of the seam that comes toward the front; the other seam need be opened only far enough to allow the sleeve to lie flat. Fig. 4 shows such a sleeve ripped in this manner with the dress-sleeve pattern placed over it in readiness for cutting. When the under-arm seam is joined, the back seam may be finished with a placket, a neat, close-fitting sleeve resulting.

37. Neck and Front Finishes.—Neck lines and front finishes frequently require especial attention because of buttonholes, or of the failure of the original lines to assume the desired outline. There are several remedies for defects of this kind. If the buttonholes cannot be disposed of either by cutting them away or by working them into the design of the dress, they may be covered by a jabot when such a feature is fashionable. A surplice front with a long roll collar or a contrasting lapel is often used as a means of covering the buttonholes. If these are not seasonal, the center front of the blouse section may be cut away and a vest of lace, batiste, or other similar material may be inserted. If a slenderizing line is desirable, both the blouse and the skirt may have a section cut from the front, and a panel of contrasting material inserted the full length of the dress. Such a panel may be buttoned down the center

REMODELING

in coat effect, or it may be in one piece, with the edges of the dress proper lapping over it in the form of plaits.

38. Using Shiny Skirts.—When the skirt of an old suit is shiny from much wear and the material cannot be turned, the effect may be relieved somewhat by pin tucking it, provided this does not interfere with the general effect of the design.

If the skirt is so shiny or worn that it no longer matches the coat, which is still in good condition, the latter may be made into a likable dress for a child by using a plaid or figured material in combination with it. One method of using this idea is to insert godets of the plaid material both front and back on the seam lines of the coat.

USING MEN'S SUITS

39. Making Boys' Suits.—When a man's old, half-worn suit is brought out of the storage chest and considered for renewed usefulness, the small boy of the family is almost sure to emerge a short time later in a new suit looking suspiciously like the original as to material and color. A man's suit seems to be made for the one inevitable end of being reduced in its last days to the proportions of a small boy's suit.

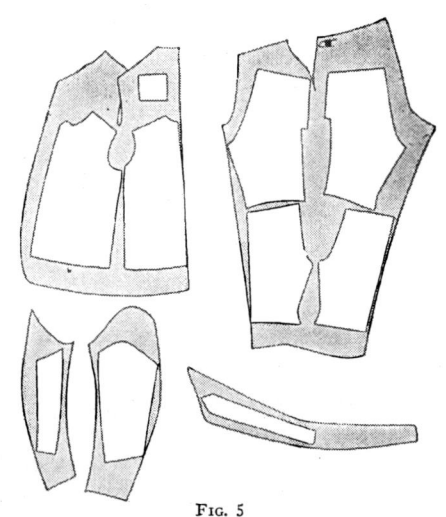

Fig. 5

If one were to follow the intermediate processes, they would be found to consist of the usual ripping, cleaning, pressing, and laying on of patterns that accompany all remodeling. The various pieces of the boy's coat are cut from the corresponding parts of the large coat. Small trousers are cut from the larger ones, and sometimes, if the boy is very small and the trousers are not too well worn, there proves to be enough material for two pairs of trousers.

REMODELING

Fig. 5 shows the pattern for a boy's two-trouser suit laid on the ripped-up suit, and Fig. 6 shows the resulting suit for the child. The piqué vest and collar give an air of fresh newness to the suit.

40. Making Girl's Plaited Skirt.—If there is no son in the household, but there is a little daughter, she may have a plaited skirt made from the trousers of a man's suit, for the piecing seams are easily concealed in the folds of the plaits. And it is quite possible that a slip-on blouse of middy type can be made from the coat. It may be brightened up considerably by trimmings of red, green, or gold flannel.

Fig. 6

Before cutting over a suit for a little girl, be sure that the material is appropriate. Serge and similar materials are splendid, but some suits cannot be cut over for little girls because the material is sure to advertise its origin. That, of course, would cause the sensitive child much needless pain.

REMODELING DRESSES

41. Features Considered For Remodeling.—Though there are a great many kinds of dresses, each with its own individual details, yet all dresses have a few features in common. The features may differ, but nevertheless they are there. For instance, all dresses have length and width, though they may vary as much as 15 inches in length or 2 yards in width. Every dress has some sort of neck finish and some kind of sleeves or provision for the arms. And every dress has its waist line characterized by some kind of belt or sash or the straight silhouette that denies the existence of a waist line altogether.

It sounds paradoxical to say that the details which dresses have in common make them different, yet this is precisely true, for it is the change in the shape of the collar, the length and fulness of the skirt,

REMODELING

the placement of the waist line, or the type of sleeves, that marks a dress as being of the mode or out of it. And so these are the features to consider when a dress is to be remodeled for the purpose of bringing it up to date.

42. Lengthening and Shortening.—Common means of lengthening a dress are as follows:

- Adding contrasting bands at the bottom or inserting them becomingly through the body of the skirt.

  Adding a section of the dress material and concealing the joining under a tuck, a band of trimming, or a touch of embroidery.

  Using the old skirt as a tunic and wearing it over a longer, narrower skirt.

  Adding hip-yokes when in vogue.

  Ripping the hem and adding a facing, if the skirt is not a great deal too short.

Skirts that are too long offer no such problems, as it is a simple matter to cut off the length that is not needed. The only time for hesitation is when you are deciding whether to take the length from the top or the bottom.

In the case of a plaited skirt, a bordered skirt, or skirt otherwise trimmed at the bottom, or a skirt with stitched-in hem that you would rather not rip out, cut off the top of the skirt.

A gored skirt should always be shortened at the bottom, unless it has become too snug at the hips and must be raised to supply plenty of room.

43. Changing the Skirt Width.—Skirts that are too narrow may be increased in width by slashing them from the bottom and inserting plaited sections or circular godets, depending on the current fashion. If panels are fashionable, the sections of the old skirt may be used as panels over a new foundation skirt of contrasting color or material. Also, gored skirts, if long enough, may be raised at the hips.

Skirts that are too wide may have their excess fulness plaited in or removed entirely by cutting some of it away.

44. Neck lines.—The most common neck lines are round, bateau (boat shape), square, V shape, and surpliced, which is just a variation of the V neck. Much variety is possible with these shapes by using collars of different types, or by leaving the neck line collarless.

REMODELING

Fig. 7

Fig. 8

REMODELING

A high neck line may be changed by cutting it lower. A low neck line may be built up by inserting fitted pieces and covering them with a collar, or by changing the shape, if necessary, and filling it in with a yoke of lace or chiffon or softly shirred net or tulle. The addition of a scarf often proves sufficient change if the neck line is not definitely out of style. Figs. 7 and 8 offer suggestions for various neck finishes.

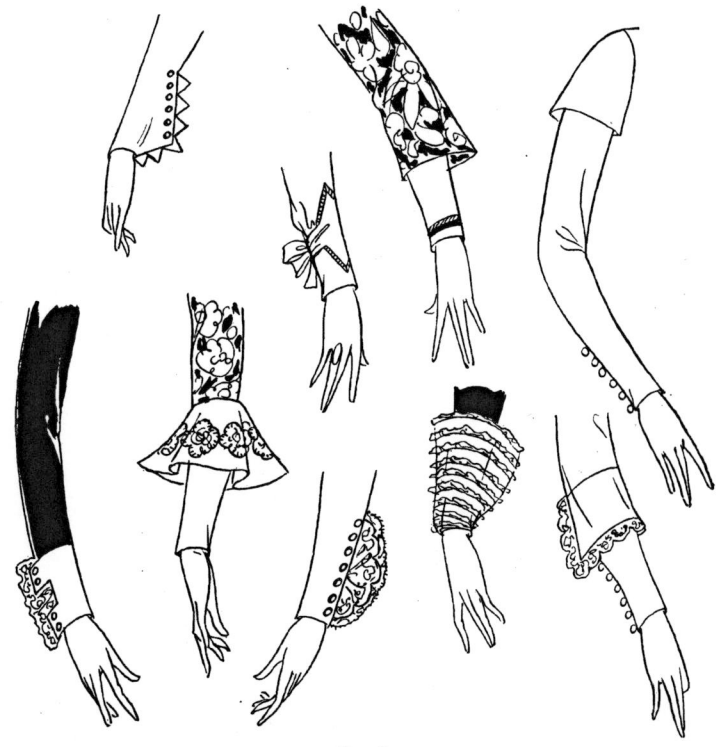

FIG. 9

The effect of a whole dress may be changed by changing its neck line. So, study the prevailing fashion in neck lines, in order that any changes you make will be fashionable. Also, before making changes, study your own type with a view to determining the most becoming shape.

45. Sleeve Changes.—Sleeves date a dress by their length and their fulness. Short sleeves may be made long by the addition of

REMODELING

transparent or heavily embroidered sleeves in bishop effect, or by joining a section of self-material and covering the joining with tucks or some other trimming feature. Three-quarter-length sleeves may be changed by the addition of full, lacy sleevelets, by adding deep

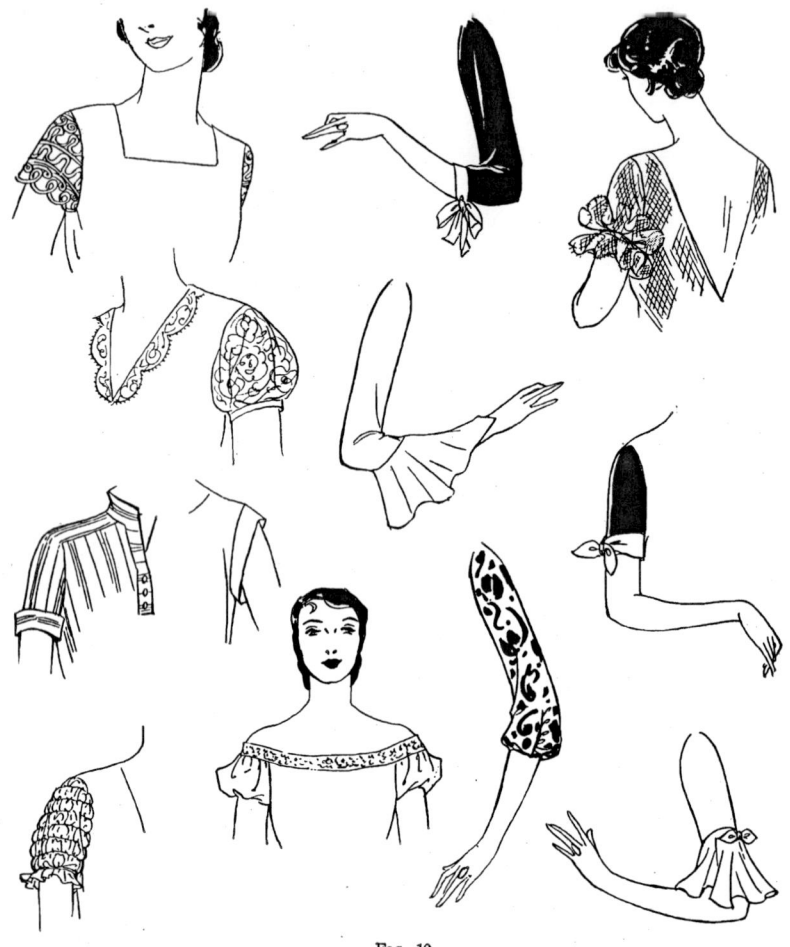

Fig. 10

cuffs, or by joining sections of self-material as just suggested for short sleeves. Or, if short sleeves are preferred, long ones may be cut off and finished to harmonize with the dress. Narrow sleeves may be increased in width by slashing them and inserting material that matches or contrasts. Plaiting this section often takes the

REMODELING

curse off a change of this kind by removing the mark of necessity. Wide sleeves may be ripped out, the seams opened, and the material recut to make close-fitting sleeves, or any other fashionable types. Figs. 9 and 10 show a variety of sleeves that offer many suggestions.

46. Changing Waist Lines.—The waist line is probably the most difficult feature of a dress to alter satisfactorily without entirely recutting the whole garment. It may offend by being too high or too low, too tight or too loose. Of course, if the position of the waist line is due entirely to the placing of a loose belt, the belt can be raised or lowered very easily. But if the dress is cut across at the waist line, the matter assumes a different aspect. If a high or normal waist line of this kind is to be lowered and there is available material, a wide, straight band, perhaps on the opposite grain, may be added to the bottom of the blouse. As a rule, however, recutting is the only remedy.

A waist line that is too low may be cut higher, provided there is some means of adding more length to the skirt. Just what this means should be depends entirely on the type of the dress. When skirt yokes are in fashion, a yoke may be used to give the needed length to the skirt.

When waist lines are drawn in too tightly, it is usually possible to let out some fulness and so produce a newer effect. If, on the other hand, the dress falls too loosely over the waist line, draw it in with a belt or with gathers, tucks, or plaits, or by taking in some of the material in the seams.

If the waist line is neither too high nor too low, too tight nor too loose, but still a change seems desirable, examine current fashion magazines with an eye to waist-line finishes. Keep in mind the type of dress you are remodeling, make note of all suitable finishes shown, and from these choose the one you wish to copy. Frequently, the addition of a smart, new finish at the waist line is all that is needed to give an appearance of newness to the entire dress. The use of matching or contrasting color at the waist line has style importance.

FIG. 11

REMODELING

When leather or other novelty belts are more fashionable than those of self-material, a dress may be made to look very different by removing a fabric belt and substituting the more fashionable novelty.

47. Making One Dress From Two Dresses.—If none of the changes suggested serve to make the dress usable, the only means that remains is to rip the dress apart and plan to recut it. Two old dresses sometimes harmonize or contrast well enough as to color and material to be combined with pleasing effect. A plain or figured silk may be combined with a plain woolen material very successfully. As a general rule, use the heavier-weight material for the skirt or lower portion of the design. Fig. 11 shows a design developed from the combination of two dresses.

Fig. 12

Fig. 13   Fig. 14

REMODELING

48. Cutting Down Dresses.—If there is not another dress to combine with the material, or if it does not seem to merit new material, cut it down for a child.

Little boys love sailor suits and they are very becoming to the child of eight or under. Many cloth dresses have in them enough material of a kind suitable for such suits, one of which is illustrated in Fig. 12. The darker colors, such as navy, brown, and dark green, are most appropriate, although tan may be used. Other light colors may be dyed a darker color if the material is good. To add to the color interest and brighten up such a suit, it may be trimmed with braid in red, blue, yellow, white. or black.

FIG. 15

49. Uses For Silk Dresses.—Unworn parts of some dresses make effective scarfs. Fig. 13 shows three of the Ascot type. Other kinds are shown in Fig. 14. Both printed and plain fabrics may be used satisfactorily in this way.

The skirts of dresses that are made of Georgette, crêpe de Chine, or any similar material and heavily beaded, may be recut and made into sleeves of the bishop type for new or made-over dresses, as is illustrated at the left in Fig. 15. The dress from which the sleeves were cut is shown in the upper right corner.

FIG. 16

REMODELING

Many silk dresses are trimmed with hand embroidery. When it comes to recutting the dress, the using of embroidery is sometimes a problem. The blouse at the lower right of Fig. 15 shows one attractive application of this trimming. Bags and hats may be decorated with embroidery cut from silk or cloth dresses. Fig. 16 shows two types of bags and a hat trimmed in this way.

Silk dresses make acceptable underskirts or bloomers if the material is strong, yet unseasonable for outer wear.

50. Uses For Lingerie Dresses.—Lingerie dresses offer endless possibilities for recutting into lovely underwear. The material must be strong, of course, to merit the work being put on it. Another use for the hand embroidery and lace of lingerie dresses is illustrated

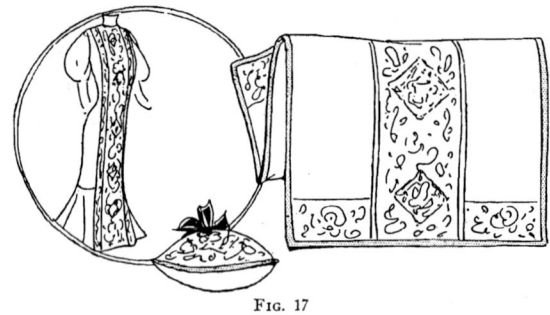

FIG. 17

in Fig. 17. This shows a dresser scarf and matching pin cushion trimmed with the elaborate front panel of an old-fashioned princesse dress. The outer edges of the scarf and cushion are bound with a color.

Very often the blouse part of a gingham dress wears out before the skirt, and the skirt fades so badly that it cannot be used again as a garment. Such a skirt may be made into bags to hold dusters, clothes pins, laundry, and the like.

USING DISCARDED BLOUSES AND WAISTS

51. Uses of Silk Blouses and Waists.—Silk blouses of dark or bright colors may be combined with old silk or wool dresses and serve as the trimming on the "new" dress. If there is good embroidery or other trimming on the blouse, it can be worked into the dress by careful planning, provided, of course, it is the type of embroi-

REMODELING

dery that is appropriate as dress decoration. A pocket and cuff and a neck finish using hand-embroidered motifs from an old garment, are shown in Fig. 18. Elaborate bishop sleeves in a blouse may be transferred to the dress without any change. It is sometimes possible to cut pastel crêpe de Chine blouses over, making brassières or other small pieces of lingerie.

52. Cutting Down Tailored Blouses.—Simple tailored blouses may be cut down for young girls who can then wear them with jumper dresses or suspender skirts or under sweaters.

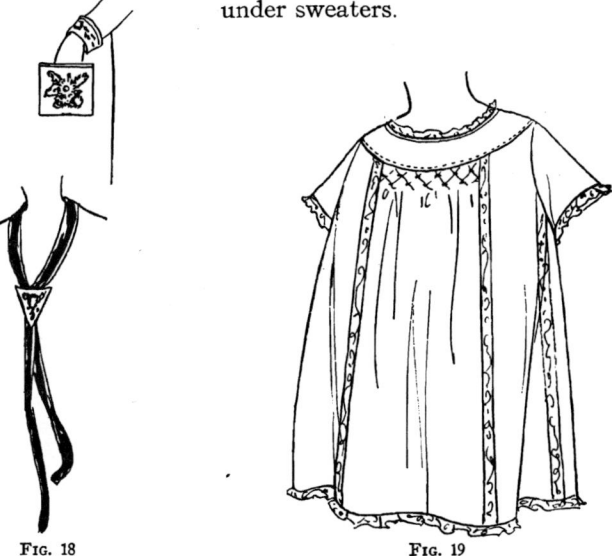

FIG. 18   FIG. 19

Fig. 19 shows a dress for a child made from two tailored pongee blouses. To give necessary length, a round yoke is used in the front. The narrow pieces obtained from the blouses are joined with lace insertion.

53. Uses of Lingerie Blouses.—Lingerie blouses are just brimming with possibilities. The fronts of hand-made, lace-trimmed voile blouses may serve as vests in cloth dresses, or as trimming for chemises or step-in suits. Both of these uses are illustrated in Fig. 20.

Never throw away good hand embroidery. If it cannot be used as it is, cut the motifs from the material, and appliqué them to some

REMODELING

other garment or household article. The list of possibilities is almost endless, but a few hints will suggest other things, and before you know it you will be originating uses for every precious scrap of embroidery in your storage chests.

Fig. 20

Time was when waists had high collars trimmed with embroidery and lace. One of these collars, sewed to baby's bonnet so that it turns back, makes a lovely frame for the dimpled, pink face. Two such bonnets are shown in Fig. 21, which shows also a baby's bib cut from an odd piece of embroidery.

Some lace collars have possibilities as nightgown yokes or trimmings for children's dresses, as shown in Fig. 22. Such lace should be firm enough to stand the strain it will suffer.

54. If there remains, from the era of the hand-embroidered shirt-waist, a relic, elaborately embroidered in front, and buttoned down the back, rejoice, for it will make a beautiful boudoir pillow. Simply cut it heart-shape, triangular, circular, or rectangular (the embroidery will suggest the shape), make a back of similar material, and edge it with Val lace. Some designs are adaptable to baby

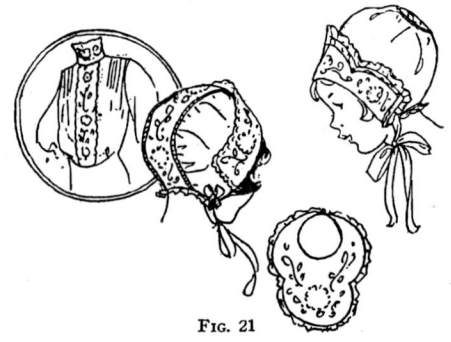

Fig. 21

REMODELING

pillows. If the embroidery is arranged in long, narrow panels, these may be used to decorate the ends of a dresser scarf and to make a matching pin cushion.

Some nightgowns are just as adaptable to the making of pillows as are blouses. Three kinds of pillows that may be made from blouse or nightgown fronts are illustrated in Fig. 23. If the embroidery is in scraps too small to make a pillow, they may be joined with entre deux, hemstitching, or lace insertion, as shown in the rectangular pillow.

FIG. 22

Another use for the embroidered shirt-waist is shown in Fig. 24, where the hand-work is used to trim the nightgown case shown at the left. Small scraps of embroidery that cannot be utilized otherwise may be joined with lace or entre deux or appliquéd to other material to make handkerchief and powder-puff cases, such as are shown at the right and the lower center.

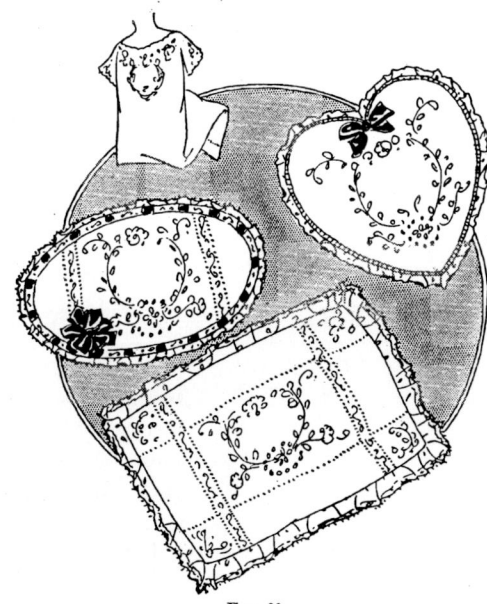

FIG. 23

REMODELING

55. Novelties From Embroidery and Trimmings.—Very "Frenchy" looking, dressing-table accessories may be made by

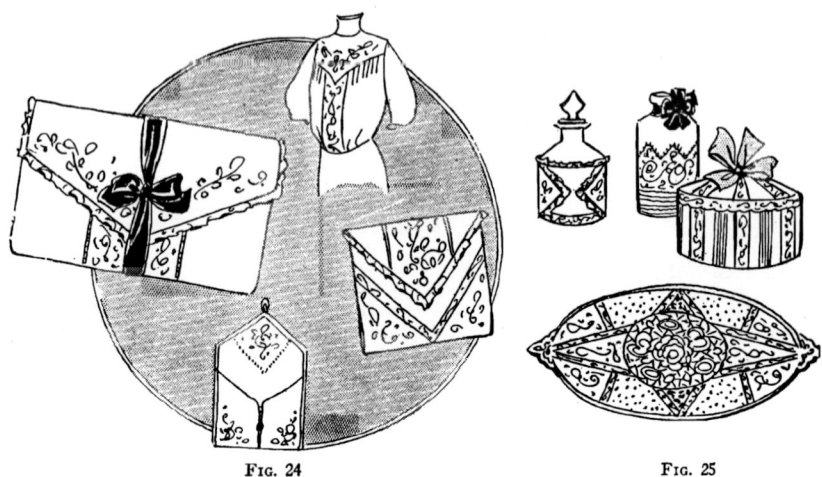

Fig. 24   Fig. 25

gluing little odds and ends of lace, embroidery, hand-run pin tucks, gold braid, tiny rosebuds and ribbon bows to powder boxes, cold cream jars, and perfume bottles. Milliners' glue is the most satisfactory kind to use. A group of these articles is shown in Fig. 25. Particularly lovely pieces of embroidery and lace may be joined together and framed in a small inexpensive frame to make a pin tray, as shown in the lower center of the illustration.

Fig. 26

REMODELING

POSSIBILITIES IN WORN SKIRTS

56. Changing the Style.—If it is desirable to make a few necessary changes and retain the separate skirt as a skirt rather than cut it over, some of the suggestions offered in Arts. **22, 42,** and **43** will be found applicable. In addition to these, there are other means of correcting defects in separate skirts. If the skirt is too tight through the hips, lift it on the belt to give sufficient ease, and then, if necessary, apply a false hem or a band at the bottom for additional length. A skirt that is too short may be dropped on a camisole or a yoke, and worn with a long overblouse to cover the joining.

Fig. 27   Fig. 28

57. Cutting Down Skirts.—A skirt that is worn may be cut down to make one of many attractive garments for a child. Fig. 26 shows a coat and a tam that may be cut for a small child from a white corduroy or a light flannel skirt.

Other garments that may be cut for children from worn skirts of suitable fabric are dresses, bloomers, and knickers, for little girls, and trousers for boys. Fig. 27 shows a dress that utilizes the good parts of two skirts, a separate blouse being made from one, and a skirt and trimmings from the other. The plaits in the skirt give opportunity for invisible piecing, if this is necessary. The skirt, being separate, may be worn with middy blouses.

REMODELING

Fig. 28 shows a child's dress made from two skirts—one serge, and the other crêpe. If the serge is shiny from wear, it may be turned, provided it is attractive on the wrong side.

58. Using Full, Plaited Skirts.—A very full, plaited skirt often provides enough material for a whole dress for an adult after it is ripped, cleaned, and pressed. Or, the plaiting may be retained, and a blouse of harmonizing color may be attached, thus producing a dress.

RECUTTING WORN COATS

59. Cutting Down Coats.—Heavy coats are restricted to a narrow field of usefulness by their very weight. The material is too heavy to be comfortable as anything but a coat. So a lady's heavy coat logically becomes a little girl's coat, and a man's overcoat just as logically evolves into an overcoat for a small boy.

Fig. 29

The coat shown in Fig. 29 is a good type for a child's coat, which may be cut from a larger coat of material that is not too heavy. Twilled weaves and broadcloth are especially well adapted to such a coat.

A heavy coat may be made into a storm cape for a schoolgirl to wear in winter over lighter-weight wraps.

Light-weight coats may be made into skirts for young girls, dresses for little girls, or even into boys' suits.

60. Making Over Coats.—There are, of course, some changes possible that will vary the appearance of a coat so that it can be worn again by its owner. Each is an individual problem, and invariably the cut of the coat in question, together with the lines of the current silhouette, suggest the possible change.

REMODELING

Fig. 30 shows a method of handling the problem of the outgrown coat. The figure at the left shows the one-time, full-length and becoming sports coat that has become too short in the skirt and the sleeves for its young owner. The figure at the right shows the same coat, again made wearable and attractive by shortening the skirt part to a becoming short-coat length, and using the material cut off for piecing down the sleeves and adding short cuffs to them.

61. Artistic Patching of Coat Linings.—It often occurs that a coat is in good style and very good condition except that its lining is worn along the lower edge of the sleeves and around the bottom. Obviously, it would be extravagant to replace the entire lining with a new one. The problem of replacing the worn section without having it look

Fig. 30

"patchy" also presents difficulties. It is a happy thought, then, that leads one to the ribbon counter to solve the difficulty. Here is the way it may be done.

Cut off the worn edge of the lining and select ribbon ½ to 1 inch wider than the piece cut off, and of a color, or colors, that blend with that of the lining. Now, 3 to 5 inches above the cut edge of the lining, slash it across and insert the ribbon. This brings a band of the lining material at the bottom, and the ribbon pieces out the necessary length, at the same time adding a touch of distinction to the lining.

When a coat lining becomes worn under the arms, instead of patching it, apply dress-shield shaped pieces of the lining material. These are double and may be interlined with muslin to give them body.

REMODELING

USING MEN'S WORN SHIRTS

62. Making Aprons.—Worn shirts have supplied the wives, mothers, sisters, and daughters of their ex-owners with aprons for so many years that no one knows whom to credit with the origin of the idea. But, although the idea is very old, new adaptations of it appear from time to time. For example, it has been proved that two aprons may be cut from one shirt, and both be large enough for a woman of average size. The accompanying figures show how this is possible.

63. Fig. 31 (*a*) shows an apron that is made from a pair of shirt sleeves, and the accompanying diagram (*b*) shows how it is

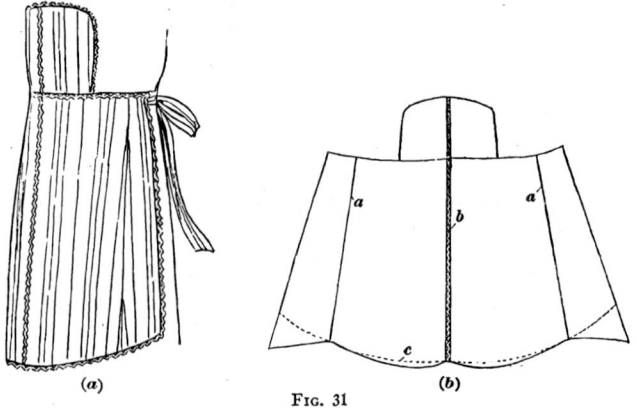

FIG. 31

done. Simply cut the sleeves open from the cuff openings instead of along the seams. The sleeve seams are indicated by *a* on the diagram. Join the two sleeves lengthwise with rickrack braid, as at *b*, and shape the lower edge as indicated by the dotted line *c*. Edge the apron with rickrack. If a bib is desired, cut it from a part of the shirt front that will not be used for another apron, as indicated by *d*, Fig. 32 (*b*) and 33 (*b*). The bib also is put together and joined to the waist line with rickrack. Strings for this apron may be cut from the shirt fronts, also, as shown at *e*, in Figs. 32 (*b*) and 33 (*b*).

64. Fig. 32 (*a*) shows a cover-all apron made from the rest of the shirt. The diagram (*b*) shows the shirt cut open on the under-

REMODELING

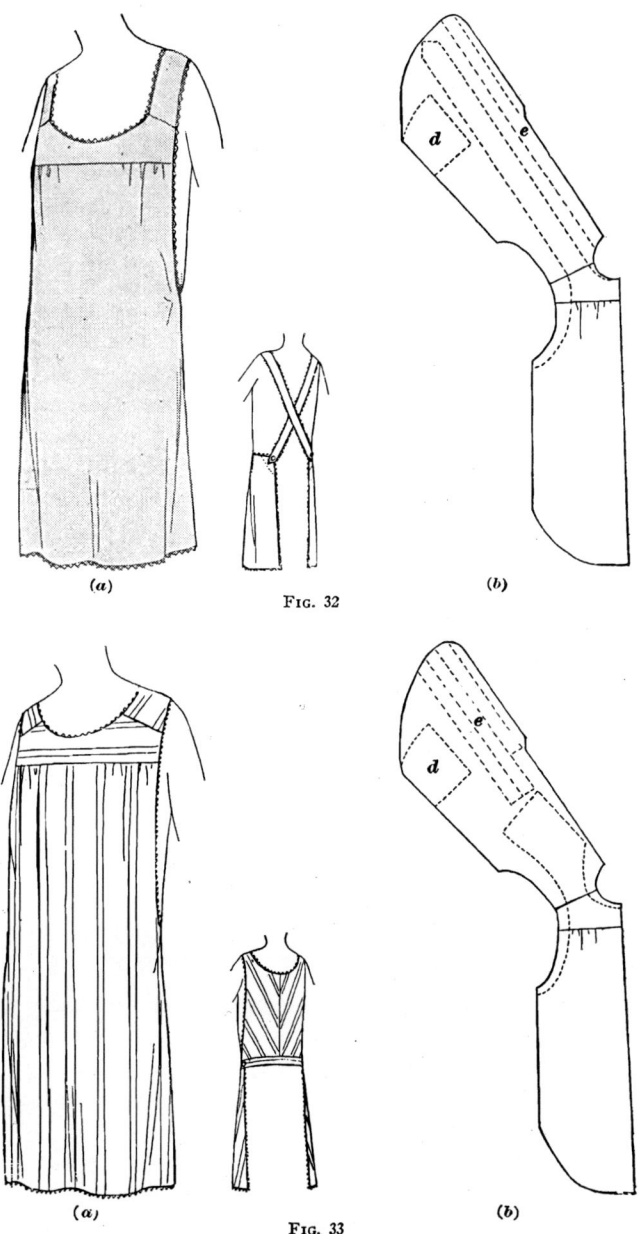

Fig. 32

Fig. 33

REMODELING

arm seam, with sleeves and neck band removed. As indicated by the dotted lines, the apron front is cut from the shirt back, and the back yoke of the shirt becomes the front yoke of the apron without the ripping of a single stitch. The straps, cut from the front, are already attached, and the only sewing necessary is to finish the outer edges with rickrack or novelty braid.

Fig. 33 (*a*) shows another apron, identical with Fig. 32 (*a*) except for the back. The diagram (*b*) shows the cutting. In this case, there is one seam at the center back.

65. Miscellaneous Uses.—Other uses for worn shirts are for a child's rompers, apron, or dress, and for a boy's shirt. In cutting down a shirt for a little boy, place the pattern on the shirt so that the original hems at the front, with their buttons and buttonholes, may be used for the front of the boy's shirt.

A worn silk shirt supplies material for a pleasing chemise by cutting the chemise front from the shirt back and the back from the shirt fronts. A seam at the center back gives an opportunity for slight fitting and an inverted plait, if desired. The top may be bound with self-material cut from the sleeves. Also, step-ins may be made from the lower part of a silk shirt by replacing the plait with a French seam and using this at the front. A 3×7 crotch piece may be cut from the sleeves. The top should be finished with a casing and the lower edges may be left plain or finished with lace or blanket-stitching. Some striped silk shirts make attractive sports blouses for young girls or dresses for children.

UTILIZING HOUSEHOLD ARTICLES

66. The thrifty housewife does not stop with the remodeling of garments. Her enthusiasm carries her over into the realm of household articles, and she finds that there are many things, often thrown away, that will give additional service if a little ingenuity is used.

67. Table Linen.—Linen table-cloths break and show wear on the lines where the folds come or where the cloths touch the table edges, while the remainder of the cloth is still very strong. From them, one may cut lunch napkins, table runners, individual mats, tray cloths, dresser scarfs, and face towels. Lovely, soft wash cloths for the baby may be cut from small pieces. The edges of some of these articles may be hemmed by hand or machine, or, as in the case of tray cloths, they may be machine hemstitched, and a

REMODELING

picot edge crocheted in the hemstitching. Cross-stitched edges will be found decorative for dresser scarfs, table runners, or individual mats.

Fig. 34 shows a luncheon set made from small pieces of linen. To increase the size of the lunch cloth, hems were applied with machine hemstitching, and, although the napkins and individual mats required only very small pieces, they were treated in the same way to harmonize. Fagoting may be used in the same way, or the pieces may be joined with feather braid, which gives an effect that is similar to hemstitching. The set in Fig. 35 has its edges finished with simple crochet. A machine-made lace may be substituted, if preferred.

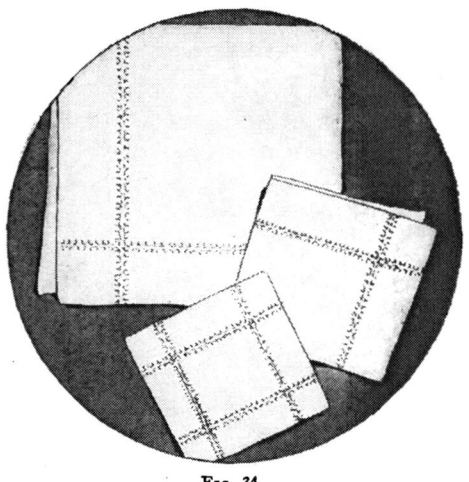

Fig. 34

68. Towels.—The good parts of worn Turkish towels may be cut into squares and hemmed for use as face cloths. Bibs for small children may also be made from Turkish toweling, and, when bound with a dainty color, they are most attractive. Linen towels may be used in the same ways as Turkish towels, and, in some cases, for small doilies finished as suggested for those of table linen.

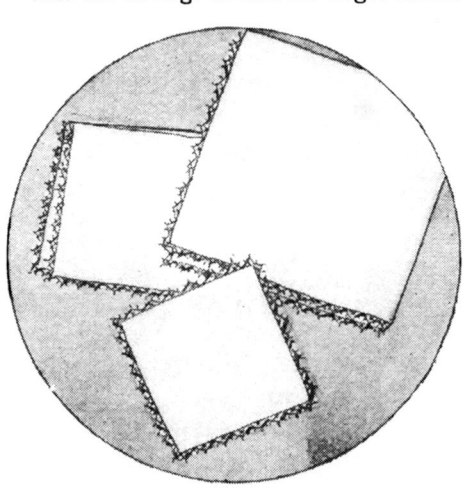

Fig. 35

REMODELING

69. Bed Linen.—Worn pillow slips may be cut down for use on smaller pillows. Soft old bed spreads may be cut up for hand towels or face cloths. The worn edges of blankets may be cut off and silk blanket binding, 2 or 3 inches in width, may be stitched on. Another method of finishing blanket edges is to crochet a shell edging, using a steel crocket hook. If the blanket is worn through the center as well as along the edges, it may be cut into squares about 1 yard square, which may be used to wrap around the baby when he is taken from his bath. Or, if there is no baby in the house, put two of these thin blankets together, cover them with pretty silkaline or similar material, tie them with wool yarn, and you have a warm and attractive comfortable that will be very serviceable. It may be laundered easily, since the blankets do not "bunch" in washing as the cotton filling, generally used in comfortables, is likely to do.

FIG. 36

70. Curtains.—Full-length curtains of Swiss, net, scrim, or dimity may be cut down for sash curtains when their edges become worn. A little design in simple darning-stitches, such as shown in Fig. 36, makes them look almost like new.

USING OUT-OF-SEASON CLOTHES FOR HOUSEHOLD ARTICLES

71. Every now and then something—a dress, a scarf, a blouse—goes out of style or meets with an accident, so that it can no longer be worn. Some of the material is good, but it is in pieces of sizes or shapes that make them valueless as possibilities for remaking into other garments. Before you discard them completely, look them over with an eye to their possibilities as sofa pillows, table runners, or lamp shades. Often, too, when the garment can be made over, there are pieces left that might well be used in one of these ways.

72. Making Pillows and Runners.—A kerchief scarf came into close contact with the ink bottle, and a big ugly stain in the center

REMODELING

left it useless as a scarf. The corners, however, were unharmed, so they were cut off and used to make the square pillow in Fig. 37.

A piece of light-brown taffeta from a dress made the foundation of the oblong pillow, and to brighten it up, small gay-colored silk scraps were cut in pieces 3 inches wide and of various lengths. These were sewed together with plain seams, gathered on both sides to form puffing, and applied to the pillow with novelty ribbon. Scraps of velvet of various colors may be used for a similar trimming on a velvet floor cushion.

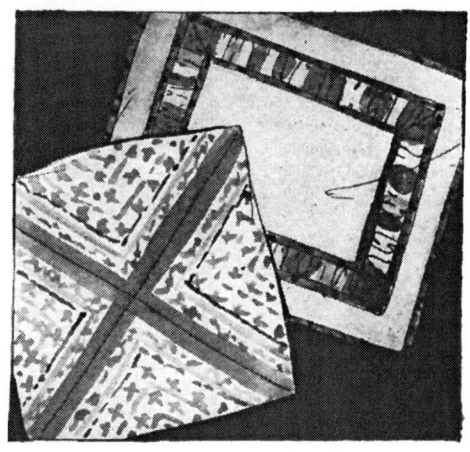

FIG. 37

In this case, however, it is better not to gather the varicolored band but rather to insert it flat.

Fig. 38 illustrates a number of types of pillows, many of which may be made from cast-off apparel of suitable material and color.

FIG. 38

An old velvet suit that is cut in small pieces so that it offers very limited possibilities for remodeling may be transformed, with the

REMODELING

aid of a little metal brocade and metallic braid, into a table runner and some cushions to match it.

73. Lamp Shades.—If you wish to make a lamp shade from parts of an old dress, consider the weight of the material first.

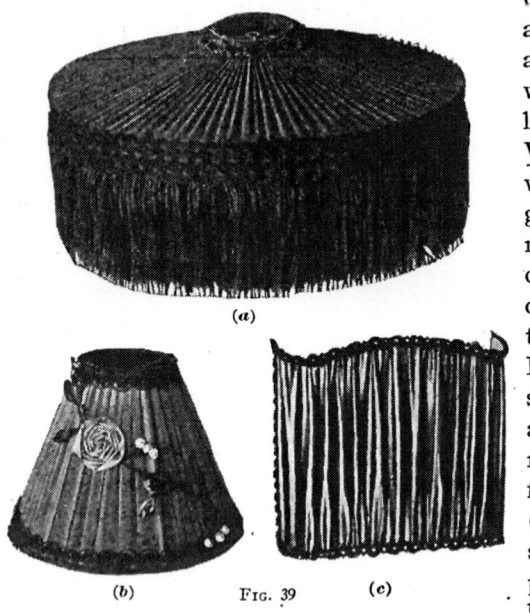

Georgette, chiffon, and crêpe de Chine are light enough in weight to permit the light to filter through. Veiling a flowered silk with chiffon or Georgette gives attractive results if both are chosen so that their colors combine attractively over the light. Fig. 39 (a) shows a shade suitable in size and shape for a living room. The small flower-trimmed shade (b) and the light shield (c) are appropriate for use in a bedroom. Any ten-cent store will supply the wire frames, and most of them also sell fringe and braid for finishing the edges. Or, it may be that you have some fringe from a dress or braid from some other article that can be used. Flower trimming is easily made from scraps of ribbon or silk.

UTILIZING REMNANTS AND MISCELLANEOUS MATERIALS

74. Laces.—Lace, whether real, handmade lace or merely a machine copy, can always be used to advantage. Wide lace is lovely for evening and dinner dresses. If only a small part of the lace from a lace dress is good, it may be used as sleeves, collar, apron, vest, sleevelets, or inserts on a new or a made-over dress. Fig. 40

REMODELING

shows how lace may be used for godets in a dress or slip. Odd pieces of narrow lace may be combined to make attractive collars, such as those shown in Fig. 41. Jabots, vests, and plastrons,

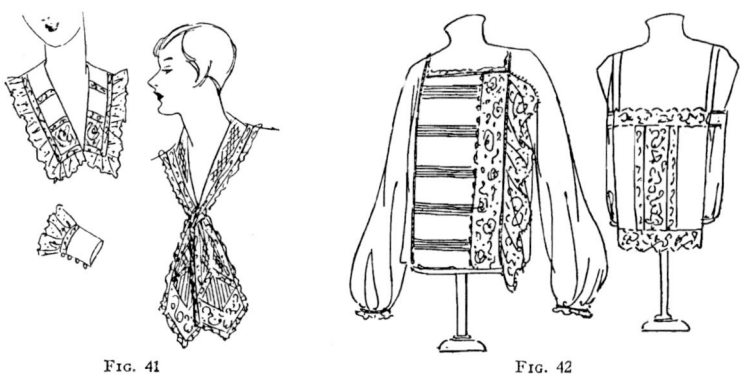

Fig. 41   Fig. 42

as in Figs. 42 and 43, are other uses for small pieces of lace in dress decoration. Then it is always possible to use them as inserts in underwear.

With a little ingenuity, fragments of coarse lace may be joined in pleasing arrangements or inserted in linen to make small mats, such

Fig. 43

as are shown in Fig. 44, for cases, candlesticks, or similar purposes. Sheer silk lace of medium width may be sewed to a tiny square of colored chiffon to make a handkerchief that gives a decorative note to a costume.

REMODELING

75. Ribbons.—Ribbons, even in very short lengths, may be made into lovely little flowers and buds for decorating under-

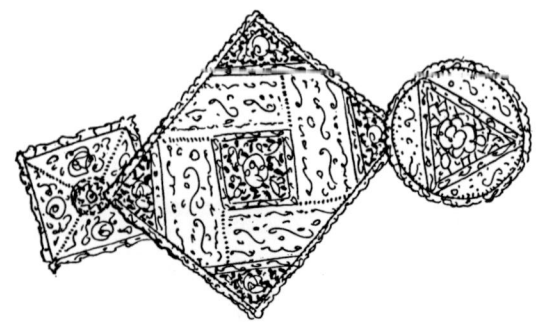

Fig. 44

garments, negligées, party dresses, and children's clothes. Fig. 45 shows several varieties. Detachable shoulder straps made of ribbon are lovely decorated in this way. Sachets may be made of

Fig. 45

ribbon or of scraps of silk and bound with ribbon. Several tied together, make a dainty trifle for personal use or a small gift. Single sachets are lovely when trimmed with ribbon or silk flowers.

NEW CLOTHES FOR OLD

IT has always been a substantial economy to renovate and recut partly worn clothes to bring them right up to date, especially where there were children for whom adult garments could be cut down. Re-modelling also had the attraction in peacetime of being a challenge to one's ingenuity and could become a really thrilling hobby.

But clothes rationing has made it a necessity as well. Coupons will not suffice to keep the family sufficiently and smartly dressed unless garments are used to the very last thread, either for their original owner or for the younger generation. No throwing away now of clothes which look a little shabby or out-of-date! Instead, they must serve again in another form until the fabric is really worn out. Much of the time women used to spend on fashioning new garments is now to spare, since we can have so few new. Then how use it better than in repairing, re-modelling and retrimming what we have in hand?

Mending is outside the scope of this book, but in this chapter you will find plenty of hints that will help you in making old clothes into new by means of dressmaking skill.

First, as it often takes nearly as much time (including unpicking) to re-model as to make a new garment, be quite sure before you start that any particular job is worth while. Anxious as we are to save coupons and expense, it is no good spending many hours renovating stuff so old that it will wear into holes almost as soon as the work is done. The fabric must have a reasonable amount of wear still left in it; the new style chosen must be possible to work out from the old garment and sufficiently becoming and up to date when finished; the cost of new materials and trimmings should not exceed, both in money and coupons,

HOME DRESSMAKING

more than one-third of the original price or coupon value of the garment.

If you intend dyeing the garment at home before renovating it, plan to cut it down to a smaller size, for home dyeing usually shrinks the material quite definitely.

It is not always a success (even when you have coupons to spare!) to buy new material to complete a renovation, as the freshness of the new may merely emphasize the shabbiness of the old. For this reason, it is often wise to use two frocks of suitable fabrics and colours to make into one new one, instead of remodelling each with the aid of fresh material. When you must add new stuff to an old garment, washing or sponging it before cutting will make it blend in better.

To achieve smart, serviceable renovations, wash or clean everything before re-making it. The old seams rarely come in the right place again. Besides, re-seaming, even if only $\frac{1}{4}$ in. away, freshens the garment, helping to give it a new look. But don't take up time carefully unpicking. Instead, cut the pieces apart close to the old seams and well press every piece. Then, with chalk, mark all worn, stained or faded patches, and avoid these as far as possible when laying on the pattern pieces for recutting (Fig. 90).

An exception to this rule of not unpicking is when a garment is to be turned—that is, made up exactly as before, but with the comparatively clean, unworn wrong side now turned outwards to be the right side. In this case, every seam and hem must be unpicked, and care taken not to cut the fabric in doing so.

Turning was the regular practice in Victorian days and it has become invaluable again now that coupons limit the new material we can buy. It is used mainly for heavy woollen fabrics which take a long time to wear out, and get shabby, faded or just monotonous while they are still much too good to throw away. This is chiefly the case with costumes or coats. Of course the wrong side must have an attractive (or at any rate a presentable) surface, which is not always the case. In fact, when ordering a

NEW CLOTHES FOR OLD

FIG. 90. Before re-cutting the old garment, unpick and press the pieces, marking worn or faded patches with chalk to avoid using them again

HOME DRESSMAKING

coat or costume nowadays, it is a wise precaution to look at the wrong side when choosing your fabric, with an eye to having the garment turned later.

Turning, though often rather a tedious job, is quite simple and gives you what looks like an entirely new garment. Merely unpick completely and re-make with the wrong side turned outermost. Skirts should have the side placket re-made so that it will still be on the left and the chief difficulty with coats is that the buttonholes are now on the wrong side. Sew them up as inconspicuously as possible—they will be unseen in any case when the coat is worn and fastened—and make new ones on the opposite side. Unless the coat material is very thick, bound buttonholes (see page 145) are the easiest to manage. Or a "little" tailor in a side street will often give the turned coat a professional pressing and provide it with expert new buttonholes, for a very modest sum.

Converting and renovating possibilities run into hundreds and vary infinitely with the existing wardrobe, the particular family and the fashions of the moment. But here is a list of suggestions which any home dressmaker can adapt and add to, according to her particular needs. All items listed in the first column are women's garments, unless otherwise stated. Helpful notes on the actual work of converting follow this list for those suggestions marked in it with an asterisk.

Original Garment	*Possible Renovation*
Cotton frock	Frock for little girl.
	Summer suit or knickers for little boy.
	Blouse or jumper for yourself or child.
	*Overall for yourself or child.
	Housework apron.
	Cut up into household articles, such as laundry bag, "shoulders" for coat-hangers, dressing-table or informal lunch mats, kettle-holders, dusters, curtain ties (see Fig. 91).
Woollen frock	Warm jumper or bolero.
	*Skirt to wear with knitted jumpers for yourself or little girl

NEW CLOTHES FOR OLD

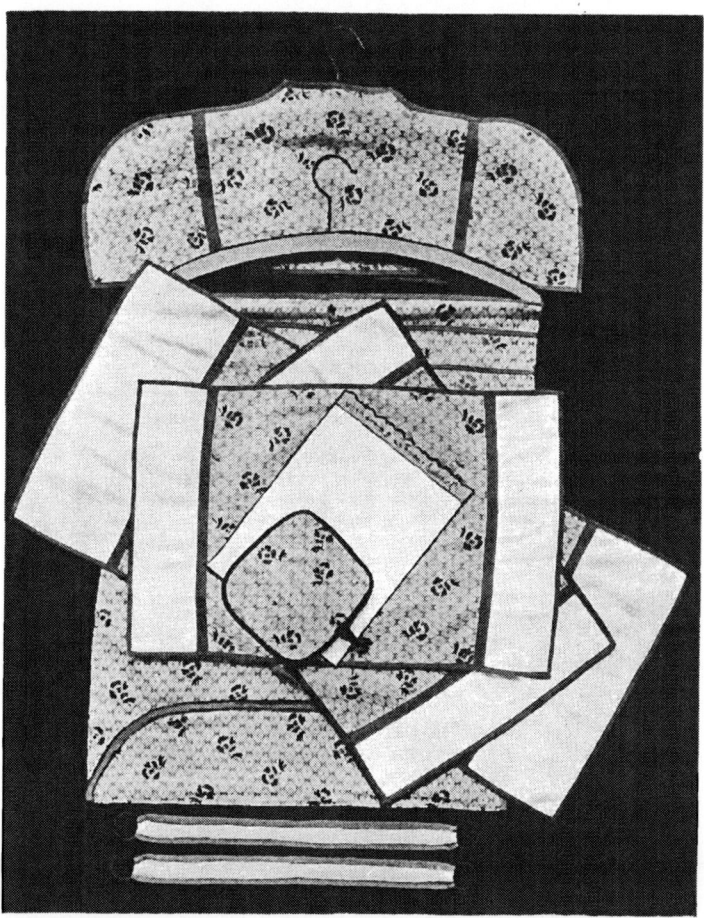

FIG. 91. All these items—laundry-bag on hanger, "shoulder" for hanger, runner, two mats, modesty vest, kettle-holder, and pair of curtain ties—were made from one old-fashioned cotton frock

HOME DRESSMAKING

Original Garment	Possible Renovation
	Frock for little girl.
	Summer coat for little girl.
	Summer knickers for little boy.
	Pinafore frock to wear over blouses.
Silk washing frock	Blouse or jumper.
	Child's blouse.
	Frock for little girl.
	Slip to wear under frocks.
	Panties, knickers or cami-knickers for yourself.
	Nightgown for yourself or little girl.
Silk frock (non-washable)	Slip.
	Blouse for yourself or child.
	Frock for little girl.
	Coat lining.
	Scarf.
Full-length housecoat (varying the list according as it is silk, wool or cotton)	Dressing-gown for yourself or child.
	Pyjamas for yourself or child.
	Frock (with matching headband).
	Two blouses for child.
	Overall for yourself or child.
	Skirt and bolero.
	Skirt.
Woollen or tweed skirt	Frock for little girl.
	Skirt for little girl or schoolgirl.
	Knickers for little boy.
	Pinafore frock for little girl.
	Hat or cap.
Coat and skirt	Coat-frock for yourself or child.
	Bolero.
	Knickers or suit for little boy.
	Hat or cap.
Long coat (woollen or tweed)	Coatfrock for yourself or little girl.
	Overcoat for little boy.
	Knickers for little boy.
	Skirt for yourself or schoolgirl.
	*Skirt and bolero.
	Pull-on hats (several).

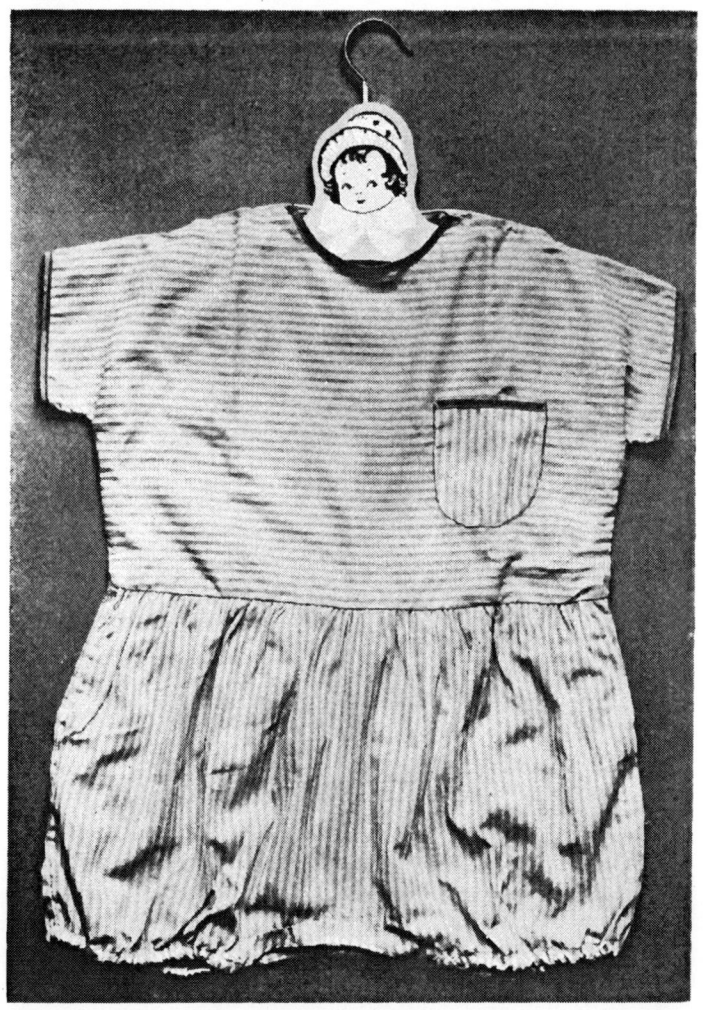

FIG. 92. Strong rompers for toddlers may be economically made from the best parts of a man's old shirt

HOME DRESSMAKING

Original Garment	Possible Renovation
Long coat (silk or linen)	Skirt and bolero. Slip. Lining for woollen coat (if silk). Frock for little girl. Summer suit for little boy. Tennis shorts or skirt. Overall (if linen). Coat-frock for yourself or little girl. Scarves (if silk).
Evening gown.	Best blouse for yourself or schoolgirl. Evening coatee (from skirt). Party frock for little girl. Party blouse for little boy. Dressing-jacket. Slip for day or evening. Coat lining Scarf; cushion cover. Panties or cami-knickers.
Blouse	Blouse for child. Headband or scarf. Decorative handkerchiefs Trimmings for a new dress. Panties.
Two-piece (frock and matching short or long coat—woollen)	*Remodelled frock for yourself. Frock and coat for little girl. Skirt and bolero. Suit for little boy. Coat for little boy with matching knickers.
Man's suit	Suit or knickers for little boy. Bolero or jacket for yourself (from coat). Pull-on hats.
Man's shirt (when neck and cuffs are worn or frayed)	*Housework pinafore. *Housework apron. Child's overall. Child's rompers (see Fig. 92). Shirt blouse for yourself or schoolgirl. Shirt for boy. Dusters; laundry and shoe-bags.

With the following hints to help you over some of the less obvious conversions, you will get your hand in, see the general

NEW CLOTHES FOR OLD

idea and be able to attempt the others with confidence. If the renovation is at all a drastic one, buy a suitable paper pattern for it. Don't waste your precious material trying to cut out by guesswork.

Cotton Frock into Overall. Choose a frock of fairly straight up-and-down cut, and slit it right down the centre-front from neck to hem. To get enough width for fastening over, add a wide wrap to each front, cutting this from any odd cotton you have by you or from a second cotton frock too old for further wear. On a printed material use plain wraps, if possible, on a plain colour flowered or check wraps. Fasten with press studs.

Woollen Frock into Skirt. This is a good renovation when, as often happens, a dress wears under the arms or becomes too tight across the bust, while the skirt is still good and well-fitting. Unpick the join of skirt and bodice at the waist, then, using the frock belt, if this is at all suitable, finish the skirt waistline as described for a soft-finished skirt waist on page 136.

Silk Washing Frock into Slip. Cut off the top part of the dress just under the armholes all round and finish the cut edge with self binding or insertion. Remove all trimmings that prevent a flat, sleek fit and narrow the garment at the side seams if required. Make shoulder-straps from the sleeves.

Long Coat into Skirt and Bolero. Cut the coat in half at a rather high waistline. Remove the collar and revers from the upper portion, shorten the sleeves if wished, remove the lining. If too loose when worn without a lining or frock beneath, achieve a snugger fit by re-stitching a little inside the sleeve, shoulder and underarm seams. Round off the lower front corners and bind all round the edges with silk braid or contrasting bias strips. Lap over and stitch together the fronts of the lower coat portion, fit in to the waist by taking in the side seams and taking up darts at side-front and side-back and finish with a belt as described in page 156.

Two-piece into Smart New Frock. If the dress part of a two-piece goes first in the bodice, as usually happens, use the coat to

HOME DRESSMAKING

re-model it. Discard the old bodice altogether. Fit the upper part of the coat in more closely to form a new bodice, removing any typically coat trimmings, such as fur, and re-trimming with braid, contrasting material or whatever is in fashion and coupon-free. Then join the new bodice to the skirt. If the coat is a long one and the skirt rather shiny at the back, a new back panel may be cut from one of the coat facings—these, being inside, will be in almost new condition—and inserted to freshen up the skirt part of the remodelled dress.

Man's Shirt into Housework Pinafore and Apron. Use the whole back of the shirt, including the yoke, for the front of the pinafore. Cut long straps from the sleeves which go over each shoulder, cross at the back and button on to the pinafore edge under each arm. Add a patch pocket. Bind all edges and the top pocket edge with a bright cotton bias binding. From the lower part of the shirt front (if this is not the coat type, opening all the way down) you can cut and shape a short apron, mounting this on a belt with long tie ends which fasten round the waist.

Nightgown into Slip. This conversion, not given in the above list, is very useful when a nightgown wears out in its lace top part, but is still perfectly good in the fabric skirt portion. Cut away the worn top part, narrow the nightgown suitably, finish the top edge with binding or lace and provide ribbon shoulder straps.

Your Mending Routine

IF YOU HAVEN'T a wholly satisfactory mending routine, plan one now. Every woman has her share of mending to do, and it depends upon you whether you enjoy doing your mending or have it forever hanging over you, depriving you of the use of articles and apparel that need only a few stitches to make them really satisfactory. Sooner or later, almost everyone meets mending problems, such as resewing seams, taking tacking stitches, sewing on buttons, or sewing down parts of a garment that have become frayed. Do you keep your mending up to date?

The Mending Basket. Tuck into your mending basket all the necessary time-saving articles: a darning egg, small sharp-pointed scissors, a safety-razor blade, darning needles, sewing needles, darning thread, pins, tape, buttons, snaps and hooks and eyes. Your mending basket or box should also be large enough to hold the garments to be repaired.

Darning-Stitch. The stitches most used in mending are darning-stitches. These look like weaving. Just use the running-stitch, alternating over-and-under-stitches in each successive row, and then pick up with stitches made in the opposite direction, so that the weave is replaced. Darning-stitches are a substitute for the original material, so the thread should be as nearly as possible the same color and texture as the material. In mending wool or linen, it is an excellent plan to unravel a thread of the material itself and darn it into the worn place. Weave the stitches into the material, so that they blend into it without bulk or seam.

Darning-stitches are used for mending holes in stockings, tears in table linen, and worn places in garments of wool and linen. When an otherwise good garment becomes thin at the knee or at the elbow, its life may be prolonged by reinforcing these points by a net of darning-stitches on the wrong side. If the hole to be darned is very large, it is sometimes advisable, as in the case of knitted underwear, to baste a piece of fine net over the hole and darn through. This will keep the hole from stretching, and give the darned portion a flat and permanent appearance.

Mending Dainty Garments. Dainty lingerie and baby clothes should be carefully mended by hand with fine thread and small stitches. Lace should always be mended with tiny overhand stitches.

Machine Mending. The machine is best for mending firmly woven cotton material such as muslin, drilling and firm shirtings. A silk stocking with a long run may also be mended by machine. To mend, crease the stocking lengthwise of the run on the wrong side and stitch the length of the run. Be sure your stitching line comes just outside the run portion, stretch the stocking slightly as you stitch to give sufficient length in the stitching line to prevent its drawing or breaking. Then overcast the seam with loose stitches to give it the appearance of a line rather than a seam. This same method may be used for runs in most knitted garments.

Mending Shirts or Blouses. To mend a shirt that is worn across the shoulder or at the front, place a piece of sturdy light-weight material, such as net, underneath the worn surface, and stitch back and forth with very fine thread on the machine, or mend by hand with running-stitches. Men's shirt cuffs and collars that are worn should be ripped off, reversed, and stitched on again.

Patches, Make-Overs. Mending and altering are akin, because both are usually made on garments that have been worn. There is economy in making over clothes for children, but the design, the fabric and the color must be suitable. Do not merely shorten mother's skirt for daughter; rip it, and make it fit as it should. Dye the material if the color is not suitable.

Altering Garments for Children. Garments of growing children often need alteration. The skirt and sleeves may be lengthened by inserting a band of contrasting material to give the necessary length. The hem may be let down to the proper length. If the bottom of the hem is worn, let it make the top of the new facing line and put a narrow tuck at the top to conceal the worn edge.

Lengthen a short-waisted dress by inserting a strip of material at the shoulder line or around the blouse three or four inches above the waistline, or use a new yoke. The strip may be of contrasting color or of the same material, washed and left in the sun if necessary, to take off the new look.

To make an armhole larger, insert a 1½" to 2" square gusset at the underarm. If more fullness is needed through the body, insert a piece the full length of the underarm seam.

Salvage Materials. Good materials may be redyed, recut, and remade. Keep the scraps of new fabrics; they may be used for trimming, facing, lengthening, making new collars and cuffs, pockets—in fact for many things that will save your time and money. See information on storing such items, page 4.

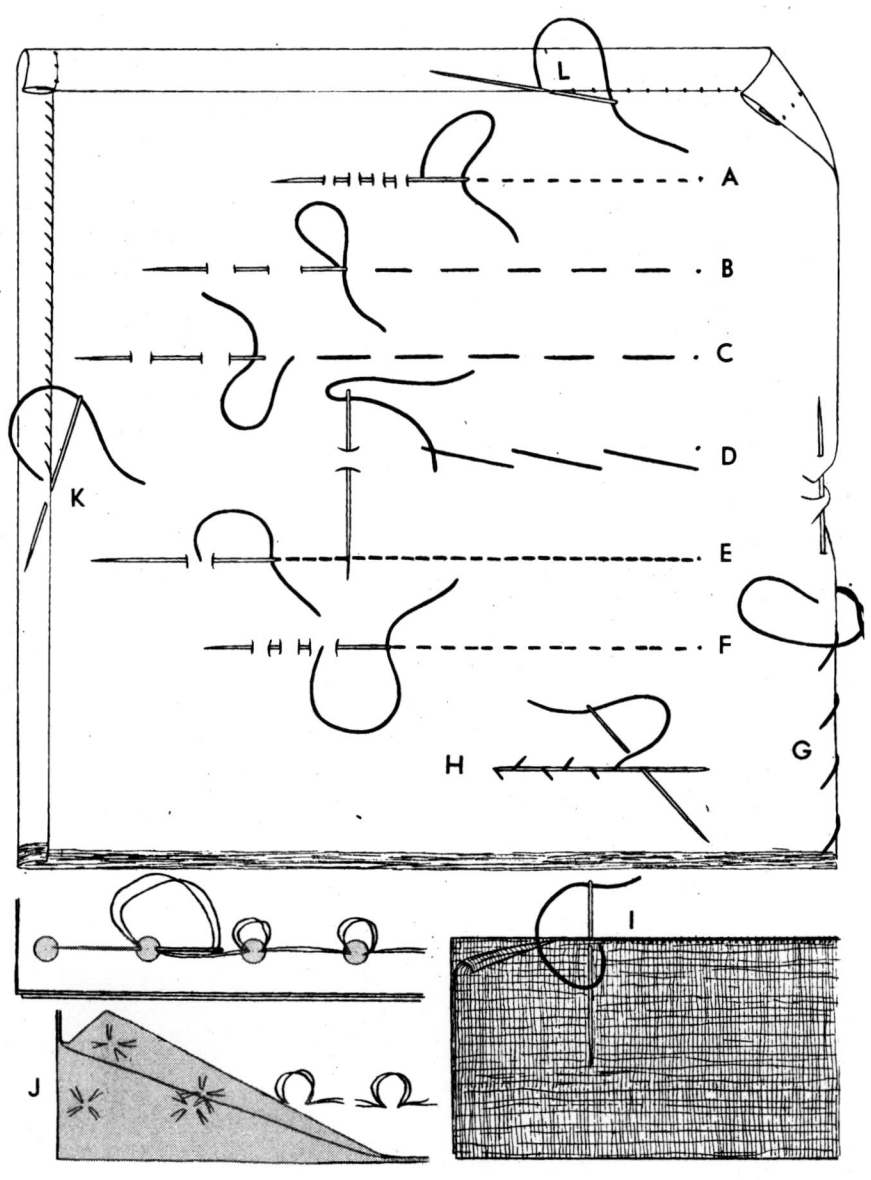

MENDING AND KNITTING

MENDING

The two main methods of repair are patching and darning. Very roughly speaking darns are applied to knit fabrics and small holes on unknitted undergarments; while patching (or combined patch and darn) is applied to outergarments and large repairs on undergarments. Use gusset patches where a tear has been due to strain rather than wear as these are cut on the bias and give; machine-darning for household repairs and undergarments not worth hand-mending: re-inforcing for places subject to special strain, or wear and tear.

In all repair work TIME, the general condition of the garment, and the cost of replacing it, are factors in governing choice of method, which are as important as suitability of method to material, etc. Re-inforcing before, or in the early stages of wear, is one of the most profitable ways of expending the time available for mending; and next to this the repair of household linen by machine darning. Worked close it is strong, done scattered over a large thin area or across a slit, a very few minutes at the machine may easily give an old towel, sheet, or teacloth (rubber), weeks of extra life.

DARNING

Definition.

Darning is a method of replacing worn *threads* as distinct from patching which inserts whole pieces of material. It can often be more invisible than patching.

Types.—The web darn is the ordinary method, and is applied to unknitted as well as to strictly web fabrics. Variations are given for cloth (Hedgetear, Fine Drawing, Stoating), also a special darn for table linen—the Damask. Loom darning is a quick method for large holes on coarse garments. Swiss Darning and Machine Darning are alternatives to the web, the former a very perfect repair only worth doing in special cases.

General Rules for the web and its variations.

1. Choose thread suitable as regards thickness, texture, and colour.

2. Leave loops at the ends of rows, to allow for stretching in wear, and shrinking in wash.

MENDING AND KNITTING

3. Darn thin places before they wear through into holes.
4. Cover all thin area round holes so that the edges of the darn reach firm material.
5. Replace selvedge threads first. On web of knitting pick up loops first, then cross the darn.

To make the most invisible darn do not pick up garment when crossing, only the threads just inserted.

6. Work on the *WS*. Stockings are sometimes darned on the *RS* (for tender feet); also the combined patch and darn.

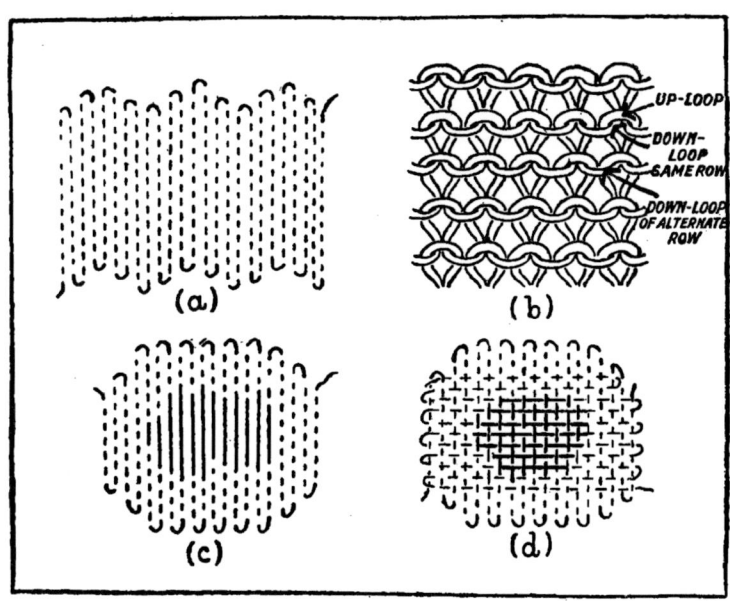

FIG. 79.

7. Shape darns so that the edges do not pull on one thread of the garment, i.e. wavy edge, hexagonal, diamond but *not square*.

8. Pick up loops, or tiny pieces of material, so that space and stitch fall alternately in succeeding rows.

Web Darn.
THIN PLACE. Fig. 79 (a).
1. Darn with a wavy edge.
2. Darn loosely and leave large loops for elasticity of web.
3. Take up-loops on the needle when pointed away from the worker, and down-loops of the *alternate row* when towards worker (Fig. 79 (b)). But do not count loops on *fine* web.

4. The darning should hardly show on the RS. Leave no space between the rows.

HOLES. Fig. 79 (c).

1. Begin darning ¼ in. beyond the hole, or more, according to the size of the thin area round it.
2. Make the first row equal to the length of hole.
3. Increase the length of each row at both ends until the hole is reached.
4. Keep rows of equal length across the hole on a small darn, but make a wavy edge on large darns.
5. Decrease on the other side.
6. Take care to pick up all the loops round the edge of the hole to prevent subsequent laddering.

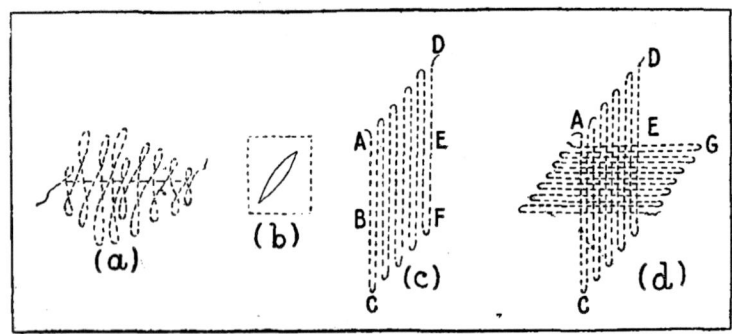

FIG. 80.

7. *Crossing* (Fig. 79 (d)).—Begin just above the edge of the hole and darn over and under, lattice fashion. Be careful to pick up, without splitting the thread. On large holes it is often best to put the first thread through the centre and work up to the firm edge and then start from the centre again and work down.
8. Press on both sides, through damp muslin unless there is danger of watermarking.

NOTE.—Leave smaller loops˙ on ordinary material than on actual web.

Damask Darn = Cross-cut Darn.

USE.—Small repairs on table linen in good condition.

1. Catch the slit together with fishbone stitch.
2. Use a soft stranded Moravian Cotton (two or three strands only). This sinks into the damask and actually *shows* less than a linen thread which *matches* better in sheen. Stitches hardly appear on RS at all in double damask.

MENDING AND KNITTING

3. To PLAN SHAPE (Fig. 80 (b)).—Tack or crease on the straight thread ; make a rectangle with sides ½ in. from the ends of the cut.

4. Mark a corner A *opposite* the cut *not* at either end.

Make $AB = BC$ and $DE = EF$. This gives the outline for the first block of darning and should be tacked.

5. Darn the first block (c).

6. To SHAPE SECOND BLOCK (d). Make $EG = AE$. Darn second block.

NOTE.—The two blocks are unequal unless the slit chances to be on the direct cross.

Hedgetear Darn (Fig. 81).

USE.—Three cornered tear on cloth.

1. Use ravellings from the material, or fine sewing silk.
2. Draw edges together with a hair using fishbone stitch (a).
3. Begin darning ½ in. beyond the end of one arm of the cut.
4. Make the rows about ¾ in. long and keep them of equal length. since the material is strong and unworn (b).
5. Darn till half the length of a row short of the corner.
6. Do the whole of the second arm (c).
7. Thread up from the first arm across the corner only, unless the sides are ravelled (d).

NOTE.—This method of working from both ends towards the corner makes the latter easier to keep in place.

Combined Patch and Darn.

USE.—Where darning is less visible than a patch would be, as on exposed parts of an outergarment of plain material. Strength is given by placing material matching garment, or nearly so, behind the darn.

METHOD.

1. Tack material to *WS* with way of thread following that of garment.

2. Darn frayed ends of tear on to material with ravellings or fine silk. Darn from the *RS* but at the ends of rows take the needle to the back and bring to the *RS* again in position for the next row leaving a loop on the *WS*. If the tear is not complete i.e. one set only of the threads is broken, it is not usually necessary to cross.

3. Trim down turnings and round off corners at the back, and neaten edge of " patch " with loopstitch or overcasting, on thin and medium materials, or lightly hem to the *WS* of heavy materials.

NOTE.—On transparent materials such as voile, trim away close to the darn (made as small as possible) on the *WS*.

ADAPTATION FOR STOCKING KNEES.
   1. Tack net dyed to colour of stockings, to WS.
   2. Darn as described above, but fill the hole with chainstitch worked in close rows to the foundation of net. *Or* darn across in the ordinary way.
FURTHER APPLICATION to
GARMENTS.
   (i) Elbow of frock or boys' coat.
   (ii) Seat of trousers.

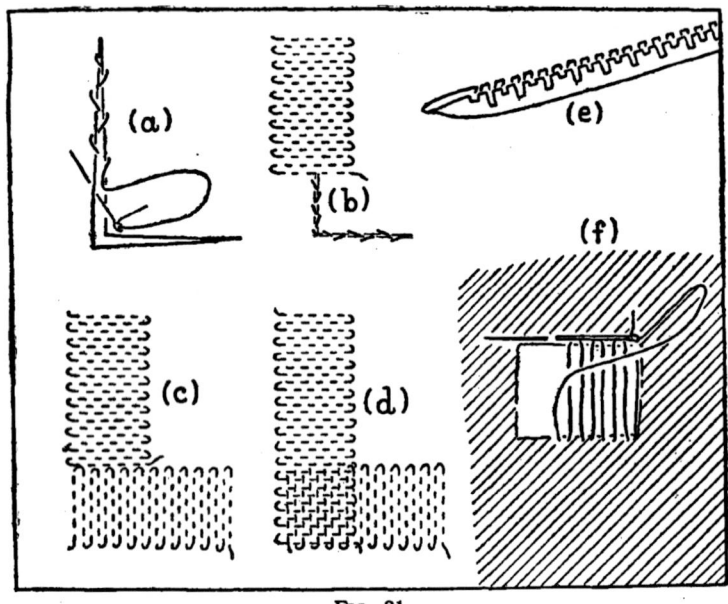

FIG. 81.

   (iii) Back of frock torn out from armhole seam.
   (iv) Torn buttonholes darned on to material (or tape on undergarments), and hole reworked, at least at the end.
HOUSEHOLD.
   (i) *Tape.*—Slits in sheets, etc., darned to tape.
   (ii) *Net.*—Large worn area on turkey towel, etc., darned preferably by machine, on to net which gives strength without bulk.
Machine Darning.—See Machine Attachments under Stitches.
Loom Darning.—A rough repair, but quick (Fig. 81).
   1. Cut the hole square or rectangular and strand across (*f*).

MENDING AND KNITTING

2. Take the thin triangular piece of metal (the so-called loom) with alternate deep and shallow slots on two of its edges (Fig. 81 (e)). Place it beneath the strands which run through the slots on one edge only, one strand to each slot.

3. The threads in the deep slots are depressed and those in the shallow slots are raised, i.e. a shed is formed (see page 13).

4. CROSSING.—Pass needle straight through the shed (i.e. the gap between the two layers of threads) without any darning over and under. Give the loom a slight turn so that the other slotted edge is now taking the threads. Those which were raised are now depressed. Return the needle through the new shed. Repeat till the hole is filled.

USE.—The method is quick but cannot be used on fine material which it would strain. It is suitable for use on children's holiday garments, e.g. jerseys, stocking knees, etc.

Grafting.—See Knitting also. Page 249.

DEFINITION.—Joining a new piece to an old, edge to edge, by an invisible join (or two edges without inserting a new piece). The join is made by (i) Swiss Darning or (ii) Fine Drawing.

Swiss Darning. Fig. 82 (a).

This is a method of joining two pieces of web by imitating the knitting stitch with ordinary needle and thread.

Take the needle into a loop and out of its neighbour on one side.

Repeat on the opposite side.

Return to the first side and go into loop already containing a thread and out of its neighbour (without one).

Repeat.

Sometimes a thin place on a garment of coarse knitting is strengthened by *following* the original weave in the same manner.

FILLING A HOLE BY SWISS DARNING. Fig. 82 (b).

Unravel the sides to obtain a square or rectangular hole. Strand with cotton going into one loop and out of its neighbour, first at the top then at the bottom, but always go into a hole containing a strand and out of one without (Fig. 82 (b)).

Now do the filling with thread to match the garment. Go into the loop from which the thread comes, and out of its neighbour. Take needle and thread round the back of the two strands which run into this loop, before re-inserting needle in same loop and out of the next.

Fine Drawing.—USED : (i) On a straight slit, (ii) to let in a cloth patch of thick material. Fig. 82 (c).

1. Cut patch to exact size of hole. Fix with fishbone stitch.

2. Set one edge of patch along forefinger with thumb holding edges together.

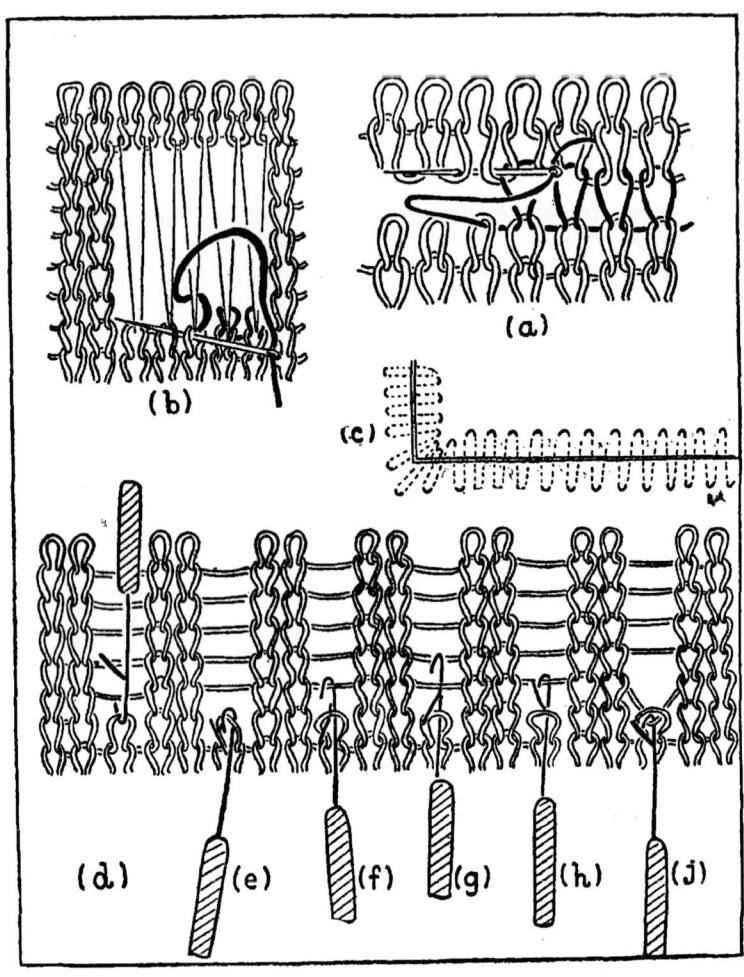

Fig. 82.

3. With needle pointing away from worker slip *in* the edge of the patch and bring out ⅛ in. from edge. Re-insert needle again picking up only half thickness of the cloth, point towards worker and bring to surface ⅛ in. from edge of garment (Fig. 82 (c)).

MENDING AND KNITTING

Stoating (Fig. 80 (*a*)).—Darn across the slit with fine silk or ravellings. The rows are not side by side, but cross each other in figures of eight and are very uneven in length. The stitches are taken in the thickness of the material and do not show through to the RS.

Stocking Ladder. Stretch over hand and crochet as shown in Fig. 82 (*d*) to (*j*) with ladderknit.

PATCHING

The standard patch is the Cotton or Calico Patch, but variations are made from it where it would be too visible or too bulky.

Classification.

General Characteristics.	Name.	Individual Characteristics.
1. Double row of stitching	COTTON	Special strength.
2. Strength	FLANNEL / DAMASK	Flatness and avoidance of bulk.
Invisibility	DRESS / (Print) / CLOTH	Single row of stitching, which must, therefore, be strong and close, i.e. Oversewing.
	COMBINED	Hole darned to foundation.
	GRAFTED.	No overlapping.
Strain on the bias	GUSSET	Variable shape, round, oval, or square.

Definition.—Cutting away worn material and replacing by a stronger piece.

Reasons for Patching.

1. TO PROLONG THE USE OF THE GARMENT.

Patching is used in preference to darning when :—

2. The garment suffers heavy wear or constant laundering, since it is a stronger method.

3. The garment is an outer one. *But* outergarments of plain material are often repaired by combined patch and darn.

4. The area to be repaired is a large one in which case it is quicker than darning unless machine darning is used.

General Rules.

1. The material of the patch should match that of the garment as far as possible in colour, age, and texture. The older the garment the more undesirable is the use of new material which imposes a strain on the weaker material. If the patch is new it must be washed and colour faded, if material will wash.

2. The size must be large enough to cover the thin area round the hole or tear, and reach firm material.

3. Cut the patch straight by the thread (exception is the gusset patch if round or oval). It is therefore square or oblong except when shaped to correspond with the shaping of the garment,

e.g. the curve of the armhole or slope of a seam. This shaping is not usually done until the patch is fixed to garment on its straight sides.

4. The patch is generally placed to WS of garment. *Exception*, Dress Patch (Print).

5. The way of thread on patch matches that of garment, i.e. warp follows warp, and weft goes with weft.

6. The position of patch may be marked out on garment with tacking or tailor's chalk (on cloth).

7. METHOD OF ATTACHMENT.

The selection of method depends on the strength and the degree of concealment required.

(i) On strong everyday garments the wearing qualities are of great importance and the patch is attached with a double row of stitching. The Cotton Patch (Calico) method is applied to cottons and the Flannel Patch to woollens.

(ii) On outergarments and dainty undergarments, only one row of stitching is used for attachment, though turnings are neatened with loopstitch or overcasting. The attaching stitch must, therefore, be strong and close *and* as little visible as possible. Use oversewing. Apply the method of the Dress (Print) Patch to patterned or easily-fraying material, and that of the Cloth Patch to heavier materials.

(iii) Darning is used as a method of attaching where the defined shape produced by a seam would be too visible. The method of the Damask Patch is applied to table linen, and that of the Combined (Patch and Darn) to plain materials mended in prominent position.

(iv) The finest results are to be obtained by grafting a patch into the garment edge to edge without turnings. This can be done on very thick cloth.

8. *After* the patch has been attached to the garment by its straight sides, shape the remaining sides by the old part which is only then cut away, leaving sufficient turning for the second stitching or the neatening.

9. Re-stitch any seam or hem unpicked to let in the patch.

Order of Work.

1. Unpick seam, etc., as necessary.
2. Prepare patch, sides straight by the thread.
3. Place and fix.
4. Do first stitching.
5. Shape remaining sides.
6. Cut away worn part of garment.
7. Do second stitching or neatening.
8. Re-stitch seams.
9. Press.

MENDING AND KNITTING

Cotton Patch = Calico Patch. Fig. 83.
CHARACTERISTIC.—Strength and, to some extent, flatness.
  1. Cut the patch straight by the thread. If the garment is pulled out of shape the patch is pulled diagonally from corner to corner to make it correspond. Crease small turnings to *RS* of patch. Place patch *RS* against *WS* of garment. Fix and hem (Fig. 83 (*a*)).
  2. Turn to *RS*. Make a pinprick exactly $\frac{1}{8}$ in. diagonally from

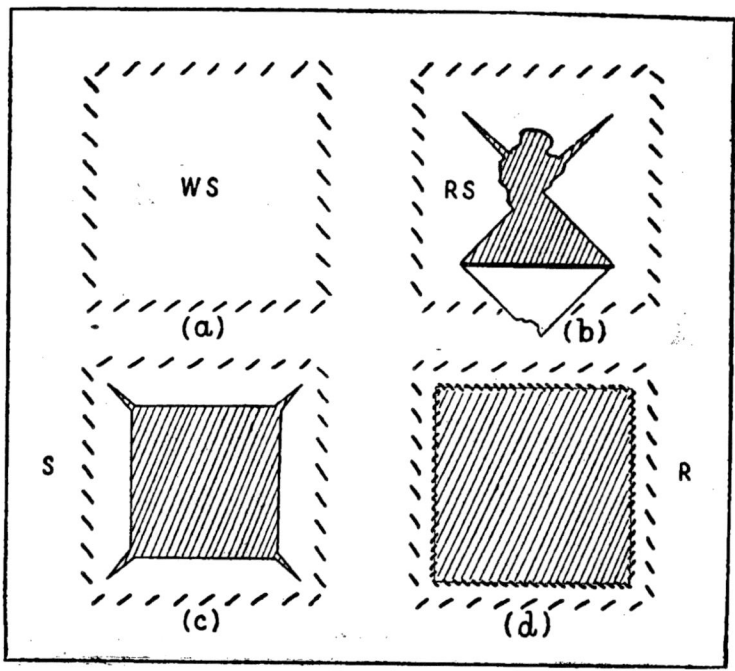

FIG. 83.

each corner. From the hole cut to each prick. Fold back the triangles so made, and cut along the resulting crease (*b*).
  3. Snip a little further into each corner to allow the raw edge to be turned under (*c*).
  4. Turn under the raw edge and oversew to the patch with patch held nearest to the worker (*d*).
  This Patch may be applied equally well by Machining in place of Hemming and Oversewing.

Flannel Patch.
CHARACTERISTIC.—Avoidance of bulk on thick material.

1. Place patch with *RS* to *WS* of garment without turnings.
2. Herringbone over the raw edges to the garment. Begin near the botton left-hand corner but not *at* the corner (Fig. 84 (a)).
3. OUTER CORNER.—Make an upper stitch one space short of the corner. For the next upper stitch turn and insert the needle as for the first lower stitch of second side (b).
4. Complete all sides of patch.
5. Cut away garment on *RS* by method given for Cotton Patch,

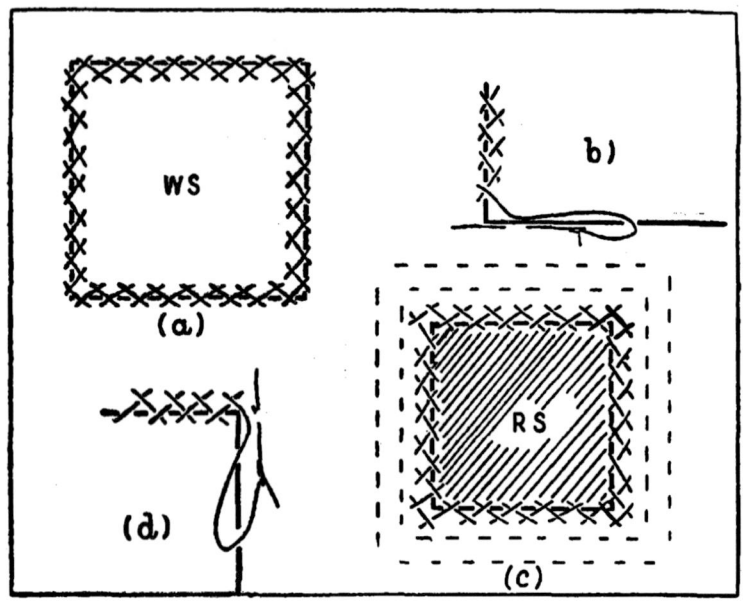

FIG. 84.

and so as to allow space between previous row of stitching, and that now to be done (c).
6. Herringbone edge of garment to patch.
7. INNER CORNER.—Make a lower stitch come close into the corner. For next lower stitch turn the needle and insert as for an upper stitch of the next side (d).

APPLICATION.

To flannel and knitted (stockinette) undergarments. The latter if not thick are often machined or closely hemmed on the *RS* with edge turned under. Leave garment turning a little wider than patch turning and herringbone to *WS*.

MENDING AND KNITTING

Damask Patch.

CHARACTERISTIC.—Avoidance of bulk and of defined shape.

1. Cut a sufficiently large patch of similar quality damask to the article to be patched, and of the same pattern if this should be possible.
2. Place with RS to WS and without turning, so as to avoid a bulky ridge which would show when ironed. Tack diagonally.
3. Make coloured lines of tacking ¼ in. inside and outside edge (Fig. 85 (a)).

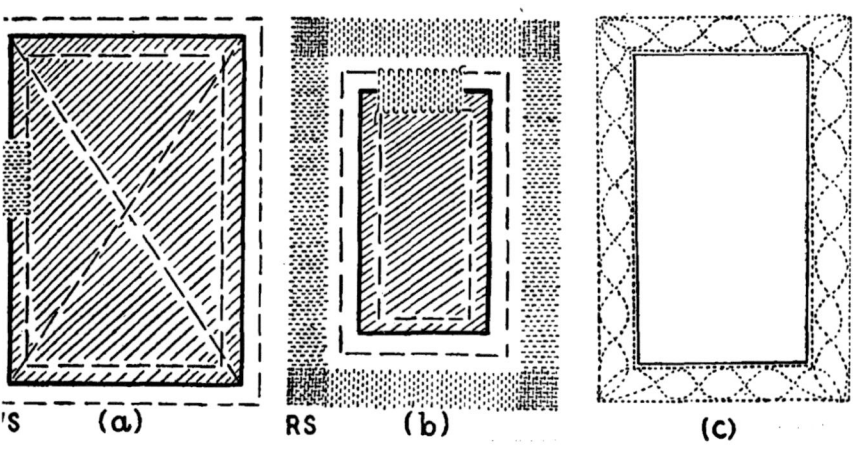

FIG. 85.

4. Darn between tackings.
5. Remove all tacking and cut away worn material on RS to within ½ in. of darning. Darn down this turning (b).

ALTERNATIVE METHOD.

The patch may be applied with one band of darning across both turnings. This method is quicker but much more difficult, since the worn material must be cut away before the patch can be placed and the fixing is difficult.

NOTE.—Much the most invisible method is to insert the patch by grafting, but it is not easy and takes more time than the busy woman can usually spare.

EASY QUICK METHOD. Fig. 85 (c).
Apply patch to WS and machine near raw edge.
Cut away on the RS to leave a ⅜in. turning and machine near the raw edge. Trim down the raw edges against the stitching and wave machine twice between the two rows of machining.

Dress Patch = Print Patch. Fig. 86.
CHARACTERISTIC.—Invisibility with fair strength.
This is the chief outergarment patch. It is specially suitable for patterned material which is most easily matched by a patch

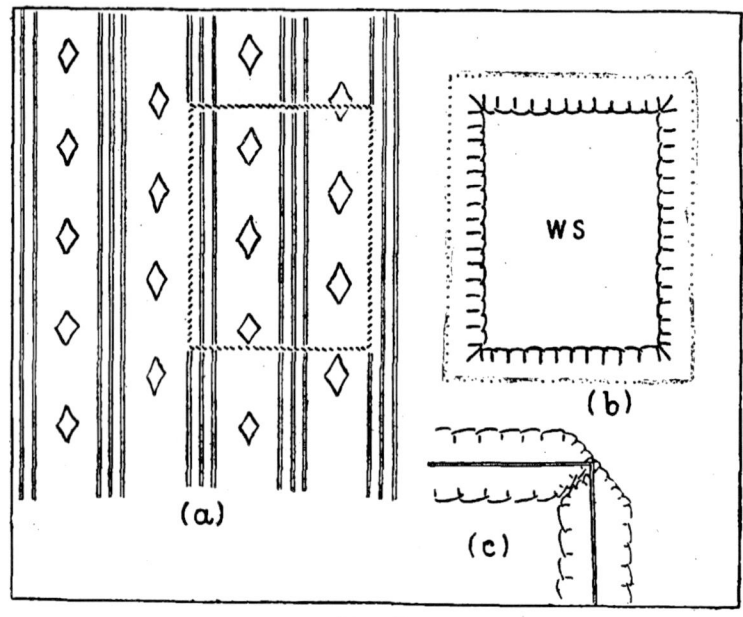

FIG. 86.

placed on the RS. It can be used on plain materials and on fine undergarments.

1. Cut patch to match the pattern if any, and allow ¼- to ½-in. turnings all round and crease these on any straight line of the pattern.
2. Place patch to RS of garment (WS to RS). Oversew the two together holding patch nearest worker (Fig. 86 (a)).
3. Cut down all turnings to ¼ or ⅜ in. and loopstitch the raw edges together (b).

MENDING AND KNITTING

NOTE.—On all but thin materials it is better to open the turnings and loopstitch raw edges separately. The extra folds of the turning will be cut away at the corners, and care taken not to catch these when oversewing (c).

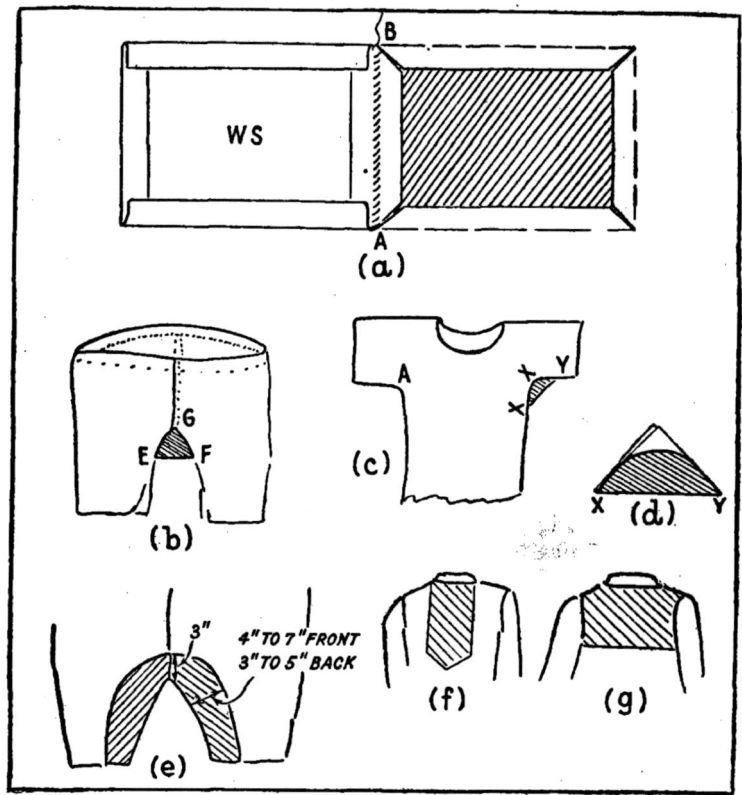

FIG. 87 A.

Cloth Patch. Fig 87 A.

CHARACTERISTIC.—Invisibility.

In contrast to the ordinary outergarment patch, the oversewing worked from the *WS* is much less visible on the *RS*. The corners are more difficult to match on patterned materials.

1. With chalk, mark on the garment the position which the patch is to occupy, and inside this mark ½-in. turnings. Cut out by the *turning* line (Fig. 87 A (a)).

2. Cut patch to finished size *plus* turnings. Fix turnings to WS of patch, damp, and press.

3. Apply patch to garment RS facing and one side of patch to the corresponding Fitting Line on garment (AB of diagram) and in such a way that the patch is ready to close into the hole like a door. AB is the hinge.

4. Snip the garment turnings diagonally into the corners at A and B.

5. Oversew from A to B and leave thread hanging.

6. Close the patch into the hole and oversew the remaining sides, snipping into the corners as necessary.

7. Open seams cutting away surplus at the corners and finally damp and press the whole.

Coat Lining Patch = Machine Dress Patch. Fig. 87 B.

Two patches for each armhole are usually necessary.

METHOD.—Unpick the lining armhole and side seam to 2 in. or 3 in. beyond area needing repair. Mark the outline and cut the piece to be inserted to same size and shape *plus* turnings. Cut away worn parts leaving turnings inside the stitching line. Apply the patch on the " door " principle of the Cloth Patch, i.e. place, fix, and stitch along one side first, with RS facing. Stop with needle down *exactly* at corner A. Pivot the work on the needle to bring second edge AB in position for stitching. Pull round the corner C of the patch so as to meet B. Let everything above A go. Pull both layers from the needle and stitch the first inch or two without fixing. (Turnings cleared from corner A with a strong needle or pin.) If the side is a long one, fix the remainder before completing the stitching. Insert the second patch and re-stitch the side seam. Open the seams and counterstitch from the RS for flatness and to strengthen the corners otherwise rather weak. It is common practice to show up an insertion thus giving the impression of intended ornament. To sustain this idea, make the patches on right and left sides match although the wear may not be the same.

When there is no spare material for repair it may be obtained :—

(a) From an inside patch pocket.

(b) From the bottom, the lining being shortened to half or three-quarter length and the exposed seams neatened separately.

(c) From the sleeves, these being replaced by a near match or an absolute contrast, e.g. navy lining but sleeves pale or patterned. For underarm repair only, the top portion of the sleeve is sufficient and can be replaced by purchase of $\frac{1}{4}$ yd. or $\frac{3}{8}$ yd. If the sleeve itself requires repair at top $\frac{1}{2}$ yd. is needed ; $\frac{3}{4}$ yd. replaces whole (of both sleeves).

MENDING AND KNITTING

Take a pattern of the lining before cutting up for patching. It may be a one or two piece sleeve. Unpick completely, lay out on paper, and re-outline. It is certain to be pulled out of shape by wear, and the aim is to restore it to its original shape before outlining. Rule two (guide) lines at right angles on the paper. Lay the sleeve piece on the other side of the paper and begin by pinning along the straight grain first lengthwise and then across, the pins coming through just on the ruled lines.

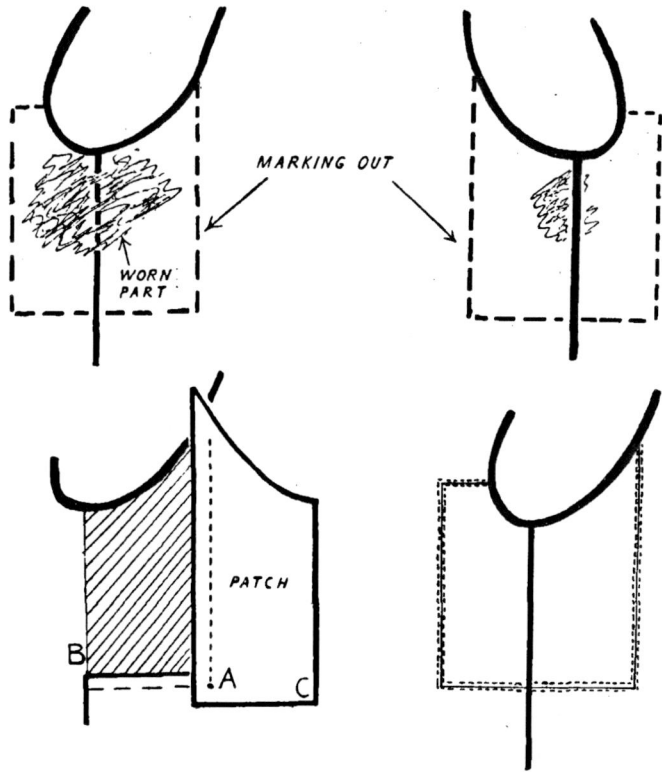

FIG. 87 B.

Gusset Patches.

A gusset is a piece of material, usually square or triangular, used at the *angles* of seams for the purpose of strengthening, by throwing the strain on the bias; and also of neatening. *Patches* of this type are used where the damage to be repaired has been caused by strain rather than ordinary wear. The patch replaces worn material, but often adds to the size of the garment as well.

Oval Patch on Magyar Garment (Fig. 87 A (c)).

On a badly-cut garment too sharp an angle at A would cause splitting in the underarm seam. The patch has made the curve less sharp, has provided bias material in the direction of greatest strain as well as replacing the torn part of the garment.

METHOD.

1. Cut a square of suitable size and straight by the thread. Fold diagonally and round off the corners opposite the fold XY (d).

2. Unpick the seam. Mark the centre of the hollow on both back and front of the garment, and centre of both curves on patch.

3. Seam one side of patch to front of garment with marked centres matching. A seam to match that of garment is generally used. It must be made sufficiently far in on garment (by cutting away worn material) but leaving turnings.

4. Cut away a similar amount on the back. Do up the whole seam unpicked which will now include the patch.

Square Patch for Knicker Fork (Fig. 87 A (b)).

This is usually double for strength.

METHOD.

1. Cut a sufficiently large square and fix turnings to WS.

2. Place on RS of garment with a point to each of the four seams which meet at the fork, all equally distant from it, and so that the edges of the patch will lie smoothly on the garment. The distance from the fold to G may be larger on the patch, than the distance from G to fork on garment, which will therefore pucker behind patch till cut away. But the *edge* of patch must lie smoothly from the beginning.

3. Cut away worn material leaving $\frac{1}{4}$-in. turnings.

4. Place second patch on the inside.

The inside patch is usually hemmed. The outside patch may be machined or oversewn.

Adhesive Patches.

Material of various colours is now sold prepared in such a way that it can be stuck to a garment to fill up a hole. The general method is to place the patch with RS to WS, and with hole closed up as much as possible; pass a slightly warm iron over, which melts the gummy preparation on the patch; then leave a few minutes to set. The particular instructions sold with the patch should be carefully studied. Examples are " Mend-a-tear " for mackintoshes, cloth, motor car hoods, etc., and " Lustru " for heels of stockings. (Good stockings should always be darned.)

MENDING AND KNITTING

LACE CURTAINS.
Starch a patch when starching curtain. When ironing place damp patch over hole and it will stick by means of the starch. Do not turn edges under.

Reinforcing.
This is a method of strengthening some area of a garment which receives special strain, as a preventive measure, before use.

BOYS' TROUSERS.
Place patch at seat on the *RS*. When these wear through they can be removed and the garment is good underneath. If the garment is not made at home, tailors are quite prepared to do this, with some it is a matter of course.

KNICKERS. (Fig. 87 A (*e*).)
Some women are so heavy on these that they find it worth while to follow a similar practice. If two pairs of same material and colour are bought, then, when one pair is worn, its good parts are used to reinforce the second pair. The chief wear is not at the seat, but either side of the leg seams and mostly to the front. The diagram shows the shape of the pieces. The thread follows that of garment. Take pattern as for shaped facing. The width on the front is 5 to 7 inches, and on the back 4 to 6 inches.

STOCKINGS.
The old habit of running the heels, the sole over the ball of the foot, and top of the toe, has largely died out. But for children it is well worth doing, unless they go to a boarding school where the mending is unusually well looked after.

FORK OF TROUSERS.
This is reinforced by 2- or 3-in. triangles of interlining.

PYJAMAS. Fig. 87 A (*f*) and (*g*).
Some men invariably split the coat down the centre back, others at back of armholes. On home-made garments reinforce either outside or inside, on bought match material as nearly as possible and place inside.

SKIRTS.
If these bag at knee, line front breadth only.
If these bag at seat, make a $\frac{3}{4}$-length lining a little smaller than skirt and hanging free from waist to take the strain.

MENDING ETCETERAS

Gloves.
Wool and fabric gloves are darned. *Skin gloves*: draw slits together with fishbone stitch worked in silk, or loopstitch edges separately and then draw together.

Holes.—Obtain a small piece of skin by shortening at wrist, cut to exact size and shape of hole, and graft in with fishbone stitch. *Seams.*—Most easily re-sewn with a curved glove needle.

Glove needles, straight or curved, have sharp edges for piercing holes in skin.

Slits on Undergarments.

Whip together edges of slit from *WS*, thus giving the appearance of a seam on *RS*.

The method is suitable for dainty undergarments not subject to heavy wear, and on which a less visible method than darning is desirable. It is also used as a quick method on garments not worth the expenditure of time on patching, or darning. It is also applied to ladders at the *back* of cheap stockings.

Sheets.

When worn in the middle only, cut down the centre and turn sides to middle. If the selvedges are good oversew these together producing a very flat join ; otherwise join with machine fell seams. Neaten the sides using the machine hemmer unless the edges are too stretchy. If necessary cut away worn parts making the sheet fit a smaller bed. It is a great saving to do the turning before the worn area is large ; the wear on the tucked in sides is slight, but two or three weeks may render much of the centre not strong enough even for this.

Ends and Edges of Towels, etc.

All tears running in from the edge must be darned, preferably by machine, and sometimes on to a backing of tape or net.

WORN SELVEDGES.—If these are mainly good, then, after repairing bad parts, turn down once to. *WS* and herringbone. Bad edges should be loopstitched with coarse D.M.C. (No. 12 single or No. 18 double). The whole turned over portion must be included in the depth of stitch.

WORN FRINGES.—Loop hemstitch at the base. But if badly torn cut off and neaten with a hem.

Frayed Cuffs, Collars, etc.

CLOTH.

The frayed edge is a fold. Cut through the fold right round the cuff, and trim away any long frayed ends. Turn the edges in to face each other but with inner layer slightly lower. Press (under damp cloth) and secure with top hemming (tailor's hemming).

FOLD-BACK CUFF as on shirt or blouse. If the inside is good, turn the whole cuff ; otherwise cut through and seam together again through all layers. Herringbone the turnings closely to one layer.

MENDING AND KNITTING

That the seam may be just under the edge of the fold when turned back, make the distance from the upper buttonhole to the seam only *slightly* less than from the lower buttonhole or the buttonholes will not match sufficiently well for links. On striped material the seam must be very accurately fixed.

COTTON STRAIGHT CUFF.—As for cloth. On a shirt and, when suitable, on a blouse or frock, secure by machine edgestitching from *RS* instead of hemming on *WS*.

COLLAR worn at edge of roll. Make an ornamental laid-on strap of similar or contrasting material.

WEAR AT BASE OF SHIRT NECKBAND.—Often due to rubbing by stiff collar. Unpick neckband and let in a dress patch. This can be a very invisible repair well worth doing unless the garment is very old, when fishbone slit together and darn on to tape.

Shortening a Knitted Skirt or Frock.

The simplest method is to turn up a hem. The stitches must be loose otherwise they show as a tight line on the *RS and* the thread snaps the first time the skirt is stretched. Being loose they must in compensation be very close together to hold the hem effectively and avoid providing opportunity for catching on shoe heels. A deep hem looks clumsy on short frocks so a portion is usually cut off.

Never cut off the whole amount of shortening.

The amount cut off must allow for :—

(a) Removal of weight of piece cut off which itself provides further shortening.

(b) Hem, if any. A cast-off edge is perfectly neat but some people prefer the look of a hem. There is no neatening turn.

(c) Two or three rounds of unravelling after cutting. This is necessary to get a straight line of loops which can be picked up on knitting needles for casting-off.

After cutting off the piece, unravelling and picking up the loops, unpick on the needles, one more row, so making sure that the stitches are the right way on the needle, that there are no dropped stitches, and no stitch picked up from the previous row with a thread from the present row above it. Pick up short distances at a time, i.e. use a large number of needles. Only the pair used for actual casting-off need be a true match in size. With the unravellings, cast-off, not very tightly especially if there is to be a hem.

Bought Knitwear.

Cut off the required amount and immediately machine all round near the edge to prevent unravelling.

TO NEATEN EDGE.

1. Have lockstitched at a shop and hem as described above.

2. Make a neatening turn by first pressing and then passing through the machine well stretched. Then turn up full depth of hem.

3. Make a narrow hem held by three parallel rows of stitching done from the RS. The edge may be closely overcast or given a neatening turn to be caught by the third row of stitching.

To Straighten Unravelled Wool for Re-knitting.

Wind on a lath of wood, and steam over a saucepan and press under a cloth. Stretch as you wind, though not very tightly, and keep depth of winding to ½ in. or ¾ in., or the steam and iron cannot affect the deep layers.

CARE OF CLOTHES

1. Keep coats, skirts, frocks, and blouses on hangers. These should be padded for thin garments. A good type for skirts is the crossbar on the coat hanger.

Shoulder covers of celophane for blouses are quite good if used carefully. They tear rather easily.

2. A much-flared garment with level hem should not be kept hanging but lying in a drawer, otherwise the bias seams will stretch. Stuff sleeves with paper.

3. Frocks with ruffles should hang upside down from loops concealed beneath the lowest ruffle if these are on the skirt, or hang over the skirt bar of a coat hanger if the ruffles are on the bodice.

4. Light-coloured garments, and those which are kept only behind a curtain, should have bag dust covers with side openings, fastening with zip or press studs.

Transparent boxes of celophane nearly as stiff as cardboard are sold in a variety of shapes and sizes, including round hat boxes. Thinner celophane bags are available for lingerie.

5. Keep hats on stands. This preserves the shape of both brim and crown. Buy different heights so that hats fit into one another on the same shelf, at different levels.

6. Remove stains while fresh. Brush hats and cloth garments before putting away. Fasten coats, especially inside fastening of double-breasted garments, to prevent creases forming.

7. Heavy cloth garments should be periodically spread on a table to be brushed and cleaned. Brushes (10s. 6d.) which hold a cleaning fluid in the back are helpful. Brush silk with flannel and velvet with velvet. Repress pleats. Shrink away bagging at knees and in seat of skirts.

8. Keep boots and shoes on trees. Dry slowly on trees in a warm room away from the fire. Sports boots are rubbed with linseed oil when not in use.

9. Pull out fingers of gloves.

MENDING AND KNITTING

10. STORING.—At the end of summer and winter look through for garments not worth keeping till another season. Store the others so that drawers and cupboards in daily use are not overcrowded. Put away washing garments rough dried. (Never starched.) Woollens should be scattered with naphtha and kept in brown-paper parcels or moth-proof bags sold for the purpose. Garments hanging through a season should have sleeves stuffed with paper.

FOLDING

Method I.—Light Coats and Mackintoshes.

Lay the two front edges together with *WS* facing, collar turned up, revers opened and sleeves straight. Lay the right hand on the armhole and raise the collar at right-angles to the table. Now fold lengthwise in front of the sleeve. The section above the armhole will now lie flat again. Turn up the bottom according to the space the garment is going to occupy in box or drawer. Fold over as many times as required.

Method II.—Heavy Coats and Men's Clothes.

Place *WS* down on the table, sleeves straight and collar up. Fold each front back on to the sleeves *RS* facing. Fold in half lengthwise, then across once or more according to length.

Method III.—Blouses and Frocks.

Close and fasten garment as worn. Place front down on the table. Spread any loose drapery and fold down to size of garment (also flares). Fold back each side including sleeve. Then fold sleeves diagonally to bring again straight down garment. Now fold sleeves across once or twice. Fold garment across as many times as needed.

To Prevent Creasing.

The inner layer of any fold has the sharpest crease. If a layer of paper is spread wherever a fold will come this inner layer will be paper. On lightweight garments a single layer is not sufficient, a crush is needed. Pleat tissue paper roughly (and without creasing) and twist each end to fix it. To stuff sleeves, insert end of a prepared crush and telescope in the rest of the length, following up with a second. When packing, light garments should be in the tray, well stuffed with paper. If close packing is essential, they are better rolled than folded.

CARE OF HOUSEHOLD LINEN

1. Quality always pays in household articles, which are necessarily subject to hard wear and constant laundering.

2. Mark everything with name of owner or establishment, number of articles in set, and date of taking into use.

3. Look through all linen on its return from laundry.

4. Keep in piles of a kind in a well-aired cupboard with shelves deep enough to take sheets, bedspreads, and curtains as returned from cleaners without further folding.

Piles not often in use should rest on a cloth which hangs down from the front of the shelf, and can be thrown back to cover and protect everything completely from dust.

5. Use in rotation. Put away at bottom of pile, use from top.

6. Articles seldom used should be wrapped in a cloth, so arranged that contents may be accessible without moving pile from shelf.

7. Blankets should be stored with naphtha. Those in constant use should be washed or cleaned at spring cleaning if not at autumn cleaning as well.

8. Inner covers of pillows and bolsters should be removed and washed at least twice a year.

MARKING HOUSEHOLD LINEN

Methods.

1. BOUGHT NAME TAPES specially made. Hem on.
2. MARKING INK used directly on garment or on tape.
3. CHAIN-STITCH.—Write name, etc., faintly in pencil and work over in very fine thread. D.M.C. 150 or 200 Turkey Red.
4. CROSS-STITCH.—(i) Work over bead canvas with penelope weave. (ii) Make stitches all cross the same way. Stab-stitch over canvas (but if using a transfer pick up stitches). (iii) Cut away canvas but so as to leave sufficient length of thread to hold when drawing threads from under cross-stitch.
5. MONOGRAMS AND INITIALS.—These may be in cross-stitch, satin-stitch, chain-stitch, etc. For chain-stitch use D.M.C. 40 or 25. For satin-stitch 40.

Satin-stitch.—Outline in fine sewing silk. Pad between. Work the stitch, preferably in a frame, slightly sloped.

Position is very important for initials and monograms. The centre of an exact division of the article is found, and the middle letter (or middle of space between two) must coincide exactly with this. See that a suitable margin is left for size of lettering used. The bottom of the lettering should be towards the edge on

(1) *Towels* so that it is right way up when towel hangs over a rail.

(2) *Sheets* so that it is right way up when top sheet is folded back. The bottom sheet is marked with tape.

(3) *Tablecloths* and *Dinner Napkins.*

But on

Pillowcases the top of the lettering is usually towards the edge. The arrangement is often diagonal across a top corner.

MENDING AND KNITTING

USES FOR OLD BLANKETS AND OTHER WOOLLENS

1. UNDER BLANKETS.
Cut down and either loopstitch the edges single or turned once. Or lay several layers together, quilt through the middle, and loopstitch or bind all the edges together.
2. SMALLER BLANKETS.
For single beds, or for children's cots. Bind with 2-in. satin ribbon or loopstitch.
3. PATCHING.
4. FELTS.
For ironing-boards or to go under stair carpet, or to make cushions for window seats. Quilt several layers together for the latter, cut just smaller than the cover.
5. NURSERY APRONS.
Skirt.—Length 30 inches, width 54 inches.
Bib.—16 by 10 inches and hollow out for the neck.
Band.—Two strips of long cloth or calico $2\frac{1}{2}$ in., including turning.
To Make.—Neaten raw edges with herringbone stitch or flannel binding. Pleat skirt into band. Pleat down bib to 7 or 8 inches in middle of band. Sew tape to band to tie in front, and a tape loop to the bib to go over the head.
6. HOT WATER BOTTLE COVERS.
(1) A bag with buttonhole tab, and button.
(2) A shaped cover, consisting of a strip with width equal to the length of the bottle, and two round or oval ends. Length, sufficient to go round the bottle and overlap 3 inches. Fasten with three sets of tapes. Neaten or ornament seams with binding or loopstitch.
7. ETCETERAS.
   (i) Lagging to prevent pipes from freezing.
   (ii) Hay box lining and padding.
   (iii) Iron holders.
   (iv) Floor polishers. Pad an old broom and cover with velvet or velveteen.
   (v) Stockings are suitable for making coal gloves, and shoe-polishing pads.

Tape Mending.

USES.
1. To strengthen and mend torn corners of sheets, towels, tablecloths, etc.
2. Buttonholes, as a backing for reworking part of hole.
3. For whole new ends on bands of aprons, etc.
4. As a backing for darning slits. On underclothing use ribbon, e.g. Cash's which is soft cotton and usually preferable to silk.

SETTING TAPE TO A CORNER. Fig. 88.
A wide piece of tape folded in half and set to a corner, on one side of the corner is the fold. On the other side the edges are over-sewn. The remaining edges are hemmed. On a pillow slip be careful not to catch more than one of its layers when hemming (*a*).

A narrow Tape set to a Corner.—Fold in half lengthwise and set in position. Mitre at the corner by folding (without cutting away surplus inside) and hem (*b*) and (*c*).

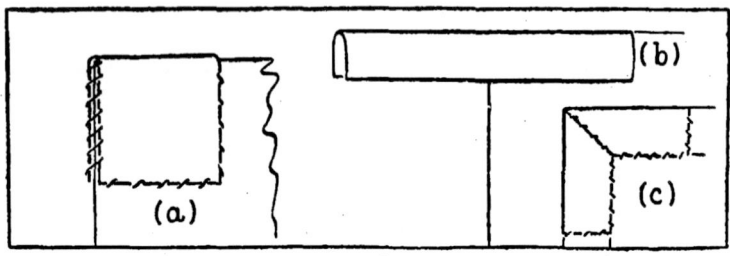

FIG. 88.

Uses for old Sheets.
1. DUST SHEETS.—Join pieces with Fell seams to required size.
2. IRONING SHEETS and shaped covers for skirt and sleeve boards. There must be no seams.
3. BAGS for boiling.
4. CLOTHS for rolling up half-dried articles before ironing, and for other household purposes.
5. PILLOW AND BOLSTER INNER COVERS.
6. PATCHING other sheets.

Linen Sheets should be kept for bandages, and all kinds of polishers for glass and silver.

KNITTING

Patterns of garment or weave are not dealt with here, there are many publications which treat of these in detail. A few fundamental facts and general principles are stated for convenient reference.

Materials.
Use good wool *and* good needles. Test the latter by a reliable gauge, e.g. the Bell, to be sure all of a set are true to size. Circular knitting is done on four needles, socks and glove ; or on one flexible needle with two firm ends, good for vests, but *not* for skirts and frocks which get out of shape without seams to give firmness. Use specially short needles (in sets of four) for glove fingers. Pins, i.e. needles with a knob at one end, are useful for loose, heavy

MENDING AND KNITTING

work liable to slip off the ordinary needle. These can only be used for flat knitting, not circular.

Tension.

Garments are best made from instructions which give measurements, not number of stitches and rows. To knit on this plan it is necessary to know exactly how tightly you knit with the particular wool and needles in question. No two people knit exactly alike. Knit a trial piece of at least twelve stitches in each of twelve rows. Then count the number of stitches to an inch. By this calculate the number of stitches to cast on and the number of rows to knit, to obtain the required measurements given in the pattern.

Casting On.

A LOOSE EDGE.—German Method.

Make a slip knot and draw up on the first needle. Hold wool over fingers of left hand. Draw thread through loop with second needle and place on the first. Very elastic and so suitable for vests. Also used when casting-on is needed in the course of knitting the garment, e.g. second edge of a buttonhole or pocket. In a glove for fork of thumb immediately after transferring thumb stitches to a holder.

FIRM EDGE.

Take enough wool from the ball for the number of stitches required, the amount varies, but 1 inch per stitch is a good allowance. Lay the wool (loose end) across the left thumb and wind once round thumb and across end. Knit into the loop on the thumb using thread from the ball. Take out thumb and draw the stitch home. Repeat.

FOR A CIRCLE.

Use the first method and cast a third of the total number of stitches required on the first needle, then one more but do not transfer it to needle 1. Drop needle 1, take up needle 3 and cast on another third of the stitches. As before, knit one stitch too many and do not transfer. Take needle 4 to complete the casting on. Arrange the needles to make a triangle and see that the work is not twisted before continuing the knitting.

Casting Off.

Knit first two stitches together and put resulting stitch back on needle. Repeat till all are cast off, break off wool, draw end through last loop and darn in on the back (Swiss Darning is best).

RIB CASTING-OFF.

Alternately plain and purl (one and one, or two and two, etc.), according to the rib. This maintains elasticity.

LOOSE CASTING-OFF.
Convey stitches to a crochet hook with hook at ball end. Hold hook in right hand, wool in left. Draw through one stitch, then through two, alternately till all are cast off.

TO JOIN WOOL.
Unravel the ends 3 to 6 inches according to looseness of knitting, and cut out half the strands from each. Place ends overlapping, slightly damp, and roll together between fingers or palms of hands.

To Increase.
WITHOUT MAKING A HOLE.—(i) Knit first into the front and then into the back of the same stitch, or (ii) knit into the stitch of row below, or (iii) pick up thread between stitches with left needle and knit into the back of this.

MAKING A HOLE.—Pass the wool round the end of the right hand needle without knitting a stitch. This increases. To make a hole without increasing the number of stitches, first knit two together, then pass thread round needle without knitting.

To Decrease.
With decrease turned to the right ; knit two together.
With decrease turned to the left ; slip 1, knit 1, pass the slipped stitch over.
Or knit two together into the back of the stitch. In this way the decreasings are paired.

Edges.
To make a smooth edge slip the first stitch of the row—plain in purl rows and purl in plain rows. This is the proper method for free edges, i.e. both edges of a scarf, the front fastening edge of a coat, or the side of a heel flap where the slipped stitches will be picked up later. An edge to be seamed needs, above all, firmness, and does not have the first stitch slipped.

To Pick up Stitches on an Edge.
e.g. side of heel flap on a sock, or a sleeve knitted on to shoulder instead of seamed.
An even edge is already made by slipping the first stitch in each row—plain in a purl row, and purl in a plain.
Pick up the absolute edge from the WS with a spare needle ; when knitting the first row off this needle, knit into the SHORT side of the stitch. On a sock the back of the stitch will be short on one side of the heel flap, and the front will be short on the other side. This twists the stitches of the first row and prevents holes occurring.

To Make a Buttonhole.
Cast off two to four stitches or more according to the size of

MENDING AND KNITTING

the hole required. In the next row cast on loosely the same number of stitches opposite those cast off.

When knitting these cast on stitches (in the next row) insert the needle from the back, which makes the second edge as firm as the first.

Shoulder Slope.

The same method is suitable for the waist of knickers and other slopes.

Example.—Shoulder of 32 stitches.

RIGHT SIDE.—On a plain row knit to 8 stitches from the end. Slip one, bring the wool forward, put the slipped stitch back and carry the wool back; turn and purl (wool slack for first stitch to prevent slipped stitch being drawn against the next leaving a gap the other side). Turn next time at 16 stitches from the end, then at 24, and finally cast off the whole shoulder. This gives a smooth continuous cast-off line at a slope, instead of the old step method of casting-off eight at a time in succeeding rows.

LEFT SHOULDER.—Do the turns on the purl rows. At 8 from the end, slip 1 purlwise, carry wool back, put slipped stitch back, and bring the wool forward. Turn and knit plain. Repeat at 16 and 24.

To Calculate Number and Position of Turns.—Decide how many rows the slope is to affect. With 9 or 10 rows to the inch, a $\frac{5}{8}$ in. slope will affect 6 rows. This means three turns since a turn takes 2 rows. To find the spacing divide the total number of stitches by *one more* than the number of turns, e.g. 32 stitches and 3 turns, $\frac{32}{4} = 8$; 40 stitches and 4 turns, $\frac{40}{5} = 8$.

Seaming.

First Method.—Hold the two parts of the garment with edges even and *RS* facing and crochet the two together, i.e. draw thread through two loops, one from each side of the garment, then through one.

Second Method.—Seam together as a plain seam using ordinary sewing *silk* used double. Take very small turnings—$\frac{1}{4}$ in. or less —and press these open. This is the best method for outer garments. It gives and helps to retain a good tailored appearance.

Third Method.—Oversewing with wool. Simple and quick, but results not as good as the first two methods.

Strengthening.

On coats and jumpers, but especially the former taping is a great help in maintaining shape in wear. The most important thing is to counteract stretch in shoulder seams *and back neck*. Hem a piece of Paris Binding or luteen binding along one shoulder seam, across the neck, and down the other seam. Test the two sides so that two seams and two halves of neck really match. Stay the fastenings on the front edges of coats also. Binding is sufficient to support the buttons but rarely wide enough for the buttonholes; a strip of silk hemmed to the wrong side is better. It gives much more satisfactory wear if the holes are worked in the ordinary worked buttonhole way to a slit in the backing. In this case they must be made full large when knitting as the buttonholing contracts them markedly.

Knitting in Several Colours.

While knitting in one colour the threads of the others lie along the back until needed. To prevent formation of long loops which catch and break, these are twisted. To do this by crossing over the balls each time is so laborious a process that multi-colour knitting by the amateur has been largely restricted to jumper borders and stocking tops. But all-over patterns can be knitted *quickly* in several colours bringing flecked, small lozenge, and diaper designs within reach of the hand knitter, by knitting either into the left hand or the right as desired.

Double Knitting.

For belts, scarves, etc., cast on an even number of stitches and twice as many as required for the width. Slip the first stitch of every row purlwise. Then alternately knit one and slip one purlwise. The slipped stitch of one row is knitted in the next.

KNITTING MAN'S SOCK

Wools.

(1) Heather mixture four-ply fingering for ordinary wear.
(2) Yarn which is harsher for heavy wear, e.g. service socks.

Quantity.

5 oz. of 4-ply fingering make one pair and supplies mending. A set of four No. 15 or 16 steel needles, with (1) or 13 with (2).

Proportions.

The basis for the proportions is the length of the foot. Before casting on it is necessary to knit a small piece of web to discover how many stitches go to the inch (width) with the wool used. Average is 12.

1. LENGTH OF LEG.—Usually once and a third foot length.

2. NUMBER OF LOOPS.—Cast on = Number of stitches required for 1 inch multiplied by width at widest part of leg. Average, ninety-two or ninety-six with heather mixture, but 72 for service socks.

MENDING AND KNITTING

This is for width of 8½ in.
Choose a number divisible by four.

3. Sizes.

	Small.	Medium.	Large.
Foot length	9¼–10 in.	10–11¼ in.	11¼–12 in.
Width	8¼ in.	8½ in.	8¾– 9 in.

Welt.

The welt equals one-third length of foot.
If desired the welt may be made longer and the plain part of the leg shorter (4 in. for service socks).
Knit in ribbing.

> Knit 3 purl 1.
> *or* Knit 2 purl 2.
> *or* Knit 4 purl 2.

Leg.

The leg is knitted plain for one-sixth length of foot. Then

DECREASE.

(1) Make a measuring gauge = one-third length of foot.

(2) Number of decreasings = Number of stitches divided by 16.

(3) Divide the gauge. The number is one less than number of decreasings.

(4) Mark the centre back in centre of one needle with thread of contrasting colour.

(5) To DECREASE.—Knit to within three stitches of the centre. Slip 1, knit 1. Pass slipped stitch over, knit 1, knit 2, knit 2 together.

(6) Knit every round plain to the depth of one division, then decrease. Repeat till stitches are reduced as required.

Ankle.—Knit plain for one-sixth length of foot.

Heels.

FRENCH = Gusset heel.
DUTCH = Square heel.

FRENCH HEEL

1. Put half the number of stitches on to the back needle, now called the heel needle.

METHOD.—Knit to the end of the heel needle. Calculate the number of stitches to be moved to it. Knit half this number from the next needle. Transfer the other half from the previous needle (on to the other end of the heel needle).

2. Flap.

(i) Transfer the remaining stitches to a second needle.

(ii) Knit on the heel needle about as many rows as there are stitches on the needle. The return rows are purl.

(iii) Slip the first stitch in every row plain or purl as required.

3. To Turn the Heel.—(Continue to slip first stitch in every row.)
  (i) *Knit* to the centre and 2 beyond : decrease (slip 1, knit 1. Pass slipped stitch over) and knit 1.
  (ii) *Turn.*—Purl back and 2 beyond centre. Decrease (purling 2 together). Purl 1.
  (iii) *Turn.*—Continue decreasing by taking one stitch from each side of the gap and knitting or purling one after decreasing.

TO TURN A DUTCH HEEL

  (i) Knit to the centre and 3 or 4 beyond. Decrease.
  (ii) Turn immediately, purl to the centre and 3 or 4 beyond ; decrease. Turn.
  NOTE.—No stitch is taken *after* decreasing.

4. Picking up Side Stitches.

The last row of the turning must be plain. If the ball is the wrong side, knit an extra row.

There are half the number of edgestitches that there are rows.

In picking up take the edgestitch of web when flat. Begin at the bottom and insert the needle from the WS.

Do not take the top stitch already knitted into when turning heel.

Knit the picked-up stitches on the side of the flap on to the heel needle, being careful to knit into the front short side of the loop, as this turns the stitch and prevents gaps.

Knit the instep stitches.

Pick up the stitches from the second side of flap as before, i.e. from the bottom. Knit into the back of the stitch or turn each stitch on the needle before knitting it as usual from the front. Knit on to this needle also half the heel stitches. *Note.*—Be careful that the same number of stitches is picked up from the second side of the flap as from the first.

Gussets.

There are now two foot needles and one instep needle.
1. Count the stitches while knitting one or two plain rounds.
2. Reduce the number to equal that of the ankle.

Decrease at the end of the first foot needle and at the beginning of the second. There are therefore half the number of decreasings that there are stitches to be decreased.

Up to the eighth decreasing put two plain rows between.

After the eighth decreasing put one plain row between.

METHOD.

Knit to within three stitches of the first foot needle.
Knit 2 together.
Knit instep.
Knit 1 on second foot needle. Slip 1. Knit 1. Pass slipped stitch over.

MENDING AND KNITTING
REINFORCED HEEL

Knit the plain rows of the heel flap as usual. In the purl rows, alternately slip and knit the stitches, but always finishing with a knitted stitch. To allow for the reduction in width of this method there should be more stitches on the heel needle than the instep.

ALTERNATIVE METHOD.

Knit heel flap as usual but at the same time knit in No. 8 D.M.C. or Star Sylko. Carry this on till the heel is turned.

Foot.

Knit plain rounds until decreasing for the toe. A flat toe occupies about 2¼ in. and a pointed or French toe occupies 1½ to 2 inches.

Toes.—*Flat.*

Decrease 4 stitches in each decreasing round, i.e. on the foot needles as for gussets *and* at both ends of the instep needle. Reduce to 12, 16, or 24 stitches.

Do 3 plain rounds between the first 2 decreasings.
Then 2 ,,   ,,   ,,   ,, next 3   ,,
     1 ,,   ,,   ,,   for the remainder.

French Toe.

Decrease six stitches in decreasing round, i.e. three decreasings of two each and equally spaced. Rearrange stitches on needles for this.

Grafting Toe of Sock.

In effect, this is the same as the Swiss Darning already described, but the presence of the needles makes that description a little difficult to apply.

HAVE READY

A tapestry needle with eye large enough for the wool.

The stitches evenly divided on two needles (but any odd stitch to the front), and the wool coming from the back needle.

REMEMBER

(i) The wool needle passes twice into every stitch.

(ii) At the second time the stitch comes off the knitting-needle.

(iii) Stitches on the front needle come off plain ; on the back needle come off purl.

Thread the needle and pass through first front stitch purl. Pass through the first back stitch plain. Draw well home.

*Take off the first front stitch passing through plain, and at the same time pass through the next front stitch purl.

Take off the first backstitch purlwise and pass through the next backstitch plain. Repeat from *

Treatment of Wool for Re-knitting. See page 238.

Sewing and Mending for the Family

MANY a girl starts married life with only one thought about sewing for the family. She will turn the worn collars and cuffs of her husband's shirts! This is certainly a worthy ambition—and one guaranteed to impress a new husband with his bride's capability! But as time goes on this young homemaker will find more and more ways in which her ability to sew will help her to keep her family well dressed. Sewing for the family can be divided into three classes:

1. **New clothes.** Decide what clothes you should make for yourself, your husband, and children, and what clothes it would be wiser to buy.

2. **Remodeled clothes.** Decide which clothes are good enough to make over. There is no point in spending time and energy in sewing on material which is too worn to be worth the work involved. (See Chapter 15 for more information and instructions on made-overs.)

3. **Clothes to repair.** See that buttons and hooks are fastened on clothes, socks are mended, torn spots are patched or rewoven.

If you are a practical mother you will encourage your little girl to share the responsibilities of the family sewing and mending. A little girl of six or eight usually enjoys doing what Mother does and this is as good a time as any to begin teaching her to sew. She can learn to make clothes for her doll as well as little aprons for herself. And she can even learn to darn.

As her teacher, you will have to be patient with her, for you cannot expect her to be quick or perfect in her work. Nor can you expect her to sit still for more than fifteen or twenty minutes at a time. She will do better work if she is allowed to stop sewing when she begins to tire of it, and you will find that as her interest grows she will spend longer periods at her task. One last word: Don't forget to praise your little girl's work. Judge it by her age and ability, not by your own, for nothing will do so much to encourage her interest in sewing as the feeling that she has earned your praise and recognition by her effort.

CLOTHES TO MAKE FOR CHILDREN—By all means make your children's clothes. Prices asked for ready-made children's clothes are often very high. Of course there's no denying that many a woman has almost stitched herself blind making baby clothes when she would be doing herself and the baby more good by taking a walk outdoors. But the average mother will make some baby clothes for sentiment's sake and

Incidentally, if you are interested in having your small daughter turned out in the right way, her shoes will be

will make most of her small children's dresses, rompers, play suits, and sun suits if she wants attractive clothes at a budget price.

The finest children's clothes are made in cotton, linen, and lightweight woolens. Only for very special occasions should a child's dress be made of silk or rayon crepe, and these are not recommended for general wear. A child is dressed in good taste for summer best in white or pastel linen, voile, or organdie; and for winter best in a velveteen basque dress with gathered skirt, or a dark velveteen jumper with a sheer white guimpe or blouse.

The velveteen might be a princess dress, with short puffed sleeves. A velveteen dress with no other trimming can have a small collar of Irish crochet lace. A more delicate lace can be used to trim an infant's very best dress.

Mary Jane pumps—black patent leather with one strap—worn with white socks when she's dressed in her

best clothes and oxfords or loafers with school outfits. Keep her hats simple—a cloche or Breton sailor in felt or straw, with a ribbon band and streamers down the back. Beanies, little berets, and Scotch caps are good

too. Keep her clothes short—above the knee until she is ten or twelve. Children—both boys and girls—usually wear clothes halfway up the thigh until they are five or six years old.

Make corduroy or denim overalls for hard, rough play. These sturdy cottons wash and wear like iron.

Another increasingly popular trend is to match your daughter's outfit to yours. Mother-and-daughter outfits are charming and easy to make. Select a pattern which is becoming to you yet simple enough so it will look well on a tiny figure. A pinafore style is good. If you use eyelet ruffling, which can be bought by the yard, the time it takes

for the sewing of the shoulder ruffles will be cut in half. Make mother-and-daughter aprons too. Your daughter will love to wear hers when she is helping you around the house.

Don't forget the rightness of the buttoned-down-the-front princess coat for any little girl. Then there is the straight coat so often made in navy or gray chinchilla cloth or melton for winter. This may be worn by either boys or girls. The girl's coat is buttoned from right to left and the boy's from left to right.

CLOTHES TO MAKE FOR GROWN-UPS—Whether you are the mother of a family or the daughter who sews, in the section which follows you will find suggestions for making things for the members of your family.

Home dresses—Somehow the name "home dresses" makes them sound prettier than just plain house dresses. At any rate, every woman—even a business girl—finds she has use for several. They can be bought ready-made, but most of them—at least those within reach of the average budget—are poorly finished and are of an inferior material. It is much more satisfactory in every way to make your own dresses. After you have made a few, you will have a pretty good idea of about how much material such a dress takes and will be able to take advantage of a yard-goods sale, buying up several remnants at a time. This practice is not recommended for any other type of garment, but for home dresses it is seldom wasteful, since you will probably want several dresses in the same pattern and since the scraps can be utilized for quilts, pot holders, aprons, and other utilitarian articles.

Another advantage of having a piece of material on hand is that it offers the perfect outlet for that rainy-day urge to sew.

Aprons—There are aprons and aprons. They can be strictly utilitarian for housecleaning and gardening or gaily elaborate for serving when you're a hostess at a tea or a cocktail party. You can use remnants or leftovers from your other sewing, or even that old standby—a man's shirt that is no longer serviceable. Aprons have no age limit—from tots to grandmothers —and you will enjoy making them for gifts as well as for your own use.

You can buy patterns with directions for cutting and sewing. But you may also devise your own patterns and may combine two different materials if you are using short lengths. Aprons can be finished with contrasting bands and pockets, ruffles, appliquéd designs, rickrack braid, bias bindings or lace.

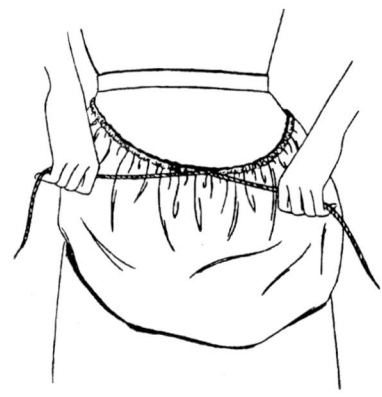

The apron shown in the illustration is usually called a "basket apron" because of its carrying capacity. It is useful in the house or back yard, for small working appliances or clothes-pins. Use a strong cotton fabric. Make a one-inch hem, turn it over and stitch on the right side of the apron. Using a buttonhole stitch, make two eyelets an inch apart in the center of the turned-up hem. Through each eyelet draw a cord or a shoelace to serve as a drawstring. Pull each string through at the open top. Cut a belt of double thickness of material. Baste the belt to the top of the apron, including the two ends of the pulled-through drawstrings. Stitch the belt at the top and the bottom. Untie the strings and flatten the apron when laundering.

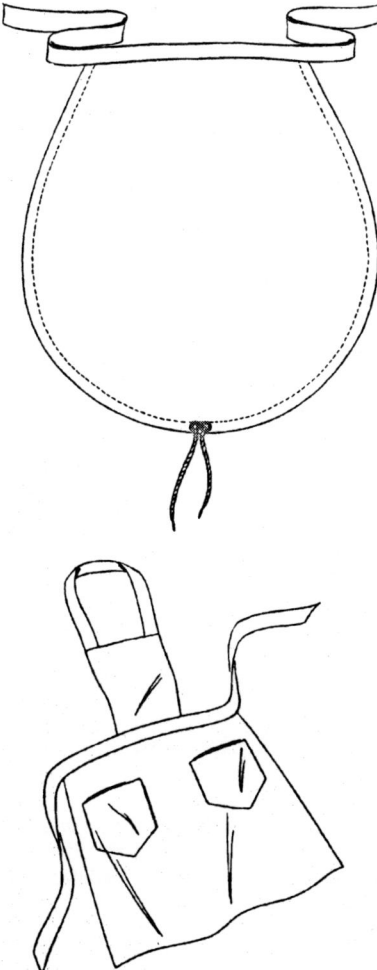

A bib apron with a strap to go around the neck is easy to cut and sew. Use a heavy cotton fabric, with wide tape or a double thickness of self fabric to be sewed on for the neckband and the two side belt pieces. A pair of pockets can be added in contrasting material if desired. This apron can also be made of plastic material, or of heavy canvas or oilcloth for the man of the house to wear when puttering around the garage or for other household chores or hobbies.

Here is an ideal apron for the home sewer or the knitting and crocheting enthusiast. It has handy pockets for her spools of thread, thimble, needles, and eyeglasses. Cut it from a straight

piece of material, allowing six to eight inches additional length at the bottom if the material can be used on either side. Make a hem, turn up and stitch on the right side. Now turn up the extra length which you allowed. Stitch it down the center to form two pockets—or, if it's a wider apron, make two stitchings, several inches apart, to form three pockets. Hem the sides of the apron. Gather the top into a straight band made from two thicknesses of material. Stitch down. This band, of course, should have enough length at each side to allow for tying in the back. If the material is not reversible, cut an extra piece of material to be seamed together at the bottom before turning up for pockets. You may, of course,

prefer to use contrasting material for the pockets and for the band too.

Little girls especially will love aprons

made from colorful scarves and large handkerchiefs; they are attractive for the woman of the house as well. You can make an apron from a single scarf or you can work out colorful designs by stitching two or more together or by arranging handkerchiefs on solid-color material and using a scarf or handkerchief as a bib.

To please the eyes of your family or guests you may indulge in aprons made in gay or pastel colors, of delicate patterns and materials, such as organdie or dotted swiss. You can even make aprons of silk or rayon taffetas or moirés to wear when you are entertaining at home. The latter, however, may not be washable, so take that into consideration before you spend too much money and effort in making one. Gift aprons, as a rule, fall into this dressy class.

Plastic material, which can be bought by the yard, is also used for aprons. Since plastic does not fray, it is not necessary to turn under a hem; the edge can be left straight or cut with a pinking shears for that little saw-tooth edge trimming. Do not sew by hand. Stitch by machine. Place a piece of tissue paper beneath the plastic on the side next to the machine. Use a fairly long stitch (try ten or twelve to the inch). Of course you know you don't launder plastic material—you wipe off the surface with a damp cloth to clean it. And don't put large pockets on the apron—the plastic might not be strong enough to hold the weight if you are inclined to fill the pockets heavily.

Lingerie—Handmade lingerie adds luxury to any feminine wardrobe, but few women can afford to buy it. If you have always wished you could wear the dainty handmade underthings you will find they are easy to make and inexpensive as well.

SEWING AND MENDING FOR THE FAMILY

LINGERIE FOR THE TROUSSEAU—Whether it is for your own hope chest or for some member of your family who is happily planning a trousseau, intimate apparel made at home has a sentimental value which no ready-made things ever have. What can or should go into a trousseau is a matter

to be decided by the woman who is assembling it. To a great extent it depends upon her taste, her pocketbook, and her own needs. Obviously it is quite impossible to say that any specific item must be included. Generally speaking, however, a trousseau usually includes the following:

TAILORED SLIPS, NIGHTGOWNS, PANTIES, PAJAMAS, BED JACKET of nylon, silk, rayon, or cotton.

LACE-TRIMMED OR EMBROIDERED SLIPS, NIGHTGOWNS, PANTIES, BED JACKET of rayon, nylon, silk, or sheer cotton.

EVENING SLIP, full length, of nylon, rayon, or silk.

TAILORED HOSTESS GOWN AND HOUSE COAT of cotton, quilted cotton, wool, or corduroy. The shortie brunch coat comes in this category, since it is really a house coat cut short.

DRESS-UP HOSTESS GOWN, HOUSE COAT, NEGLIGEE of silk, rayon, velvet, or sheer wool, trimmed with lace or other types of trimming or with self fabric.

LOUNGING PAJAMAS—If you're the type who looks glamorous in them make them of the same materials as above.

BATHROBE—One made of terry cloth or candlewick cotton material for mild weather; a woolen one for colder weather.

BRASSIÈRES—Made of cotton, rayon, nylon, net, or lace. If your figure is large enough to require a bra with substantial reinforcement, you will probably be wise to buy ready-made brassières.

STYLES OF LINGERIE—Whether your lingerie is simply tailored or trimmed with lace and ribbons depends entirely on your own taste and the kind of clothes you customarily wear.

It is best to stick to the classic styles when choosing a house coat or hostess gown because their styles tend to follow the changing modes in fashion and you don't want yours to be outdated before you have enjoyed wearing it for any length of time. If you avoid extremes of cut, such as pinched-in waistlines or dipping hem lines, and designs and colors which shriek and will make you (and the groom) very tired of look-

ing at them, then there is no reason why these garments can't always be fashionable without being faddish. It is poor economy, in a trousseau, to make anything from a temporary high-style pattern.

Slips, too, should follow simple lines, even though you may trim them elaborately. You will be thankful for their simplicity should it be necessary to make alterations later—widening or narrowing them, turning up the hem, or adding a longer hem line of matching material or lace to meet dress-length requirements.

An evening slip will last for years if it is made correctly. It should be cut along simple lines, tailored, and long enough to reach to about an inch

above the hem line of a long evening gown. It should also be cut as low as possible in the back to permit you to wear the lowest-cut dress.

Nightgowns and pajamas, as a rule, should be very long, for they are ungraceful when they are that awkward length somewhere between the knee

 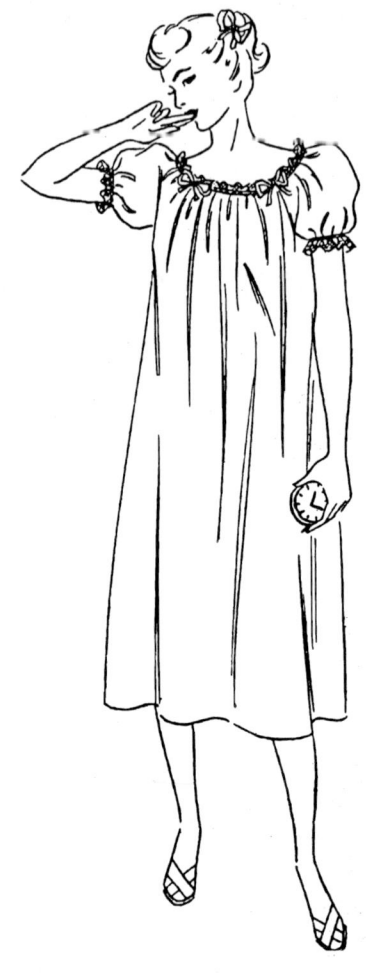

and the ankle. The shortie nightgown, which has recently begun to increase in popularity, is, of course, an exception to this rule.

Bed jackets have no particular style to them—whatever you prefer in the matter of style is all right at any time. When you're on a vacation or a visit, the prettier the bed jacket the better. Indulge your whim for all the fluff and lace trimmings you like. If you're an avid reader in bed and use a bed jacket constantly at home, keep it simple so there will be little or no trimming to get easily soiled or wrinkled and require too frequent launderings.

A serviceable tailored bed jacket can be made from the pattern for a pajama top or a coolie jacket.

MATERIALS FOR LINGERIE—If only for sentimental reasons, you will want your trousseau to last a long time so that you can enjoy wearing the things you made. Therefore, do not practice false economy in buying materials. Look for remnants, yes, but not for cheaper quality. These are the best choices you can make in materials:

Cotton—Batiste, crepe, nainsook, lawn, voile, fine broadcloth.

Rayon, nylon, and silk—Crepe, crepe de Chine, jersey knit, crepe-back satin, chiffon, georgette.

Wool—Sheer crepe, fine challis.

For a house coat or hostess gown use wool fabric, such as flannel, jersey, lightweight gabardine, or any other light woolen dress material. Velvet, velveteen, and corduroy are also suitable.

Self trim, applied in bands and stitched down flat, is always good, because it eliminates the laundering problems which arise when two different types of material are used in one garment. An effective lingerie trimming is satin bands on crepe, or vice versa. Whatever your choice, make sure you use the same type of fabric; that is, rayon satin and rayon crepe, or silk satin and silk crepe. Remember this even when buying ribbon for trimming. Lace trimming, applied in bands, edging, or appliquéd, should be carefully selected; a good cotton lace is preferable to rayon lace. It will withstand laundering better and retains its strength longer. NOTE: If you use a lace trim on rayon, nylon, or jersey knit lingerie which does not require much ironing, the lace will look quite well without ironing after the garment is washed.

When you've decided on the materials and the trimmings you want to use, make certain they will not fade or shrink and are not of an inferior grade which will come apart after a few launderings. Those materials which you will have dry cleaned, such as the velvet or wool house coat, should also be the best quality you can get for your money, because you want them to be attractive for a long, long time.

SEWING HINTS FOR LINGERIE—If you are not an experienced sewer, start by making lingerie that is cut on the straight grain of the material; later on you can make the bias-cut slips and nightgowns which require more intricate cutting and sewing. Bear in mind that when you wear bias-cut lingerie it is apt to get much shorter as you move in it, for slips have a habit of "riding up" when you sit down. For this reason it is best not to wear a bias-cut slip under a sheer dress.

The same holds true for the evening slip, and if you plan to wear it under a lace dress, you won't want it to slip up to your knees when you sit down or creep up when you dance. While we are on the subject of evening slips, if you have a strapless evening gown, you can make detachable shoulder straps to be snapped on and off the slip, and if you're afraid the slip won't stay up, use a few stays from an old girdle and sew one under each side of the seam of the slip, from the waistline up to the top of the slip. These should hold it up.

Lingerie which gets frequent laundering must have strong, flat seams and no exposed edges to fray. (See Chapter 6 on seams.) The hems, especially on bias-cut garments, should be very narrow, and preferably rolled. (See Chapter 7 on hems.) Lace edgings, appliqués, and all other trimmings and decorative stitching must be put on as flat and as securely as possible. (See Chapter 17 on appliqué and decorative stitching.)

In making the more delicate lacy outer garments, such as hostess gowns or negligees, use the same care as in making underwear. However, for the less intimate outer garments, such as the hostess gown and the house coat of velvet, wool, or other heavier material, you can use the same cutting, fitting, and sewing methods as you use in sewing your dresses.

CLOTHES TO MAKE FOR THE MENFOLK—Small boys' suits can very well be made at home if you wish to save money. They are simple to sew and require little tailoring skill. You can also make the short trousers worn by the older boy of six or seven. And even though you may think it is easier to sew for a girl, you can also make the chinchilla box coat which is standard equipment for little boys. Mothers can sew sports shirts for the boys and men of the family. Pajamas for men and boys are almost like tailored pajamas worn by girls and are no harder to make. Men's lounging robes and smoking jackets also can be made at home.

Many women sew for men as a labor of love—making something very special and monogramming it for a gift. A hand-hemstitched handkerchief in fine linen and a scarf in heavy white rayon or pure silk are typical gifts. However, they must be simple and made to perfection for the man to like them.

MENDING—The mending, darning, and sewing-buttons-tighter-before-they-pop-off, can be greatly simplified by looking over all clothes before they are washed or sent to the cleaner. If worn spots are reinforced before they go through the washing machine, the hole that is about to appear is usually warded off for another few washings.

For directions for sewing on buttons, snaps, hooks and eyes, see Chapter 10.

HOW TO AVOID SLIDE FASTENER TROUBLE—Close all slide fasteners in washable clothes before putting them in the water in order to keep the slide fastener from spreading and to keep the garment in shape. The other two chief causes of slide-fastener grief are: (1) pocketbooks filled to the top, with a handkerchief just waiting to be caught in the fastener; and (2) edges of material which catch in a dress slide fastener. When a slide fastener has jammed, patience and a hairpin are helpful. But if the teeth of the slide fastener are bent, you may have to replace it. Directions for inserting come with all slide fasteners.

GIRDLE REPAIRS—Save good elastic garters from your discarded girdles, so that you will have a supply of garters on hand to replace those which wear out. Notice how the old garters were stitched to your girdle. Usually the end of the elastic is stitched between two two thicknesses of material, or between the girdle and a piece of tape. Rip off the old garter, slip the new one into the same position, and restitch by hand or by machine.

Never tighten an old girdle by taking a seam in an elastic panel, because the elastic threads will be cut by the machine needle. Stitch on the fabric. When you find a loose end of an elastic thread in the girdle, fasten it securely by wrapping the end with sewing thread. Knot the sewing thread to the elastic. Thread a needle with the sewing thread and reweave the elastic thread in and out of the section from which it was torn. Then fasten the end of the elastic in place by stitching it down with the sewing thread.

MENDING RIPS AND TEARS—Mend a rip by stitching it on the wrong side —by machine, if possible; otherwise with small hand stitches. Stitch beyond the place where the rip began and fasten the threads firmly. If the stitching is done by machine, pull the bobbin thread through and tie it to the thread passing through the needle. If the stitching is done by hand, take three small stitches, one on top of the other, to fasten.

Mend a tear by stitching a narrow dart on the wrong side of the material. The widest part of the dart should be at the outer edge of the cloth, where the tear began. The dart should extend one inch beyond the place where the tear ends. Make the point of the dart very narrow and sharp. When the dart is pressed, the mending will often be scarcely noticeable.

USE OF MENDING TAPE—For quick and satisfactory results in mending a tear on any except sheer material, buy several inexpensive kits of mending tape in different colors. This tape is applied to the wrong side of the tear and is permanently pressed on with a warm iron. The tape stays in place through washing and dry cleaning. Directions for applying come with the tape.

REWEAVING PROBLEMS—Professional reweavers make a specialty of repairing tears, moth holes, or cigarette burns in an otherwise good garment or piece of fine household linen. Their method is to pull out threads from a hem or some other place where they will not be missed and then knot these threads to the ends of the threads around the hole or tear. The ends of the thread around the hole are raveled, in order to fasten the new threads firmly in place. The replaced threads are woven into place until the hole or tear no longer exists. This work can be done at home if you have great patience. However, repairs of this sort require skill and practice. Most reweaving shops have a mail-order repair service which you can use if you live at a distance.

DARNING—You will find a darning egg extremely useful in any kind of darning. If you don't have one, use a small cold cream jar or any rounded, smooth object which fits easily into the stocking and can be placed beneath the hole to be darned. Have the stocking right side out. Clip off any loose threads around the hole. Use matching wool for wool socks, cotton darning thread for cottons, and nylon thread for nylon hose. Do not knot the thread, for a knot will be uncomfortable when the stocking is worn. Instead, start your

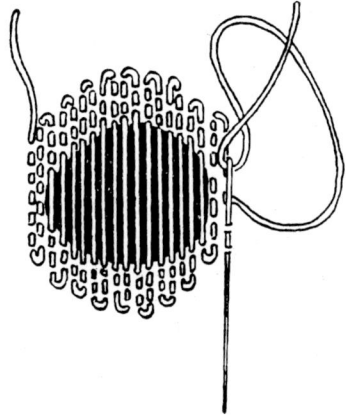

darning by taking several small stitches in the material, about a half inch from the hole. Turn the stocking and take another row of stitches beside the first one. Cover the hole with lengthwise threads in this manner, each row ending in six or eight small stitches which cover at least half an inch of the weakened area around the hole. Cut the end of the thread after the hole has been covered. Crosswise threads are woven in and out, over and under the lengthwise threads. Crosswise threads should extend a half inch beyond the worn edges of the hole, with small stitches in even rows.

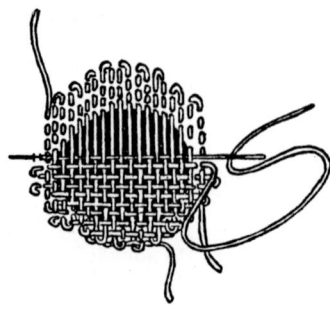

Some sewers mend runs in stockings by machine. Turn the stocking wrong side out and fold along the run. Stretch the stocking. Pin it to a sheet of paper. Stitch just inside the run with matching thread. Remove the paper and fasten the threads.

REINFORCING—This is a form of darning used to give strength to a weakened spot before a hole appears. Reinforcing is done from the right side, to keep the stitches as inconspicuous as possible, using darning cotton or wool. Long stitches on the underside of the material are anchored by tiny, almost invisible stitches which are taken on the right side. The long stitches on the wrong side relieve the material of a portion of the strain and may delay the appearance of the hole for some

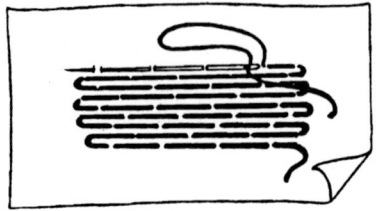

time. Darned reinforcements are most often used under the arms, at the elbows of woolen dresses or jackets, and in the knees of slacks. This type of reinforcement, however, is not suitable for thin cottons, rayon, or silk.

PATCHING—To make a neat patch on a fine material first trim the edges of the hole, to make it a small oblong or square. Clip the opening one-eighth inch at the corners, so that the edges will turn and lie flat. Then cut a piece of matching material about one inch larger than the hole on all sides. (If you are patching a printed material, try to match the print, so there will be no break in the design.) Pin the patch to the underside of the hole, working

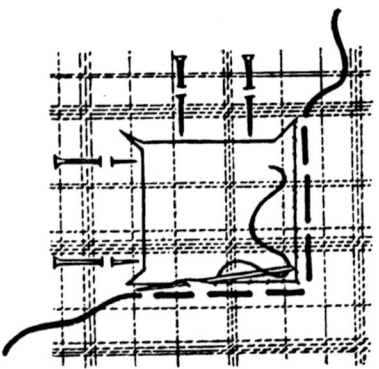

from the right side. Baste it in place if you think pins will not hold it. Bring the needle through to the right side of the garment at one corner of the opening. This will leave the knot of thread on the underside. Using the needle, turn under one raw edge of the square or oblong. If the place to be patched is small, turn under an entire edge from corner to corner, pressing it flat between thumb and forefinger. With the needle pointing toward you, take a small stitch in the patch and then slide the point of the needle into the folded edge of the hole, to make another stitch which will be invisible. The third stitch is another small one taken in the patch. These stitches (called slip stitches) are used to fasten patches to the material. The thread is fastened with three or four tiny stitches, taken one on top of the other, after the patching is completed.

MEN'S CLOTHES REPAIRS—You can use the methods discussed above in mending, darning, reweaving, and patching the clothes of the men and boys in your home. In addition to these, there are some repairs which are specifically used on masculine apparel.

Sturdy patches—On work clothes and play clothes apply patches with short hemming stitches taken close to-

play clothes worn by schoolboys, or on men's sports jackets. These patches are put on with small overhand stitches close together.

But a good jacket or coat, which has a spot wearing thin on the elbow, needs closer attention. Turn the sleeve inside out, rip the lining at the bottom of the sleeve and roll it up into the sleeve so it will be out of the way when you make the repair. Cut a piece of thin woolen material or rayon lining a little larger than the thin spot. Baste over and around the spot on the wrong side of the sleeve. Making your stitches parallel to the lengthwise grain of the cloth, tack with rows of tailor's basting, using loose stitches spaced about a half inch apart. If the cloth is worn very thin, make these lines of stitches closer to each other.

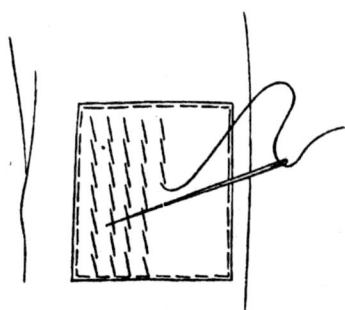

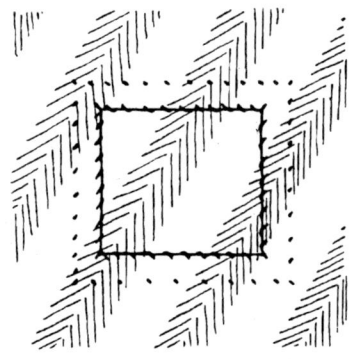

Turn the sleeve to the right side and with thread of the same color or slightly

gether. For extra strength also turn down the raw edges of the patch (which is, of course, on the underside of the garment) and hem these raw edges to the garment. This patch will not be dainty, but it will be strong.

Elbow patches—Suède leather patches can be sewn on the elbows of

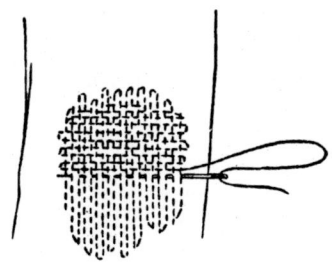

darker than the material darn over the thin spot. Catch the stitches to the patch underneath. Your vertical and horizontal darning stitches should be kept in line with the yarns in the sleeve.

Trouser knee patch—If a spot is worn thin on the knee, it can be patched by the same method as given above for the thin spot at the elbow.

Frayed sleeve—A vulnerable spot in a suit or coat is the edge of the sleeve. If it has frayed, rip the lining at the cuff and turn it up to keep it out of the way while you're sewing. Rip off the sleeve buttons. Remove the cotton interlining which is usually placed at the cuff for reinforcement. Turn down the sleeve hem and cut through the crease precisely on the line where it is frayed. Trim off very closely both the worn parts of the sleeve and the piece of facing you have just cut off.

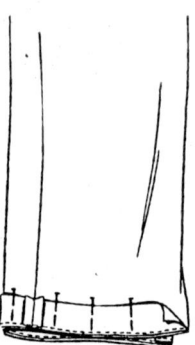

chine stitch the new seam on the facing very close to the joining to prevent this narrow seam from rolling up. Then turn the facing up into the sleeve again and baste it just inside the sleeve. Fold over and finish the corners of the cuffs as they were originally. Turn in the raw edges. Then tack the facing back into the sleeve with a loose stitch. Slip stitch the lining back into place at the bottom of the sleeve. Press. Resew the buttons.

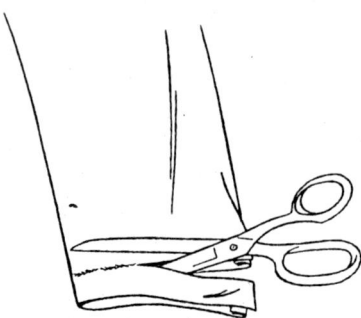

Replace this piece, matching the pieces at the seams, and pin it to the sleeve (right sides of material facing each other). Baste a very narrow seam, about one eighth of an inch. Stitch on the machine.

Press out the seam in the sleeve and facing as well as the new seam you just stitched. Turn the facing down and ma-

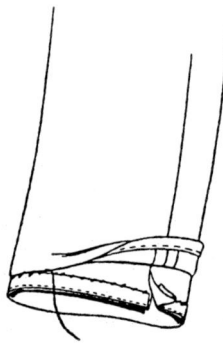

Worn coat collar—Baste with a contrasting thread on the roll line where the collar is worn.

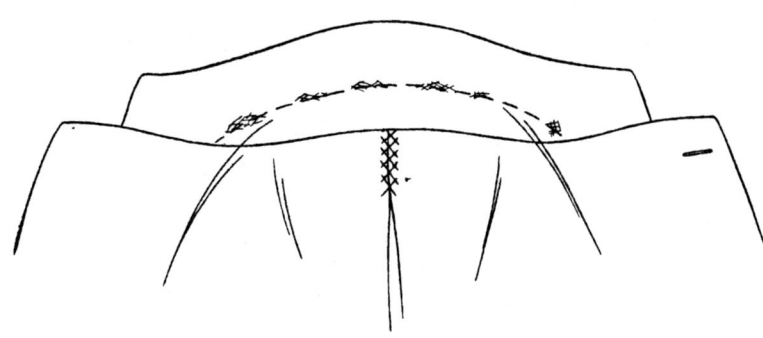

Rip the lining and the collar apart at the neckline. Turn up the inside of the collar and make a fold on the line of basting. Baste about an eighth of an inch from this fold on the inside of the collar, tapering the stitches at each end of the collar. Stitch on the machine. With sharp-pointed scissors, snip through the fold. Then press this narrow seam open.

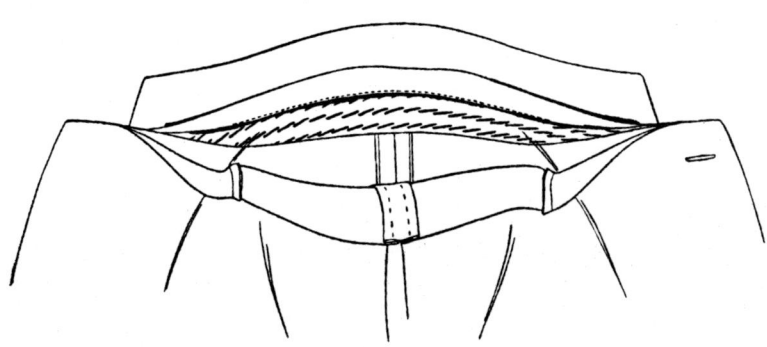

Turn the collar back, baste to the lining over the newly stitched seam to avoid stretching or puckering, then baste to the neckline and slip stitch the lining back into place. Press all seams carefully.

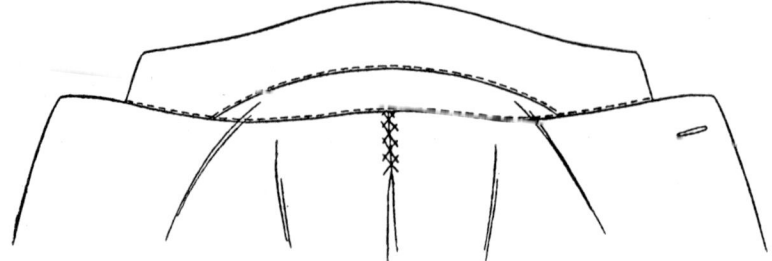

Relining sleeve—Remove the lining by ripping it at the cuff and the armhole. Rip open the seams of the lining, press the pieces flat (a man's sleeve lining usually has two pieces), and use them as a pattern to cut the new lining. Use pre-shrunk lining material. Make sure the old lining hasn't shrunk so that

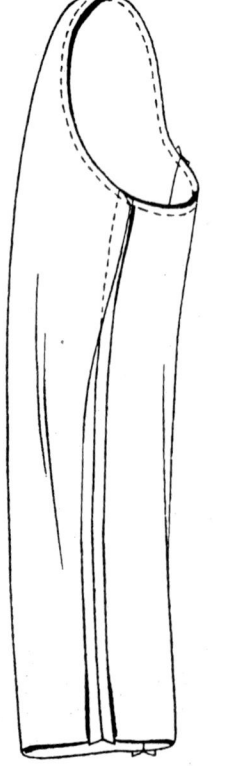
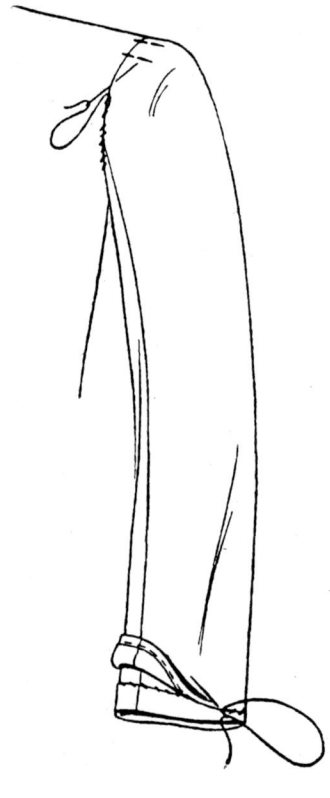

it is now too small for the coat sleeve. If it has, be sure to make this allowance in the new lining.

Stitch the lining seams. Press. Machine stitch around the top edge of the lining about half an inch from the edge to keep it from stretching. Turn in and baste the hem at the top of the sleeve lining. Pull the lining over the sleeve, wrong sides facing. Turn up the lining at the cuff line. Pin to the cuff and baste. Pull the lining up to the armhole. Pin to the armhole for a good fit. Baste. Finish with slip stitching at both cuff and armhole.

Replacing a trouser pocket—Rip the stitches from the waistband where the pocket is attached. Cut a paper pattern for the pocket. Mark the side to be laid on the folded material when you cut the new pocket. Make allowance for a three-eighth-inch seam. Cut the old pocket away from the two facings inside the pocket mouth. Leave some of the old pocketing, which is stitched back of the facing. This will make it easier to replace the new pocket.

Turn under the seam allowance of one edge of the new pocket piece. Pin it to the remaining piece of the old pocket facing, which is on the side of the trousers facing toward the back. Baste, then machine stitch twice for reinforcement.

Turn under the seam allowance on the other edge of the new pocket piece. Pin it in place on the old pocket facing which faces the front. You might have to turn under a little more of the new pocketing on this side than on the side facing toward the back of the trousers. Baste, then machine stitch

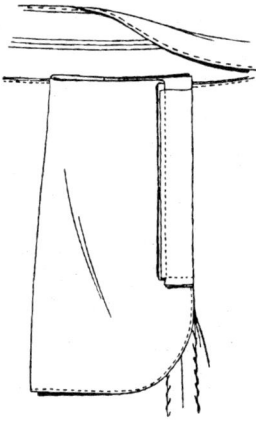

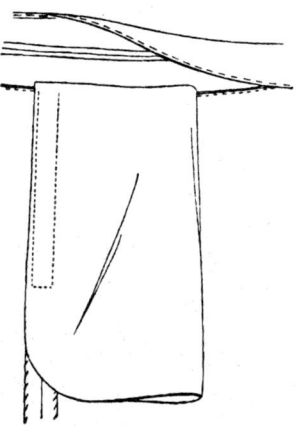

twice for reinforcement. Baste the lower edges of the pocket, stitch together with a French seam, then retrace the stitching at the corners for reinforcement.

Insert the top of the pocket under the waistband. Machine stitch on the right side, using thread to match the trousers. For a professional look you can use white thread in the bobbin to match the lining, but this isn't absolutely necessary.

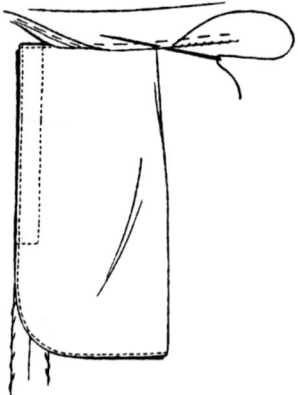

piece, allowing three eighths of an inch at the bottom for seaming and twice this allowance on the top. Stitch the new piece to the upper half of the pocket, so that the seam edges will be on the outside of the pocket. Press the edge of the seam toward the top of the pocket. Turn under the raw edge and finish with a flat fell seam.

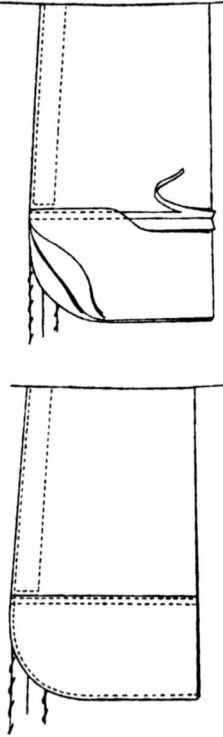

Repairing a trouser pocket—A small hole may wear through the corner of a pocket. When this happens machine stitch rows along the old stitching a fraction of an inch above the little hole. Do not cut off any material below the stitching.

If the hole is too big for this simple repair, or if the lower part of the pocket is badly worn, you can still repair the bottom half without having to take out and replace the entire pocket. Cut off the torn lower part of the pocket.

Use it as a pattern to cut a new

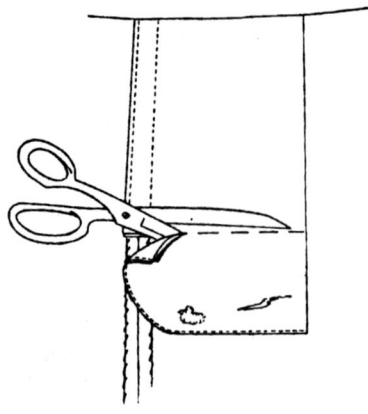

Then turn the pocket inside out. Baste a one-eighth-inch seam around the bottom and side. Stitch on the machine. Turn the pocket back into the trousers and finish with a French seam, stitching a quarter of an inch from the edge.

Replacing torn-off buttons—If the man of the house has pulled off a button, and with it some of the cloth from his coat, vest, or trousers, it's not beyond repair. If the torn spot is smaller than the button itself, slip a piece of material under the hole as reinforcement. With matching thread, darn over the spot and through the extra piece of material for strength. Then sew the button back in place.

If the cloth is torn so that the hole extends beyond the button, you will have to match the material. You may be able to do this by snipping a piece from the inside facing of the coat or vest. Make as neat a patch as possible, matching the weave of the material. Resew the button over it, but to make sure it doesn't pull directly on the patch, sew the button on with a shank. (See Chapter 10 on sewing buttons.)

Underarm patch—Cut away the worn portion of the sleeve and underarm in the shape of a square. Each corner of the square should be at a seam line. (There are four seams meeting at the underarm.) Rip the seams back half an inch, to allow for turning under the raw edge.

There are two ways of finishing this patch. It can be pinned into place, basted from the right side, and overcast by hand. This finish is used for an everyday work shirt whenever there is no machine available.

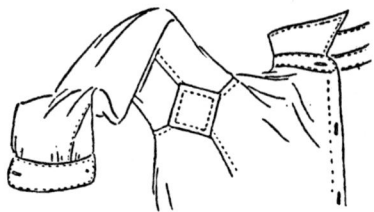

A better-looking finish is obtained by pinning the patch in place on the wrong side of the garment, with the right side of the patch face down. Baste the raw edges of the patch to the edges of the square opening.

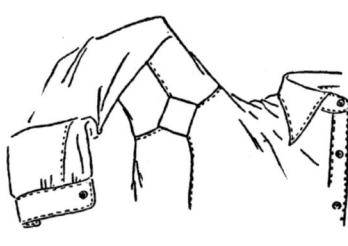

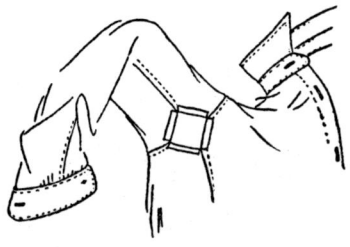

Cut the patch half an inch larger all around than the opening it is to cover.

Stitch by machine with four separate seams, running each seam off the edge of the patch at the corners. Be certain that the seam comes exactly to the corner of the square opening. This corner stitching is a bit tricky. Practice it on an old garment first, so that you will not run into trouble later.

Turning collar and cuffs—Carefully rip the collar from the neckband. (The double collar is set between the double thickness of the neckband.) Reverse the collar; that is, turn the worn side to the back. Fold the collar in half, matching the points and making a crease down the center back. Pin the center back collar into the center back neckline, matching the creases. Pin the collar into the neckband from the center to the two ends. Do not stretch or pull. Baste the collar in place, providing the same seam allowance as in the original stitching. Stitch the collar in place by machine, on inside of the neckband, using the same size stitch as originally used on the shirt.

You can turn cuffs in the same way you turn a collar, but since cuffs wear at the edges, it is not always practical to turn them unless they are double French cuffs which fold back and fasten with links.

Mending

25. Mending

Mending should be done at the first sign of wear, in order to save work, to make the article last longer, and to keep the mended place as inconspicuous as possible. It is usually desirable to mend the article before it is laundered.

Mending may consist merely of restitching ripped seams, sewing on fasteners, or replacing worn parts, such as collars and cuffs, or it may require darning or patching. In darning, the worn and broken yarns are replaced and reënforced by weaving in new yarns or threads; in patching, the hole or worn place is mended by adding another piece of cloth.

Darning

Darning by Hand on Woven Fabrics

Most darning is done by hand with crewel needles or sharps as fine as the thread will permit. The thread used should usually match the yarns of the fabric. In wool fabrics wool yarn or cotton thread is preferable to silk because it shows less. It is often desirable to use ravelings of the cloth; if there is no extra fabric from which to secure them, they may be obtained from the seams or the top of the hem.

Tears may be classified as straight, diagonal, and three-cornered. The methods used in darning will vary somewhat with the kind of tear.

Straight tears are the easiest to mend. The darning is usually done from the right side, but in very heavy materials it may be done from the wrong side, the stitches being caught only part way through the cloth. Match the torn edges as carefully as possible, use no knot, and, beginning a little beyond the end of the tear, draw the edges together with rows of fine running stitches. If the tear has frayed, darn by weaving over and under the loose yarns. These stitches should extend far enough beyond the sides of the tear to hold the edges together firmly and to reënforce any yarns weakened by the tear (Fig. 130). Do not draw stitches tightly enough to pucker the cloth. Make the rows of stitches irregular in length, and stitch back and forth only enough times to hold the edges together firmly. Extend the rows of stitches beyond the tear, and cut off the thread without fastening it.

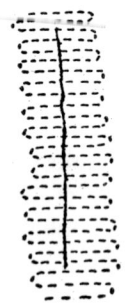

FIG. 130. Darning a straight tear

A *three-cornered tear* is mended like a straight tear, except that at the corner the rows of stitches should be slanted, as in the fan of a buttonhole (Fig. 131).

In a *diagonal tear* both the warp and filling yarns are broken at the same place. To mend, first fill in the warp yarns, as in Fig. 132. Then turn the cloth at right angles and put in rows of filling yarns, weaving under and over the lengthwise yarns, alternating as in plain weaving (Fig. 132).

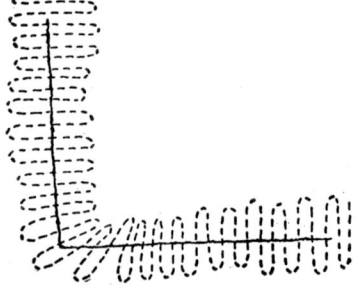

FIG. 131. Darning a three-cornered tear

Darning worn places. Worn places may be strengthened, or reënforced, on the wrong side by darning in extra warp or filling yarns or both, depending upon how much the places are worn.

Mending

Reënforced darn. If the fabric is badly worn, baste a piece of cloth under the worn place. Hold the reënforcement in place by catching through it with the darning stitches. Trim off the reënforcement close to where the lines of stitches end.

Darning by Machine on Woven Fabrics

Darning by machine is a satisfactory and quick way to mend towels, sheets, table linen, and underwear. Use thread of the same size as the yarns in the fabric. If the

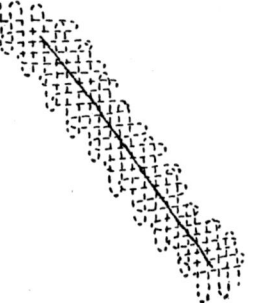

FIG. 132. Darning a diagonal tear

machine does not stitch backward, as well as forward, tie up the presser foot lever so that the foot is about $\frac{1}{16}$ inch above the feed. With a short stitch, stitch back and forth, lengthwise of the fabric, over the worn spot and holes, drawing the article back and forth with the hands. Repeat this process until the worn spot is sufficiently covered; then turn the article at right angles and stitch crosswise over the same place. This process is facilitated if the article to be darned is held taut by means of an embroidery hoop. The hoop should be slipped under the presser foot upside down, that is, with the cloth against the feed.

Darning on Knitted Fabrics

The thread used in darning knitted fabrics should be of the same color, size, and texture as the yarns used in the fabric. In darning silk hose, mercerized cotton may be used satisfactorily in the feet; but if the darn will show, it is better to use darning silk or thread. A darning ball is a convenience in mending places difficult to hold or reach, as the toes of stockings and sleeves of sweaters. Any of the methods that have been suggested for darning woven fabrics may be used for knitted fabrics, but hand darning is preferable to machine darning because it is more elastic. The darn will be still more elastic if a small loop of the thread is left at each end of every row of stitches.

Darning holes. Sometimes it may be desirable to trim the edge of the hole so that there are no ravelings. Put in lengthwise rows of running stitches, beginning far enough away from the hole so that the worn places are reënforced. When the hole is reached, carry the thread across it and continue with running stitches, being sure to catch on the edge of the hole each loop of the knitting. Put in enough rows to cover the hole and worn places. These rows should be about the width of the thread apart, and should be of uneven lengths. Turn the article and put in crosswise rows of stitches, weaving under and over the lengthwise threads, as in plain weaving (Fig. 133).

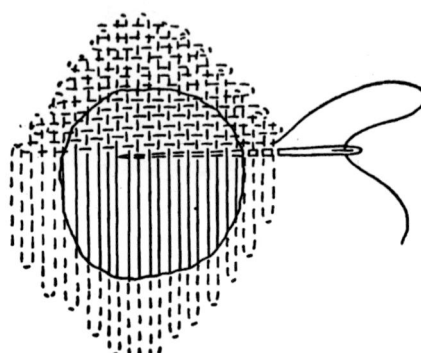

FIG. 133. Darning a hole

Runs in hose may be mended with running stitches, but the following methods are more satisfactory:

Mending runs with a crochet hook or latch needle. Pull the first dropped stitch through the loop at the end of the run with the hook or needle. Then pull the next dropped stitch through the loop thus formed, and continue in this manner throughout the length of the run. Fasten the last loop to

Mending

the loop at the other end of the run with several overhand stitches. This method is comparatively easy if the garment has rather coarse yarns; it can be done on silk hose, but it is a very laborious process.

Mending runs with overhand stitches. This is a quick method of mending runs and rips in seams. Working from the right side, begin beyond the end of the run and draw the edges together with overhand stitches, making sure to catch the loop of the last dropped stitch. Continue to the end of the run and extend beyond the end as in the beginning. Care should be taken not to draw the stitches too tight.

Mending Leather Gloves

To repair rips in seams, use overhand stitches or backstitches, depending upon the effect desired and the kind of seam used. Use cotton rather than silk thread, because it is not so likely to cut the leather.

To repair tears, blanket-stitch each edge of the tear; then draw the two edges together by catching the purls on each edge with overhand stitches.

Patching

The fabric for the patch should match the article to be mended as closely as possible. New fabric to be used on a faded or shrunken article should be faded and shrunk to match. When no extra cloth is available, a pocket or a piece from the under side of a hem or some other inconspicuous place in the garment may be used.

There are several methods of patching. The method used will depend upon a number of factors, such as the kind of cloth, the type of garment, and the location of the hole.

Hemmed Patch

This patch is used on light and medium-weight fabrics when strength is very important, as in wash garments. It may be stitched by hand or by machine. Since saving of time is an important factor in mending, hand hemming should be used only when machine stitching is too conspicuous, and in places difficult to stitch by machine, such as the knees of pajamas or overalls.

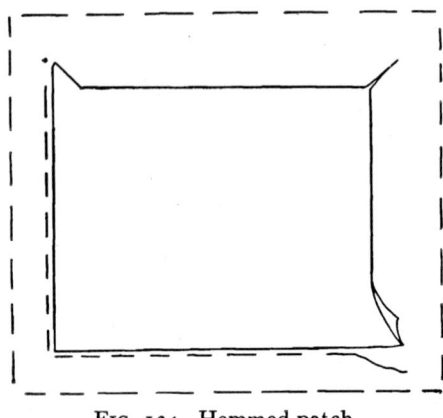

FIG. 134. Hemmed patch

Preparation of the article to be mended. Trim away the worn or torn parts. Square or rectangular patches generally show less than round or irregular ones, and since they are more easily made, it is usually better to trim along the yarn of the fabric.

Preparation of the patch. Place the patch to the wrong side of the article, making sure that the patch laps beyond the edge of the hole the same amount on all sides, and that the design and yarns of the fabrics match. Pin in place and baste if necessary. Clip the corners of the hole diagonally to the desired seam line. Turn in the raw edges, pin in place, and baste if necessary (Fig. 134). Stitch by machine close to the edge on both the right and wrong sides, or hem by hand.

It may be more convenient, if the hole is quite large, to pin in place the fabric from which the patch is to be cut, before trimming out the hole. Finish the right side; then cut away any extra fabric on the wrong side and finish the edge.

Mending

Variations of the Hemmed Patch

The raw edges may be held in place in one of the following ways when the fabrics used are too heavy to be turned under (as blankets), or when the material does not fray or ravel (as some knitted underwear and stockings).

Catstitch is used on either woven or knitted fabrics and is desirable for the latter because of its elasticity (Fig. 135),

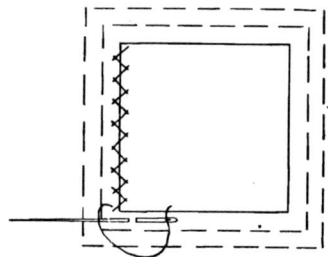
FIG. 135. Catstitched patch

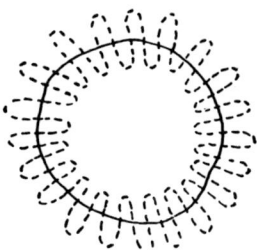
FIG. 136. Darned patch

but it is more conspicuous than the other stitches. For the method of making see "Decorative Stitches," p. 68.

Darning may be used on either woven or knitted fabrics. Since it requires considerable time to make a good-looking darned patch, darning is used only where neither catstitching nor hemming is satisfactory, as on men's trousers or the elbows of coats and dresses (Fig. 136). For the method of darning see "Tears," pp. 169–172.

Hemming stitch is used in knitted materials where the catstitch would be too conspicuous, as in stocking legs (see "Stitches," p. 290). This is a good method for some lace fabrics. The torn place should be trimmed in an irregular line following the design in the lace. The design in the patch and the garment should match exactly. Hem around the raw edges on the right side; then trim the patch, following the design, and hem the patch on the wrong side; or trim quite close and finish with overhand, buttonhole, or blanket stitches taken through the two thicknesses.

Glued Patch

A quick and practically invisible method of patching woolen and silk fabrics is the use of mending tissue, mending cement, or glue. These are generally used on a tear or a split and to reënforce worn places; they are seldom satisfactory when the edges of the tear are frayed or when there is a hole. Neither are they satisfactory on thin fabrics or on garments which are to be dry-cleaned frequently or laundered.

With mending tissue. Working from the wrong side, match and draw together the torn edges as carefully as possible. Then place over them a piece of mending tissue just large enough to extend a little beyond the edges of the tear. Cover the mending tissue with a piece of the fabric, matching the lengthwise and crosswise yarns of the article and the patch. Press with a *warm* iron to make the tissue and the cloth hold together. If too hot an iron is used, the tissue will become hard and rubbery, and a stain may appear on the right side of the article. Let the tissue dry thoroughly before handling or wearing the article.

With mending cement or glue. Working from the wrong side, carefully match and draw together the torn edges. Brush over this space a light coating of glue or cement. Cover with a piece of the fabric, matching the lengthwise and crosswise yarns. Place a cold iron or any heavy object over the patch until the glue or cement sets. If too much glue or cement is used, a stain will appear on the right side of the garment, and the patch will be stiff.

Mending

MENDING IS A TERM THAT COVERS ALL SORTS OF FABric repairs—replacing broken stitches, reinforcing places that have worn thin, filling in holes, joining tears, all the little jobs that prolong the life of worn, but still valuable articles. Your machine can save you much time and effort in mending; use it to darn, patch, reinforce and restitch, and see how it speeds the task and restores the fabric.

Threads and Needles. A fine needle is usually best for fine mending. Thread should match the fabric as nearly as possible in color and weight. Two-toned fabrics, such as woolen tweed, may be mended almost invisibly by using dominating color in needle and secondary color in bobbin. Warp threads of a fabric may often be used to darn small holes by hand. For a fine stocking darn, separate the strands of darning thread and use only one or two strands in a crewel needle.

Machine Darning. Use the Singer Darning Foot and either drop the feed or cover it with the special Feed Cover Plate, as shown in **A**. Consult your machine instruction book for details on installing these. Use the Darner for stockings and the Flat Darner or embroidery hoops for linens, towels, etc., so that the place to be darned is held taut as you stitch.

A

Flat Darning. Trim away frayed edges around hole. Center hole in darner frame or in embroidery hoops, right side up, as in **B**, and place under needle. Turn balance wheel slowly by hand, hold upper thread and pull up under thread. Take several stitches until threads are securely locked; then cut off loose ends. Hold frame with both hands and move it in time to the needle. First stitch three times around hole about ⅛" from edge. Then stitch back and forth across the hole from one side to the other, as in **C**, covering the whole opening with stitches running to the outline stitching.

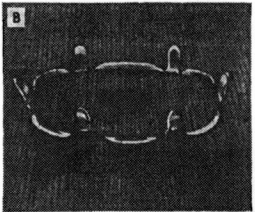

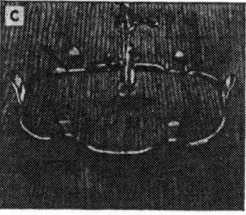

Complete the stitching in one direction; then turn frame so as to stitch across at right angles to first darning. Cover hole from edge to edge within the outline as before. Thread should be strong, but not so heavy as to pull away from thin or weakened fabric around hole; fine mercerized cotton is usually satisfactory for linen darns. If fabric is sheer, looser texture of darn can be made by moving hoop enough to make long stitch; for heavy, closely woven fabric, move hoop less so as to make short stitch. This type of darn is good for towels,

D

sheets, table linens. A cigarette burn is mended almost invisibly on damask if fine thread is used, as in **D**.

Darning Stockings by Machine. Put the stocking on the Darner in this way: Run your hand inside the stocking to the place where the darn is to be made. Grasp the frame of the darner with the hand inside the stocking, as in **E**, and turn the

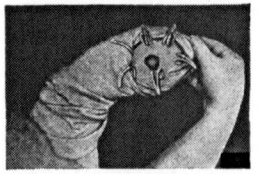

E

stocking inside out over your hand, rolling the excess length softly under the anchoring hooks. Turn over and apply the Darner spring, as in **F**. Bring

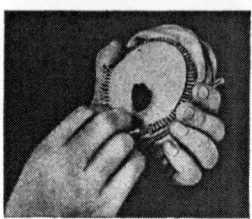

F

hooks to position, as in **G**. The right side of the stocking should be inside the Darner, with the hole to be darned in the direct center, as in **H**.

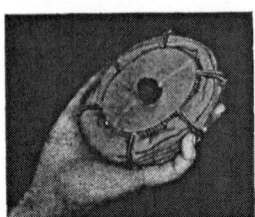

G

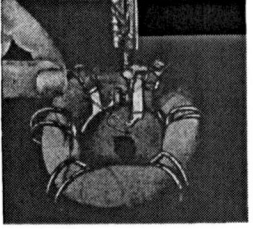

H

Ease edges of hole gently toward each oth that grain of stocking is straight up and down across. Using darning cotton, run line of stitc around edge of hole. Trim edges away. The for flat darning, stitch back and forth in one c tion across hole inside outline, as in **I**. Try to stitchings connect chain lines of stocking. and stitch back and forth the other way a darn to complete, as in **J**.

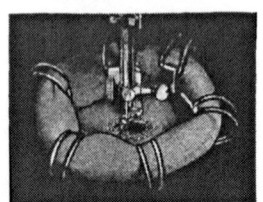

I

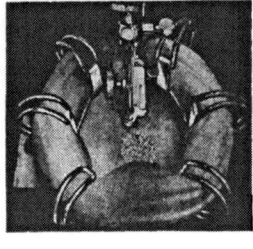

J

Darning by Hand. With small running-stitche begin about ¼" from edge of hole and work acros to a few stitches beyond opposite side, layin thread over opening in parallel lines until hole filled. Then turn and work across these thread weaving alternately over and under in paralle

K

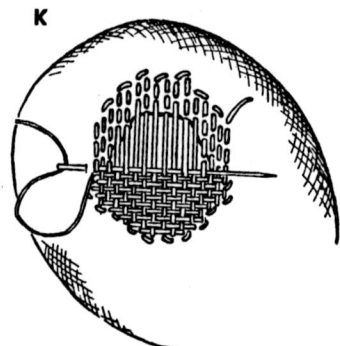

until fabric is replaced, as in **K**. For stockwork over darning ball so that darning ls are not drawn so tight as to pucker edges n.

ht Tear. Stitch back and forth across the ıs in **L**, making about five stitches on either nd beyond each end. If tear is long or on

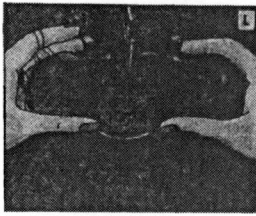

ıs, draw edges together first by hand, as in **M**, baste over paper to prevent slipping. Tear paır away when stitching is complete.

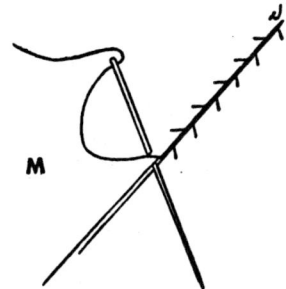

ıree-**Cornered Tear.** Smooth edges toward each her. Stitch back and forth across edges, beginng a little outside one end and going slightly ıst corner, as in **N**. Cross stitchings at corner for inforcement and continue stitching across edges tear to a little beyond other end. If fabric lacks ıdy, baste paper to wrong side before mending. ıper will tear away from under stitches.

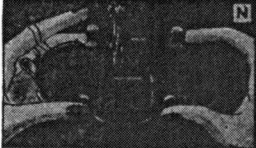

Stocking Runs. To mend by machine: Turn stocking inside out and fold along run. Pin edges along run, placing pins at right angles to the fold and spaced an inch or so apart. Make machine-stitch very short and use mercerized sewing thread of correct color. Begin stitching about 2" above beginning of run, slanting the seam gradually in from edge to take in full depth of run. Stretch stocking slightly as you stitch to allow sufficient "give" in seam. Stitch down alongside run and taper seam off to edge about 2" below end of run. Sometimes using paper under the seam helps to make a truer stitching line.

To mend by hand: From right side, whip edges together with small close stitches. Stretch lengthwise to prevent drawing seam.

Patching. When a hole is large, use a patch instead of trying to fill in with darning. Use fabric of the same piece if possible. Cut a patch piece from a facing, under a collar, or some place where it will not show. Patch this place with any similar fabric and use the piece for the part that shows. If there is no piece of the same fabric available, match the color, weight and texture as nearly as possible. Trim away ragged edges around the hole, cutting a square opening exactly along the fabric threads.

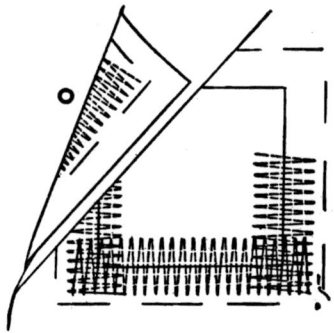

Darned Patch. Cut patch about 1" larger than hole. Baste under hole, matching grain of patch to garment. Darn on right side, stitching back and forth across each edge of patch, running about five stitches beyond on each side, turning and crossing stitchings at corners, as at **O**. Remove bastings. Trim off edges of patch close to stitching on wrong side.

Inserted Patch. Good for heavy fabrics because it eliminates extra bulk. Cut patch to fit squared hole exactly and to match grain of fabric. Place patch in hole, as in **P**. Cut a square of old net, cheesecloth, or curtain mesh about 1" larger than the patch and baste under it on wrong side. Thread machine with thread matching color of fabric. Darn on right side as for darned patch. When stitching is finished, trim off edges of mesh and pull out threads of mesh under stitching if desired.

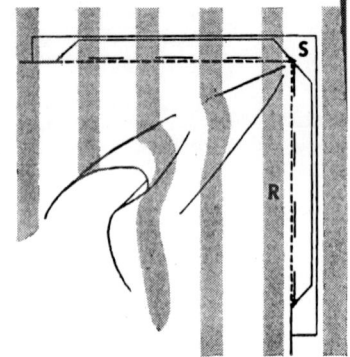

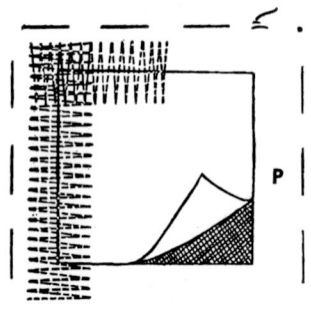

of hole. In wool, catch-stitch down on wrong as in **T**, making sure stitches do not go all the

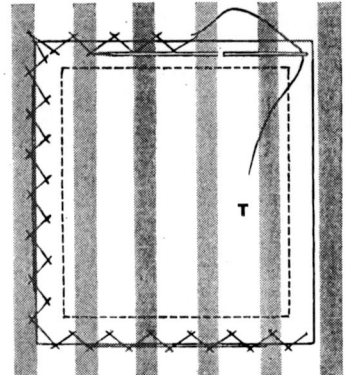

Tailored Patch. Prepare hole by clipping diagonally at each corner, as at **Q**, turning edges to wrong side and pressing. Cut patch about 1"

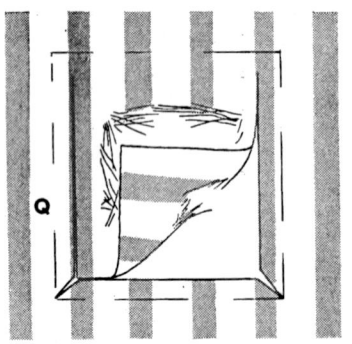

through to right side. In cotton, overcast edge The right side of patch should appear as in **U**.

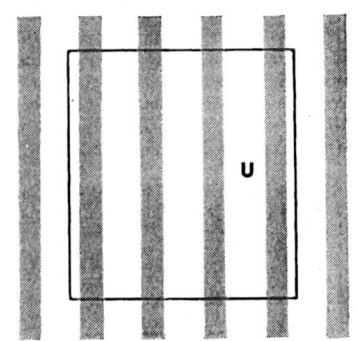

larger than hole, matching fabric grain to that of garment. Lay patch under hole and, from wrong side, baste it along pressed crease. Take a small back-stitch at each corner to hold in place while stitching. Then stitch along basted line on all four edges of hole, as in **R**. Make a few small overhanding stitches at each corner for security, as at **S**. Trim edges of patch to width of turned-back edges

ell Patch. Trim edges of hole to square or ngle. Cut patch about 1½" larger than hole. under hole, matching fabric grains. Turn r raw edges of patch and baste flat, trimming rs away, as at **V**, to prevent bulk. Turn to ment. Baste in place, as in **X**. Catch-stitch edge of hole to patch, using strong thread and small stitches. Turn to wrong side and catch-stitch around edge of patch, as in **Y**.

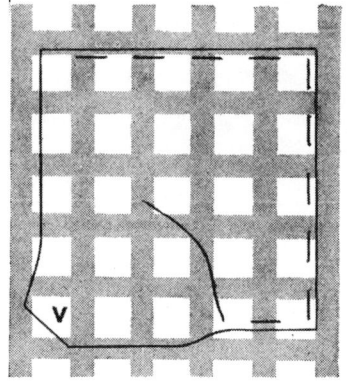
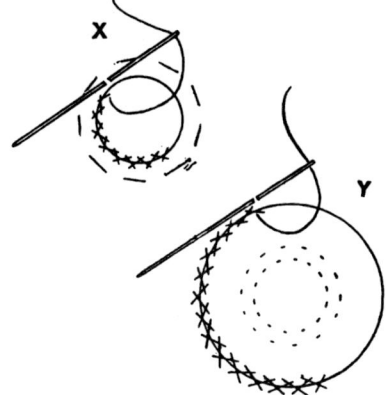

ght side. Clip corners of hole diagonally and rn under raw edges, as in **W**. Baste. Stitch close turned edges on both sides. If finished by hand, rned edges are hemmed on both sides. This is so known as a *hemmed patch*.

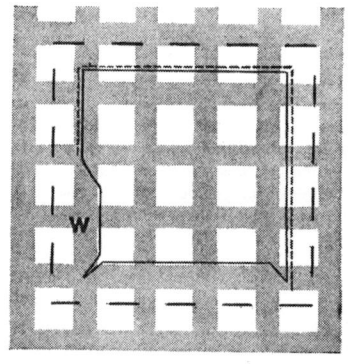

und Underlaid Patch. Good for knit-wear and undation garments made of material that has nsiderable stretch. Trim ragged edges of hole to rm circle. Cut patch piece of same type of fabric, aking it about 1" larger in diameter than hole. ace patch so that knit ribs match those in gar-

Decorative Patches. Sometimes patches can be made to seem a decorative feature of a garment rather than a mend. On a blouse, for instance, use an appliqué motif or series of motifs to cover holes, placing with care so as to give impression that design was planned purposely. Finish with decorative stitches, if desired, to carry out design. On tailored garments, sometimes applied bands may be used to hide holes or tears. Plan and apply these also so that they carry out a decorative line. Even if only one is needed, say on one half of a skirt front, apply a matching one opposite to give the planned appearance. Hobo patches, panels, borders—all may be used to do the work of patches without betraying that they are really mends.

Reinforcing. Fabrics that have not torn or broken through but simply worn thin can be reinforced by backing with another piece of fabric. For elbow reinforcement, use a fabric with some "give" for reinforcing piece, so that elbow movement will not be restricted. Chiffon, net or sheer stocking piece will serve well for wool dress. Nylon stockings no longer wearable make excellent reinforcement pieces, especially under the knees of trousers or elbows that have worn thin. Heavier fabric may be needed for heavy garments. Place piece over all of thin spot on wrong side and pin. Make a small running-stitch around edge of patch, as in **Z**. Start with a few back-stitches, then take tiny stitches through both fabrics so that those on right side barely show, while those on wrong side are ⅛" to ¼" long. Keep stitches in rows lengthwise on fabric, spacing rows about ⅛" apart, until reinforcing piece is securely fastened under whole thin area, as at **A**. If necessary, make a few rows of stitches in opposite direction for extra body. Press.

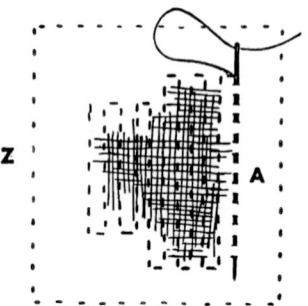

Terry Darn. Torn edges of towels, wash cloths, etc., can be repaired by placing a piece of paper

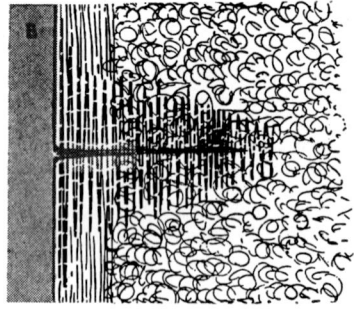

under the tear, drawing edges together and ing back and forth across them and through as in **B**. Pull paper away when edges have be curely joined all along tear. If edge is frayed back once and stitch with heavy thread.

Scallop Darn. Embroidered scallops on li garments and other articles often tear at the

ings of scallops, as in **C**. To mend, hold edg tear together and stitch across, back and

until edges are securely joined from edge to en as in **D**. Turn and stitch back and forth at rig angles to first stitchings, as in **E**.

Mending Hemstitched Bed Linen. Sheets and p low cases with hemstitched hems often bre along hemstitched line. The simplest way to ma them strong again is to tear off hem, lap it a litt over edge, pinning at intervals crosswise of t joining, and stitch in position.

Never were there more apt words assembled in a sentence than "A stitch in time saves nine." Do take stitches where needed in a slit in a garment, a break in a seam, or a torn place in a piece of linen. Mend promptly and with skill, and be proud of the mend. Your mending will not only save you money but will protect good merchandise—rightfully a responsibility of every homemaker everywhere.

Lightning Source UK Ltd.
Milton Keynes UK
UKOW042201200513

210979UK00001B/176/P